When Johnny and Jane Come Marching Home

"If we, as citizens, want to do right by the young men and women who serve in our military and fight our wars, we can start by reading this profound and moving book. By the book's end, you will be certain of one therapeutic truth: A society that sends its young off to war needs to be ready to hear their stories when they return and know that 'there is healing power in not only listening but also remembering what the speaker says.'"

—Robert Whitaker, author of *Anatomy of an Epidemic* and *Mad in America*

"The suffering of returning Iraq and Afghanistan war veterans, their families, and those whose lives they affect is likely to be the greatest mental health tragedy of at least the next decade. Dr. Caplan's passionate, eminently readable book makes a compelling case that this is about human pain, not mental illness. Dr. Caplan's critically reasoned review of the multiple dimensions of this crisis is both a call to action and a guidebook for how we can all do our part (still to be done for Vietnam vets) to welcome our American heroes home."

—Paul Block, Director, Psychological Centers, Providence, RI

"Caplan peels away the layers of myth, denial, and cliché we've used to shield ourselves from our veterans' unmet needs and our unpaid debt to them. Veterans' own stories put a human face on this book's careful research and thoughtful analysis. This book is a must-read not just for those who care about our veterans but for anyone who has benefited from their sacrifices, which is to say all of us."

—Kenneth S. Pope, psychologist, ABPP, and coauthor, *Ethics in Psychotherapy and Counseling*

"Rather than dealing with soldiers' postwar pain through denial or the distancing, detachment, diagnosis, drugs, and dis-ease of professionals, Caplan advocates that we all contribute by listening when soldiers tell their stories, and she presents a clear and convincing case that we should not recoil from or deny the horrors of war. Refusing to recognize the experiences of soldiers contributes to the continuation of both war and the debilitating impact of war on returning warriors. Caplan employs prose, poetry, literature, logic, and empirical data to convince us of our power to contribute to a community that connects with and socially supports returning veterans. It is important for all of us, laypersons and professionals, to hear what Caplan has to say and to listen to the stories that veterans have to tell."

—Maureen C. McHugh, Professor of Psychology, Indiana University of Pennsylvania

When Johnny and Jane Come Marching Home

How All of Us Can Help Veterans

Paula J. Caplan

The MIT Press
Cambridge, Massachusetts
London, England

For information about special quantity discounts, please email special_sales@ mitpress.mit.edu.

This book was set in Stone Serif and Stone Sans by Toppan Best-set Premedia Limited. Printed and bound in the United States of America.

Library of Congress Cataloging-in-Publication Data

Caplan, Paula J.
When Johnny and Jane come marching home : how all of us can help veterans / Paula J. Caplan.
    p.   cm.
Includes bibliographical references and index.
ISBN 978-0-262-01554-7 (hardcover : alk. paper)
1. Veterans—Mental health.   I. Title.
RC550.C37   2011
616.890086'97—dc22

                                                                2010036660

10 9 8 7 6 5 4 3 2 1

To the memory of my beloved, gentle father, Jerome Arnold Caplan, my hero, who so loved his family and loved the men with whom he served during World War II in the 969th Field Artillery Battalion when he was Captain Caplan

Other Books by Paula J. Caplan

Bias in Psychiatric Diagnosis (edited with Lisa Cosgrove)

Gender Differences in Human Cognition (with Mary Crawford, Janet Shibley Hyde, and John T. E. Richardson)

They Say You're Crazy: How the World's Most Powerful Psychiatrists Decide Who's Normal

You're Smarter Than They Make You Feel: How the Experts Intimidate Us and What We Can Do About It

Thinking Critically About Research on Sex and Gender (with Jeremy B. Caplan)

Lifting a Ton of Feathers: A Woman's Guide to Surviving in the Academic World

Don't Blame Mother: Mending the Mother-Daughter Relationship

The Myth of Women's Masochism

Between Women: Lowering the Barriers

Children's Learning and Attention Problems (with Marcel Kinsbourne)

Contents

Note to the Reader

Readers who want to move quickly to connect with one or more veterans and hear their stories may choose to skim chapters 3, 4, and 5 or read them later. Readers who want to learn in some detail how the most common efforts to help vets are failing may want to attend carefully to those three middle chapters.

Readers can find the full reference list at http://mitpress.mit.edu/caplanjohnny.

Acknowledgments

To those without whom I could not have written this book, I owe the deepest gratitude. In roughly chronological order:

• My mother, Tac Karchmer Caplan, for inspiring me and supporting my work for as long as I can remember, and for her penetrating comments on crucial portions of the book;

• My dear cousin, Alexis Harman Pearce, who told me the first heartbreaking and horrifying veteran's story that led me into the darkness and intense humanness of soldiers' lives;

• Caroline and Marcel Kinsbourne, for making the videotape of my father that catalyzed my need to understand more about his war experiences;

• Bob Colonna, for his marvelous directing of my play, *Shades*, which is about veterans and includes my father as a main character; for his remarkable performance of the character based on my father; and for his many thoughtful suggestions for improving the script;

• Aaron Frankel, the brilliant director and playwriting mentor, for awarding first prize in the Pen and Brush New Plays Contest to *Shades* and for his later, unfailingly patient and deep, insightful work with me on that script and another play about a soldier, *War&Therapy*, and about veterans in general, as well as for his love and moral support;

• Robert Dove McClellan, for welcoming me to the world of working with soldiers and veterans;

• Dr. Maureen McHugh, who as Collective Coordinator of the Association for Women in Psychology in 2003, just before the Iraq War began, raised in AWP's Feminist Forum meeting at its conference the question of what we could do about the imminent war and got me to think about what led to this book, and who subsequently urged me to keep working on these thoughts;

• Dr. Arthur Kleinman, for encouraging me to work on this subject and approach;

• Veteran and brave activist Stan Goff, who told me my first piece about vets was right on the mark;

• Michelle Dillow, for what she told and taught me;

• The soldiers and veterans who over the years opened their hearts and souls and spoke to me, especially David E. Jones, who moved and inspired me with his honesty, his courage, his love of humankind and of nature, and his exquisite poetry;

• My agent, Regina Ryan, who gently but persistently pushed me to think hard about the book I wanted to write and was a rich source of ideas and insights;

• Peter Yarrow and my mother, Tac Karchmer Caplan, for telling me I had to write this book;

• Jeffrey Poland and Jennifer Radden, for urging me to write the book for MIT Press and for connecting me with the Press, as well as to Jeffrey for his always profound comments on every chapter of the draft;

• Dan Bancroft, writer extraordinaire, for comments on an early chapter and for constant help with my writing;

• Teresa Wiersch for her invaluable perspective about combat veterans and her understanding of what the heart of the book needed to be;

• Trina Mascott for her insights into the experiences of World War II veterans;

• Professor Margaret Matlin for reminding me about important rules of clear writing;

• Professor Julie Johnson of Missouri State University for putting me in touch with wonderful veterans;

• John Judge, Richard Ievoli, and Franz Schneider for information about relevant articles and resources;

• David Dunlap for urging me on when the going was rough;

• Jordan Christopher Ford, whose brilliance and attention to every level of the writing, from commas to flow to logic to politics, as well as sense of humor, made it possible to get the book written;

• Tom Stone, formerly of the MIT Press, for his interest in this book;

• Philip Laughlin, Deborah Cantor-Adams, Marjorie Pannell, Johna Pico, Marge Encomienda, and Katie Hope of the MIT Press for their help, care, and attention to detail; and

• My children, Jeremy Benjamin Caplan and Emily Caplan Stephenson, for constant support and help.

Every time I write a nonfiction book, no matter how hard I try to locate and read all of the relevant work, I invariably discover wonderful things that I have missed. This time I only learned of Chaim Shatan's important work just before the book went to press, so I hope that both Shatan and anyone else whose good work I have yet to learn about will forgive me.

Prologue

What Brings Me Here

A war is a huge fire; the ashes from it drift far, and settle slowly.
—Margaret Atwood, *The Blind Assassin*[1]

The media are filled with stories about suffering veterans and what therapists and others in the military and the Department of Veterans Affairs are
doing about them. As I began to write this book in January 2010, I saw a
public service announcement urging citizens to listen to what vets have
to say. But although many people are trying to help, few have questioned
whether the efforts to help are effective or whether some may be misguided, even harmful. It is time to ask this question, to think critically
about the gigantic and still growing machinery of programs and policies
said to be serving veterans. Those who have been sent to war have suffered
enough without getting the message that if they only do what the experts
say will help them, they will surely feel better. In fact, there is no guarantee
they will feel better, and a wealth of evidence reveals that many of these
approaches have failed in the past and are likely to fail in the future.

The first war stories I ever heard came from my father, Jerome Arnold
Caplan, a veteran of World War II and captain of the 969th Field Artillery
Battalion during the Battle of the Bulge. He was white and Jewish, and the
men in his unit were black. Although this was at a time when, he recounted,
blacks were not to be sent into battle, because it was shockingly assumed
that they would be cowardly and run from the field, his men performed
so well that they were sent into combat and received a Presidential Citation
for bravery. I went to antiwar marches during the Vietnam War. I was born
in 1947, and from my youth until I was well past middle age, although I
listened with interest to my father's stories about his war—he was an
intense and compelling storyteller—I could only listen by keeping myself

at an emotional distance, and that distance made me uncomfortable. He rarely spoke about any role he played, only about how fine the men in his unit were and how lucky he had been to make it through, saying frequently that since the war, "I've been living on borrowed time." My mother had described how, after they had been married for a year, having known each other for only four months before that, he went away to war for twenty-two months, and when he returned it felt "strange" to be together again, but the strangeness quickly passed, because they talked constantly and immediately began to plan for the future. I did not know how to explain the emotional distance I felt from my father's war stories, although I sensed it was connected in some way with how hard it was to imagine my gentle, tender, graceful, loving father in connection with any war, no matter how necessary and important the war had been. However, there was more that I did not understand until 1995, when a friend videotaped my father telling his war experiences. As I watched the tape, I had to press the pause button several times, because I was weeping, overcome by terror as that lifelong emotional distance disappeared at last, and, almost as vividly as if it were a flashback, I saw my father in danger on the battlefield (not wearing his helmet, since he never did: it was too heavy to be comfortable, he said). Thus began my wish to understand how it had really been for him.

As Spokesperson for the Association of Women in Psychology at the time the United States began the war in Iraq, I wrote a white paper about what I thought people in the United States expected psychologists to be able to do—that is, make it all OK—when the soldiers from this new war started returning home, emotionally devastated. I noted how sadly misguided that expectation was. In 2004 I wrote a piece for the *Washington Post* about the need to avoid calling veterans mentally ill, about the fact that there is only so much emotional carnage of war that psychologists or psychiatrists can fix, and about the importance of every citizen being willing to listen to vets' descriptions of what they have been through:

Simply sending frightened, angry soldiers off to therapists conveys disturbing messages: that we don't want to listen, that we're afraid we're not qualified to listen, and that they should talk to someone who gets paid to listen. The implication is that their devastation is abnormal, that it is a mental illness, and this only adds to their burdens. Yet since there's intense debate even among experts about the definition of mental illness, it's all the more important for the rest of us to let returnees know that we don't consider them weak or crazy for having problems.[2]

I was moved by the many veterans from various wars who wrote to say that this article had hit home for them and to urge me to continue trying to convey this message. Further evidence that it had struck a chord was that it was rapidly reprinted in the National Military Family Association's *Newsletter*; in *The Officer*, the magazine of the Reserve Officers Association; and, under the title of "Too Little, Too Late?", in the book *Opposing Viewpoints: Mental Illness*.[3] In 2007 I wrote an article for *Tikkun* magazine titled "Vets Aren't Crazy; War Is" (later reprinted in *New Scientist*), focusing on the point conveyed by the title and describing what veterans had told me they found helpful.[4]

In the decades since the Vietnam War, the war during which I came of age, I have talked with many veterans of those battles and heard the stories of their experiences in Vietnam and in the often difficult time since they returned home. One of these vets was my cousin, Robert Alan Caplan, who volunteered to go to Vietnam as a medic and died in 2003 of an illness he had contracted from the unsanitary conditions in the medical facilities there. The year he died as a result of the Vietnam War, the United States went to war in Iraq. Since the wars in Iraq and Afghanistan began, I have talked with vets in many different contexts and have also met with people who have gone absent without leave (AWOL) from the army or taken unauthorized absence (UA), as the Marines call it, listening to their stories of how they came to feel their only option was to leave the service, as well as how they have been doing since they returned home. The veterans' stories vary in many respects, depending on differences in their premilitary histories, the families and societies in which they grew up, the specific people with whom they interacted in the military, and the kinds of war experiences they had. But what moved me to write *When Johnny and Jane Come Marching Home* is how common vets' problems and dilemmas are—some of which have been created by well-meaning people who do not stop to consider what helps and what hurts vets—and that there is good reason to believe the suffering can be alleviated.

My professional training is as a clinical and research psychologist. Although many people assume that psychologists believe everyone they set eyes on to be mentally ill, that does not apply to me or to many other therapists. In more than thirty-five years of work about mental health I have learned that, in a wide array of realms (for instance, the psychology of women, abuse, academia, dealing with authorities in any arena, and sex-differences research), *socially created* problems are often the causes of people's pain, but that pain is often mistakenly attributed to factors within the individuals. Furthermore, entire sets of tough-to-penetrate myths keep the focus on the individual and off the social ills. I have also learned what helps people in these various realms besides the two primary courses of action that most psychiatrists, psychologists, and even many social workers suggest these days, that is, (1) giving them drugs and (2) putting them in psychotherapy. Not all human suffering results from mental illness, by no means are drugs and psychotherapy the only ways to help alleviate suffering, and by no means are therapists the only people who can help. I bring these beliefs to the writing of this book. I also bring nearly three decades of experiences in encouraging people to tell their stories and listening to them. I am often moved to see how what might seem a tiny step—asking people to tell their stories—has a tremendous impact, making it clear that we value the storyteller and believe it worth our time and attention to listen. The details of people's stories can be glorious or horrific, but so often the tellers say that the moment they were asked to tell their story was the moment they began to reconnect with the listener and began, in the words of some, "to feel like a person again."

Finally, I bring to the subject of this book four decades of a critical thinking approach that I began to learn formally from Don Stanton, who coached me in debate and extemporaneous speaking at Greenwood High School in Springfield, Missouri, and continued to learn from Bruce L. Baker, who taught critical thinking about psychology at Harvard University during my senior year there. Don and Bruce built on the work of my parents, Jerry and Tac Caplan, and my uncle, William H. Karchmer, who encouraged me to question everything and especially to worry when people were harmed by unchallenged actions and programs.

I coauthored with my son, Jeremy B. Caplan, a book about scientific methods that is now in its third edition,[5] and I have written frequently about the ways that science and the use of jargon in research and clinical practice distort the truth. I feel strongly that nothing goes on in the scientific or clinical realms related to psychiatry and psychology that is beyond the comprehension of virtually any layperson. It is unfortunate that so few laypeople realize this and are therefore at the mercy of researchers and professionals, who do not always take as much care as they should in thinking how to help those who are in pain. Mark Twain said that the trade of writers has one serious purpose: "the deriding of shams . . . the exposure of pretentious falsities . . . the laughing of stupid superstitions out of existence."[6] Although I certainly would not consider the vast majority of psychiatrists and psychologists pretentious or stupid, it is troubling that many (as described in chapter 3) are bound by the straitjacketed thinking taught in most (but not all, thank heaven!) training programs. This keeps too many from ways of thinking that are outside official dogma. I experienced this myself at many points along the way. Just one example:

in my first Canadian job after getting my doctorate, a psychiatrist who was supervising me told me with great firmness that I had been wrong and unprofessional to visit the home of an aboriginal woman with whom I was working and who was too downhearted to make the trip to our clinic. It did not matter that she had suffered greatly, including losing custody of her child, in utterly unfair court proceedings. My supervisor's point was that psychologists (like me) and psychiatrists (like him) *do not make home visits*. Those are the province of social workers, he said, and he considered my impulse to reach out to a suffering woman by going to her home a sign that I was overly involved. Care and respect had somehow become wrong. In such ways are the blinders imposed when traditional therapists' training limits what we feel we are supposed to do.

A word about whom I quote in this book: I have met some vets when they have come to me because I am a psychologist, and I have met others through family or friends or in airports, and more recently, when performing in my play, *War&Therapy*, in post-performance discussions in the United States and Canada. I have read some nonfiction books and articles and some fiction about soldiers and veterans. For ethical reasons, I have been reluctant to quote directly from or tell the specifics of stories from soldiers and veterans who came to me because of my professional affiliation. But every quotation and every story in this book is one I chose because it echoes what I have heard from the people I met in the various settings. When I wrote that first piece about returning vets for the *Washington Post*, I told a specific story about one vet from the war in Afghanistan, but I immediately heard from many other vets who saw in his story something of their own. And as I increasingly talk with those from Canada and other countries, the similarities are striking. Sometimes I quote poets and novelists because they say more eloquently than I could ever hope to what the veterans have told me in conversation.

A confession: I tried for years to avoid writing this book, and I am aware of two reasons for the avoidance. One is the magnitude of the subject matter, along with its seriousness. Although immersing oneself in it is far less harrowing than actually going to war, it feels like the biggest responsibility I have taken on as a writer, and I haven't wanted to foul it up. Too many vets and their loved ones are suffering, and therefore much is at stake if I fail to make clear how seriously I take what they go through or if I say anything that could risk—or seem to risk—causing them still greater trouble. The other reason for my hesitation is that in my history of writing and speaking from what seems to me to be a commonsense, middle-of-the-road position, I have often been described (often from both ends of

whatever spectrum was relevant to the topic at hand) as an extremist or
as someone who oversimplifies issues or lacks professional knowledge.[7]

I make no secret of my opposition to every war the United States has
fought since the one in Vietnam, but I have never blamed the soldiers who
fought in them. Rather, I have been shocked by the degree to which many
truths were kept from them when they were asked to risk their lives and
their peace of mind, and I have been troubled by what I knew some of
them would face when they returned home. Nevertheless, I was unprepared, in working with vets professionally and then in interviewing more
for this book and meeting still more because of my theater work, for the
extent to which I would be shaken by up-close, unadorned views of veterans' pain. Whatever anyone believes about whether a particular war is right
or wrong, any war has a profound impact on a soldier's personal, emotional, and spiritual life, and that is what this book is about. Listening to
them has changed my world. So who is writing this book? Someone who
thought at one point that she understood what veterans go through but
who became increasingly aware that she still has much to learn.

1 When Johnny and Jane Come Marching Home: The Problem

An abnormal reaction to an abnormal situation is normal behavior.

—Viktor Frankl, *Man's Search for Meaning*[1]

I had read every word in the book of poems by the handsome, physically strong David E. Jones about his time at war in Vietnam before I met him at a Starbucks on January 19, 2010, so I should have thought of this, but it never crossed my mind. We met, and I got my drink first and went to a corner table that had one side against the wall and three chairs placed around it, one on each of the other sides. As I stepped between the seat on the far left and the one facing a wall, I was vaguely aware that Dave had come over and had somehow shifted his weight to one side. Only partly consciously, I sensed that I was about to take the wrong seat, assuming it was because we had just met, so it could be awkward for us to sit at right angles from each other. So I moved toward the seat on my left. "Fine," I thought. "Now he can sit across from me rather than next to me." But Dave shifted again, and once again, I sensed that I had gone to the wrong place, so I moved toward the seat on the right. Dave swept swiftly into the seat on the far left and sat down. Ah, yes! It struck me then: He needed his back against the wall, and he needed to face the door. I have seen this before in people who have lived in danger. Dave's war had ended three and one-half decades ago, but the psychological wounds of war can last as long as the physical ones, which Dave also has. To sit with someone whose sense of danger is immediate and palpable, who needs to be on guard even in an American coffeeshop all these years later, is to experience something most of us are graced never to have to feel originate in us. I do not believe that I can fully understand what Dave was feeling as he tried to be polite and gracious while finding a safe seat that day, but I know that if you are feeling calm while sitting quietly in a room with another person, and you suddenly feel anxious, you can be sure that it is because the other person suddenly became anxious.[2] Anxiety is communicated instantaneously and wordlessly to anyone in its presence. How much more true that is for hypervigilance—and for fear.

That day with Dave E. Jones came years after the beginning of my concern about what would become of the veterans of the United States' wars in Iraq and Afghanistan. I had already been alarmed by the building tragedy of massive proportions for the veterans, their loved ones, and many others. I had already been worried in principle that we knew too little about what would help the vets, given the appalling *current* statistics about homelessness, suicide, violence against others, relationship break-downs, drug and alcohol abuse, fear, and despair in veterans of wars from decades past. But beginning with that stunning recognition of the intensity of Dave's need to take a particular seat, I felt completely overcome by the magnitude of what war does to one person's life, for the rest of that life, and when I tried to imagine it multiplied by the millions of veterans in this country and in others, I felt the kind of nausea that arises when one feels helpless in the face of unnecessary suffering. Like many vets' actions, what Dave did just after I met him wordlessly showed me at least part of how it feels to have been in physical, mortal danger. And like many vets, when he speaks, as he did for three straight hours that day, he makes it possible for us to learn about the emotional, moral, and spiritual wounds of war.

By far the most common way Americans describe the emotional suffering of war veterans these days is to say they have Posttraumatic Stress Disorder (PTSD), a label that is listed in fourth edition of the *Diagnostic and Statistical Manual of Mental Disorders*, or *DSM–IV*, sometimes called the psychiatrist's Bible[3] of diagnoses of mental disorders. But to call the psychological effects of war mental illness is to sanitize the effects of war, to make them seem to constitute clinical entities or diseases, and to set apart those to whom we give clinical labels as different and thus separate from the rest of us. In 2005, Dr. Terence Keane, the director of the behavioral science division of the VA's National Center for Posttraumatic Stress Disorder, actually said, "the most powerful predictor of mental health problems is the intensity of the war, and this is a very intense war."[4] Consider: If "mental health problems" result from war's intensity, should we really be calling them "mental health problems," as though they were medically caused or brain-based disorders, rather than calling them "pain," "suffering," and "devastation"? Similarly, military psychiatrist Colonel Elspeth Ritchie and her colleagues have said that experiencing combat, seeing dead and mutilated bodies, and feeling helpless to stop a violent situation lead to normal reactions of emotional upset.[5] A user posting an email under the name "Cory" in response to a National Public Radio (NPR) broadcast wrote, "The human mind is not meant to bear this sort of burden."[6] Culture analyst Elaine Showalter has written that, according to "most military psychologists and medical personnel, if not generals," the emotional suffering of war is caused by the "warfare itself, by chronic conditions of fear, tension, horror, disgust, and grief."[7] Finally, Barry Romo, National Coordinator of Vietnam Veterans Against the War, notes that war trauma is a normal reaction to an abnormal situation.[8] It does little or no good sweepingly to label the wracking emotions caused by war "PTSD" or other labels for mental illnesses, and it does veterans considerable harm, often increasing their isolation and always adding to their burdens by conveying the message that their reactions to war are somehow overreactions, that they should have been "over it" by now, and that the problems arose from within them. (Are feelings of terror and a need for constant vigilance after a powerful hurricane or an automobile accident illnesses?) As a result, veterans are often unthinkingly classified as Other, as different from the rest of us rather than (in some way, paradoxically) as people like us who have been through kinds of hell that we have not. This makes it harder for us to understand and empathize with them and therefore makes it harder to hear what they really need. In chapter 2 I discuss this extensively, including some of what the veterans feel and where it comes from other than mental illness, but first it is important to look at what the sheer numbers at this stage show us so far about the magnitude of the suffering of Iraq and Afghanistan vets.

As we begin our journey, it is important to keep in mind this context: As a nation, we have failed to learn from previous wars what soldiers and veterans need to help them grapple with the emotional devastation that so many suffer. The sight of the poor and deeply troubled veterans who haunt our cities, sleeping on sidewalks and in doorways or holding pieces of ripped cardboard with signs saying "Homeless Vietnam Vet" and asking drivers at stop signs for a dollar, makes us want to look away—or give them a dollar, look away, and drive on. What drives us to avert our gaze is partly our feeling that we are powerless to help them. But we are not powerless. Let us remember that as we look at some indications of what needs to be done, realizing that all of us can help. Let us also remember that, because fewer than 1 percent of Americans currently serve in the armed forces, it has been too easy for most citizens to remain innocent of the effects of war,[9] and something similar is true in Canada and many other countries.

As waves of veterans come home from war, an emergency of massive scale is building fast. Early on, people who work with first responders such as police officers and ambulance drivers sounded the alarm. They warned that soldiers from Iraq and Afghanistan would come home traumatized by actual combat or by the terror of knowing that anyone may turn out to be the enemy, and that an improvised explosive device (IED) could blow them up anywhere, at any moment; they foresaw that the rates of suicide, homicide, domestic violence, poverty, drug abuse, and homelessness would skyrocket. So did advocacy groups, such as the National Gulf War Resource Center, whose executive director, a twenty-year Army veteran, Stephen Robinson, warned in 2004 that "There's a train coming that's packed with people who are going to need help for the next 35 years."[10] As noted above, the Association for Women in Psychology decided just before the Iraq War began to issue a warning in an official white paper. For a long time, these voices were ignored. Then the evidence of the gathering storm began to be harder to ignore. Because of the George W. Bush administration's decision to extend soldiers' tours of service and then President Barack Obama's expansion of the war in Afghanistan, only a small proportion of those soldiers who will ultimately return home have done so, yet the troubles of many are already known. We face a building disaster of enormous magnitude. To help forestall this disaster, we must look immediately and head-on at the psychological carnage inflicted on Americans involved in the wars in Iraq and Afghanistan and tell the truth about the causes and nature of that carnage, as well as the truth about what will—and will not—help.

Neither the military nor the VA has learned the lessons it should have from Vietnam and the first Gulf War, and the last thing we want is still more veterans who struggle with broken families, homelessness, drug and alcohol abuse, rage, violence, and despair. As just one example, as Vietnam vets enter their sixties, the number seeking treatment for emotional trauma from the war is actually increasing.[11] As another, as of 2008, the VA still had nearly one million veterans from the Vietnam War, more than 200,000 from the Gulf War, more than a third of a million from World War II, and more than 160,000 from the Korean War on disability pay.[12] If the alarm is not sounded, and sounded soon, we will be overwhelmed by the problems of the veterans of both sexes from current wars, as well by the problems of their families. As the vets return, and as their numbers increase and the effects of their war experiences spread through society in waves, almost no one will remain untouched by the pain, anguish, and terror that these vets bring home.[13] But we can create an "army" of Americans who can help, and later in this chapter, I will begin to look at how we can.

The realm of reactions to *physical* injuries warrants an entire book on its own, but it is important to keep in mind that many of the veterans described here as struggling with the emotional consequences of war are also dealing with the physical ones. My focus in this book is on the emotional ones because so little work has been done to uncover the limitations of the treatment of emotional trauma from war and because that realm involves so much jargon, mystification, and pseudoscience.

What Is Happening to the Veterans?

Many years ago, a woman who had for decades been a close friend (and had certainly never been to war) confessed to me that she had had a dream that made her feel ashamed, and she said that she could never tell anyone what it was about. It was just a dream. From the way she referred to it, I had the sense that it was something sexual. I told her I could not imagine judging people harshly because of a dream they had, as opposed to something terrible they had actually done, but that made no difference to her. She has never told me the content of her dream. To her, it is unspeakable. For veterans, who have confronted mortal danger and the lowest depths of what people, perhaps themselves and perhaps others, can do—purposefully or not, knowingly or unknowingly—how much more fear and shame can weigh them down, make them believe that what they experienced must never be told? They will tell you that they feel it is unspeakable partly in the sense that the stories are so harrowing that they do not want to burden friends and family even by alluding to what happened, and they feel it is unspeakable partly because they believe it reveals terrible things about them, such as that they were unable to save another soldier's life, or they discovered that the "enemy" they had killed without seeing them turned out to be infants, children, and the very old. Imagine a vet who is utterly devastated from having seen a best buddy blown to bits by an IED or from having unintentionally killed an Iraqi or Afghani child. Is utter devastation not a profoundly, movingly human response? Are nightmares and terror and guilt not understandable ways to feel? And is it not completely comprehensible for those feelings to plague the vet for weeks or months or years, even for decades? What do we gain if we call these reactions mental illnesses and send the sufferers into the increased isolation of therapists' consulting rooms? This is not to say that some therapists will not be helpful by listening with compassion and understanding and by offering insight, but one must be aware of the risks of sending vets into therapy, both the risk of calling their reactions to war pathological and the risk of treating them as Other by implicitly or explicitly encouraging them to save their talk of war for the therapist's office.[14] If their reactions to war are to be called mental illnesses, then what exactly would we call a healthy emotional response to war's shattering events? In *Man's Search for Meaning*, Viktor Frankl describes what he calls the mortification of normal reactions, the extinction of normal responses through punishment of them[15]; examples related to war would be the suppression of feelings such as fear and of certain moral considerations in the service of training soldiers. Harvard University psychiatrist and anthropologist Arthur Kleinman asks how, in the face of horrific events, one could *not* be devastated, and in this connection he suggests that many veterans' reactions are more usefully and accurately called *moral disorders* than mental ones.[16] To the extent that the vets' troubled feelings reflect spiritual or existential crises, what are the consequences of throwing emotion-numbing and mind-numbing psychiatric drugs at them, suppressing their capacity to grapple with and work through those crises? As we will see in this book, it is not that the military, the VA, and the mental health community do not wish to help. It is that far too much of their efforts, time, and money are going into initiatives that fit within the traditional box of classifying reactions to war as mental illnesses.

Because so many veterans feel such pressure not to speak of what they have been through, the following statistics should not surprise us. A 2006 article in the *Journal of the American Medical Association*[17] reveals that the percentage of vets from Iraq and Afghanistan experiencing serious emotional difficulties was by then already far higher than the percentages from any previous wars. A 2007 Army report showed suicides to be at their highest point in twenty-six years and revealed a significant correlation between suicide risk and the number of days deployed.[18] July 2008 brought the announcement[19] from the VA that 22,000 vets called its suicide hotline during the previous year. According to Department of Defense press releases,[20] eighty-two active duty Army personnel had committed suicide in the first five months of 2009, and by June 2009, soldiers were "taking their own lives in record numbers, and Army leaders [were] struggling to understand why,"[21] though the DOD cited "failed marriages, financial problems, military disciplinary actions and upcoming deployments" as possible contributing factors.[22] According to Aaron Glantz, no one really knows the numbers of former soldiers who kill themselves, because the VA refuses to track these people, even though those with military experience have been shown to be twice as likely to kill themselves as those with no military experience, and this is true for veterans from World War II, the

Korean War, the Vietnam War, and the Gulf War.[23] The Department of Veterans Affairs estimates that 107,000 veterans are homeless on any given night and that 260,000 are homeless at some time during the year,[24] and the National Coalition for Homeless Veterans reports that veterans account for about 23 percent of all homeless people.[25] About 5 percent of homeless vets are women, and roughly 56 percent are African-American or Hispanic, although these two groups account for only 12.8 percent and 15.4 percent of the U.S. population, respectively.[26] Although most homeless vets are from wars that preceded the current ones, estimates in early 2010 were that during that year, there would be 419,000 homeless vets from Iraq and Afghanistan.[27] In addition, there is some evidence that Iraq War veterans are becoming homeless sooner after their military discharge, even immediately, than those from Vietnam.[28]

According to a 2010 *New England Journal of Medicine* article,[29] warfare in Iraq and Afghanistan differs greatly from that of, for instance, the 1991 Gulf War, which ended quickly. The current wars have involved intensive combat on the ground, attacks by insurgents, and many deaths and injuries to American troops. This has increased the burden on families of soldiers and Marines, and the authors of the article say that these burdens are not as well understood as those of previous wars. For longer periods of time, spouses back at home have to maintain the household, function as a single parent, and try to cope with strains on the marriage because of the physical separation, and the duration of separation is often unpredictable. These problems have led to increased marital dissatisfaction, divorce, unemployment, and decline in emotional health.[30] And, the authors note, the strains occur before, during, and after deployment. (The Bush administration's use of "stop-loss," or cancelation of scheduled dates to return home from deployments when soldiers' enlistment times were due to end, increased those strains.[31]) In spite of this, they say, associations between these intense pressures and emotional problems of various kinds have not been studied well in military families.[32] In their own large and sweeping study, the authors note that the majority of active duty servicemen are married, and they report that wives of servicemen who had prolonged deployments were more likely than others to receive psychiatric diagnoses. Putting aside for now any discussion of the unscientific and potentially harmful nature of such diagnoses, I wish to emphasize here that these women sought professional help because they were suffering. The nature of their suffering included troubling moods, anxiety, and sleep problems.

Reports are starting to come in, including from the Pentagon itself, about children of servicemembers experiencing intense fear, anxiety, and

behavior problems, with 60 percent of military parents telling researchers
that their children feel more fear and anxiety when the parent goes to war.
This unsurprising result gives the lie to any belief that parents can protect
their children when the former are heading for dangerous zones.[33] It is
instructive to contrast the cheery broadcasts of servicemembers home on
leave surprising their children at school or sports events with the hard fact
that even young children know that their deployed parents may die, and
that even if the departing parent says, "I'll be back in time for your baseball
season," no one really knows whether or not that will be true. One out of
four of the more than 13,000 military spouses in the Pentagon study said
their child coped poorly or very poorly, and one in three said the child's
grades and behavior in school were problematic. Furthermore, research
suggests that even one year after their parents returned from combat,
nearly one-third of children continued to have serious emotional problems.[34] Since at the time of the study, nearly 900,000 military personnel
with children had gone to war since 2001, and since the Pentagon estimated that in 2009, 234,000 children had a mother or father at war, the
scale of this problem is massive. Furthermore, as of the middle of 2009,
according to Army records, about 600,000 active duty soldiers had deployed
once since 2001, 110,000 had gone twice, 38,000 had gone three times,
and 8,000 had gone four times.[35] The numbers for all of these problems in
soldiers and their families are especially alarming, because some emotional
consequences and some practical consequences of war for veterans (such
as unemployment or homelessness) arise or come to light only after a delay
of months to years, so the percentages are almost certain to increase above
those cited here.

Although the focus in much of this book is on veterans from Iraq and
Afghanistan, almost everything in *When Johnny and Jane Come Marching
Home* also applies to veterans from earlier wars. We need to learn from
listening to vets of earlier wars in what ways we have failed to help, what
has helped them, and what has made their lives even harder than they
would otherwise have been. The military and the VA had changed little or
nothing from their treatment of Vietnam vets to their treatment of vets of
current wars until the Obama administration came into office,[36] and since
then, too little has improved. The longstanding treatments include ineffective therapies and the heavy use of psychiatric drugs, including sleeping
medications, antidepressants, and stimulants, with all three kinds often
given to the same patients. According to veterans advocate Ray Parrish,[37]
the new administration has begun to do a better job of bringing on board
more peer counselors for vets, and that may be helpful; however, that has

by no means displaced the more traditional approaches. Furthermore, according to a recent article from VA Watchdog,[38] the VA is putting veterans diagnosed with PTSD on "a potentially deadly drug" that "has been linked to the deaths of soldiers returning from war," and the drug is often combined with other psychiatric drugs, increasing the risks of harm and even death from drug interactions that have been studied little or not at all. The drug is Seroquel, which is approved by the FDA to treat psychosis, not to treat PTSD, which is *not* even classified as a psychosis.

As the wars in Iraq and Afghanistan have continued, the numbers of suffering vets have increased, and even when the military and the VA have made announcements about providing additional help and implementing new policies, what they—and laypeople—have mostly continued to rely on are the old, inadequate ways of responding (see chapters 4 and 5 for more detail). That these ways are inadequate is reflected in the statistics about veterans from earlier wars. A study by Yale University professor of psychiatry and epidemiology and public health Robert Rosenheck and his colleagues shows vets from previous wars to be disproportionately more likely than nonveterans to be homeless, unemployed, substance abusers, and incarcerated (including for crimes of violence).[39] Homeless women are far more likely than women who are not homeless to be veterans, and they are far more likely than homeless male veterans to be single parents and more likely to fall through the cracks of those providing services.[40] The National Coalition for Homeless Veterans notes that what leads veterans to homelessness, in addition to the complex set of factors that can lead to homelessness for anyone, such as an "extreme shortage of affordable housing, livable income and access to health care," are often the effects of trauma and substance abuse, "compounded by a lack of family and social networks."[41] As the nation's economy fell apart while the wars in Iraq and Afghanistan continued, the *New York Times* carried the report that the "newest veterans are hit hard by economic crises, especially foreclosures."[42] Related to this was an NPR report about the many women and men who joined the military as a path out of poverty but returned to poor neighborhoods as veterans reeling from the emotional trauma from war and ended up homeless.[43]

In the past few years, a spate of media stories has reflected society's growing awareness that there is a problem, that vets are plagued by heavy emotional burdens. However, these stories, with their emphasis on diagnosing vets as mentally ill, especially using the PTSD label, lead us to pathologize the emotional consequences of war and show that there is still virtually no understanding of what the problem really is.

Unfortunately, most Americans, including those in the military and the VA, believe that all the vets need, once diagnosed, is to be sent behind therapists' closed doors, to be cured through psychotropic drugs or psychotherapy or both. But that did not work for vets of earlier wars, and it will not work this time. This is well known by many therapists but rarely discussed. Like most people, many therapists prefer to focus on the times their work is effective rather than on their failures. But the above statistics cry out that the problems of vets have yet to be solved by therapists or anyone else, and this is true for many, regardless of the severity of their suffering and degree of their disorientation. It is not possible to know how many may have been helped by the traditional methods, partly because there is no reliable tracking of vets who get help outside the military and VA systems and partly because tracking of vets within those systems is seriously flawed. The point is not that traditional methods have never helped anyone but that we know for certain that enormous numbers of vets continue to suffer despite the use of traditional therapies and of psychiatric drugs.

The current, misguided efforts of the military and the VA are simply part of our overall society's wrongheaded attitude toward and beliefs about trauma, emotions, mental health, mental illness, and the search for ways to help suffering people feel better. We live in a technologically oriented society in which we are urged to treat every feeling other than happiness as mental illness so that there can supposedly be a quick fix, usually with medication. Americans as a whole society—including therapists—long to believe the myth that therapists can mop up the emotional carnage wrought by war, and all will be well. But all will not be well unless we therapists acknowledge our limits and unless all Americans know there are many, often more effective things that ordinary citizens can do to help heal our returning veterans. This can be difficult: People who become therapists often do so because they want to help, but the mission of helping to alleviate human suffering can be daunting; it is perhaps understandable that many therapists therefore stick to the safety of the techniques they learned in their training or approaches with which they are most comfortable, finding it hard to think outside the box even when what they are doing does not work. The task is made more difficult by what most people who train therapists instruct them about the limits of their mandate and by the trainers' failure to address problems that are primarily caused by major events external to the individual, such as war.

Consider how the labels for the emotional effects of war changed during the twentieth century: in World War I they were called *shell shock*; in World

War II they were called *battle fatigue*; and after the Vietnam War they were called *Posttraumatic Stress Disorder*.[44] Note the vivid presence of war in the first two terms through use of the words *shell* and *battle*. But *Posttraumatic Stress Disorder* masks the presence of war, even more so when we use only the initials, *PTSD*. Certainly, many people know that the trauma referred to in *PTSD* is often from war. But since language helps shape thought, the precise words we use are important. Even in the VA's *Iraq War Clinician Guide*, one finds the suggestion to use the term *war-zone stress reaction*, which "carries more meaning and is less stigmatizing to soldiers"[45] It is poignant that the PTSD term, which was developed with the important and worthy aim of drawing attention to the suffering of Vietnam veterans, now helps to hide the source of so much of the suffering of servicepeople. It points us too much in the direction of thinking of veterans as individuals struggling with individual problems (stress), rather than looking at the ultimate cause of so much torment: war.

What Drives People to Believe That Therapists Can Fix the Emotional Damage Done by War?

Americans cannot bear to look at the consequences of war, especially wars that their own country has initiated and sends its citizens to fight. One devastating consequence of this turning away is that it leads us to isolate, silence, and pathologize the veterans of those wars. It is human to turn away in horror from death and damage, but for all the exhortations one hears in the United States to "support our troops," the country is engaged in a massive—though largely unrecognized—cover-up of the true nature of the damage done by our wars to our troops, a cover-up executed in the ways we decide to label, categorize, and treat the vets.[46] Even the messages from the administration and the military about the deaths of *troops* rather than *people* helps with the masking, making it easier to avoid letting it register fully within us that these are human beings with families and friends in whose lives their deaths leave gaping, gnawing holes. The administration's and the military's frequent assertions that "they did not die in vain," without necessarily making it clear exactly what they did die for, what benefit their deaths brought, can create an emperor's new clothes experience for the families of those who died. Furthermore, if they do not feel pride and elation about the sacrifice of their loved ones but instead explode with grief and rage, then they make us as a country wriggle with discomfort. The cover-up also is likely fed by what Glantz describes as the majority of Americans' belief that the Iraq War was a mistake and their wish to put it behind them, based on "a kind of collective exhaustion."[47]

It seems likely that a similar disaffection and exhaustion will characterize most Americans' feelings about the war in Afghanistan by the time this book is published, if not before. In fact, the major lobbying group for psychologists, the American Psychological Association, actually encourages Americans to look away from war: In describing what it calls the measures needed for the public to "develop resilience during the war in Iraq," the APA explicitly urges Americans to limit their exposure to war-related media coverage.[48]

It helps us ignore the effects of war if we can believe that it's fairly easy to provide the help that suffering veterans need and that therapists can do most of that work. Why do so many of us need to ignore what war does? Two major reasons come to mind, one fairly simple, the other more complex. The simpler one is that much of war is foul. No one *wants* to think about it. Why not reduce the pain in one's own life by looking away from the pain in the lives of others? And why not feel that we are safe because of being different from those Others who are mentally ill?

Related to wanting to protect ourselves from troubling images and information, there is a human need to feel that the world is safe—at least for us. In some ways, the government's reactions to the events of 9/11 and subsequent threats have played on this need: Sometimes it implements showy but often strikingly ineffectual measures, such as some security procedures at airports, reflecting our need, nearly a decade after those attacks, to return to feeling safe. With rare exceptions, Americans have gone along with these procedures, participating in the fiction that passengers' removal of shoes and belts and Transportation Safety Agents' confiscation of carry-on jars of honey and hand cream that violate the three-ounce limit will make us safe. For similar reasons, it is hard to look head-on at the nature and scope of the suffering of the war veterans who live in our midst and to recognize that many are not getting the help they need. If the world is not safe for them, perhaps it is not safe for us either.

Now we consider the more complex set of reasons for nonveterans' looking away. To begin with, no one who has much power is trying very hard to force us to look at the realities of war. In fact, those with the greatest power—the government, the military, politicians, big business, the mental health establishment, the drug companies, and many in the mainstream media—prefer for their own varied reasons that we not look. Many of their resources are arrayed in ways that enable us, pressure us, seduce us into turning away. One of the most heartbreaking techniques used to turn us away from looking at and questioning war is the citation of numbers of soldiers who have already died for the cause and the assertion that we do not want them to have died in vain. As an empathic psychiatrist in Pat Barker's brilliant World War I novel, *Regeneration*, wisely observes, "The casualty lists were too terrible to admit of any public debate on the continuation of the war."[49] Politicians and military leaders have long advocated continuing to prosecute their wars with the twisted logic that because some have died for their causes, still more lives should be sacrificed, even when it is by no means clear that still more deaths will further those causes. Indeed, soldiers themselves are encouraged to advocate the continuation of the wars in which they fight: they are often made to feel disloyal to their fellow soldiers who have died if they question the value or even the likely success of the enterprise. Big business profits from war, as the materials required for battles and troop movements increase demand for goods and services. And whatever traumas or disasters increase human suffering, the mental health establishment and the pharmaceutical companies benefit from persuading us that the suffering is best labeled mental illness and best treated through the methods of therapists' guilds and drug suppliers. It makes sense that government, politicians, and military leaders do little, if anything, to interfere with the labeling of veterans' suffering as mental illnesses requiring primarily psychotherapy and drugs rather than direct consequences of war itself. In-depth investigative journalism is rare; combined with the secrecy of much in the military and with financial reasons for journalists to avoid writing or broadcasting much about war— publishers will tell you that books about current wars do not sell—this leaves many in the media functioning as purveyors of upbeat Department of Defense press releases about the war and the military's and VA's supposedly effective treatment of war trauma.

Most people recognize most of these factors, but many cease to question or challenge them, feeling too small and helpless to effect any change. Most people are probably less aware that therapists' lobby groups and Big Pharma (major drug companies) may not have soldiers' best interests at heart (see chapter 3). Thus, in our society, although we rush to call suffering vets mentally ill, we do not take the obvious next step of saying, "*If* we are going to say all these suffering vets are mentally ill, then that means that war is causing mental illness on a massive scale, so we had better consider the implications of that. Perhaps we need to focus more on ending war, or at the very least changing some of its conditions, such as lengthy and unpredictable deployments." In the meantime, that definitely is *not* happening, so for the most part, each veteran (and, for those who are lucky to have loved ones, this applies to the loved ones as well) is left to feel, "The problem comes from within me. I need to be fixed."

What helps maintain this set of interlocking structures is the inclination (perhaps more heavily promoted in the United States than in many other countries) to believe that our country is morally superior to others and that to raise questions about it is unpatriotic and even, as some politicians claim, un-American and treasonous. As an American who loves much about her country, I was nevertheless delighted to raise my children in Canada, where political tradition dictates that the political parties not constituting the majority have an obligation to function as the loyal opposition, a term that in the United States often seems oxymoronic, because it means that if you are a good citizen and a member of a minority party, it is your duty to raise questions about what the majority wants to do. This attitude may be one reason why, for instance, Canada managed to enshrine in its Charter of Rights and Freedoms a provision declaring that everyone is to have equal rights with everyone else, something that the United States has not yet managed to do. One way that Canada achieved this was through its greater willingness to acknowledge its history of racism and sexism and thus the need for such a provision. In the United States, people are too often treated as unpatriotic or as mindless rebels if they assert that not every war we fight is a "good war" like the one against the Nazis or that we are fighting a war that may be based partly on irrational hatred of foreigners,[50] especially those whose appearance or culture or religion differs from that of the majority of Americans. Furthermore, dominant culture in the United States includes a knee-jerk defense of capitalism and the free market, often whatever the cost; this makes it difficult for those who see a profit motive as part of what drives us into war to speak up. Capitalism is often treated as though it were as sacred as freedom. For these reasons, too, then, it is important for the powers that be to drive the realities of war out of the consciousness of most citizens. Otherwise, our country runs the risk of leaving its xenophobia and the ravage of the excesses of its capitalism naked for the world to see. As Kurt Vonnegut wrote, "The darkest secret of this country, I am afraid, is that too many of its citizens imagine that they belong to a much higher civilization somewhere else."[51]

When we fail to recognize what vets need, we participate in concealing the true consequences of war. The cover-up has been remarkably easy to achieve, because to acknowledge the consequences of American wars is to risk raising questions about whether America is truly the world's greatest nation. How many people, especially starting with the events of 9/11, have feared that simply to name honestly the consequences of our wars is to risk being considered unpatriotic, even dangerous? Think of the furor senior newsman Ted Koppel caused on April 30, 2004, when his *Nightline* on ABC carried the names and photographs of more than seven hundred men and women who had died in the war in Iraq.[52] Sinclair Broadcasting Corporation had ordered its stations not to air the program, and it is telling that they did not issue such an order when *Nightline* on the first anniversary of the 9/11 attacks aired the names and photographs of those victims. What Sinclair did is an example of the greater aversion many people feel to focusing on people who have died through violent acts in wars prosecuted by their own government than on people who have died through other kinds of violent acts. Sinclair president and CEO David Smith had declared that the airing of the list of war dead was an antiwar act, because ABC did not accompany it with a discussion of the "benefits of military action and the events that precipitated that action."[53] In other words, the deaths of American soldiers must be presented in a context that justifies the war in which they died. Otherwise, many people do not want to hear about it, just as they do not want to hear about the problems of war veterans.

It is hard for most people to question what the powerful and interlocking institutions do to mask the effects of war. This is both because secrecy shrouds so much of their functioning that we often lack the information even to know what to ask and because we feel so small in the face of mighty structures, such as the government and the mental health establishment. Furthermore, once we start raising questions about what they do, overwhelming questions come up quickly: Who gets to decide when we go to war, do we want to change that, and how do we make the change happen? Who decides what mental illness is and who has it, and do those who make those decisions do more good than harm? Do we want to change that, and if so, how do we begin?

A further factor greases the path to swerving away from the effects of war. This is the belief that war is part of human nature and thus unavoidable. If we believe this, why not go to war rather than take on the admittedly onerous burdens of trying to find ways to make peace in a world run by those who deal with problems by rushing into battle? UNESCO in 1991 published "The Seville Statement on Violence"[54] with commentary by Dr. David Adams; the statement begins as follows:

The Seville Statement on Violence is a scientific statement which says peace is possible, because war is not a biological necessity. The Statement was written by an international team of specialists in 1986 for the United Nations sponsored

International Year of Peace and its followup. The Statement was based on the latest scientific evidence, and it has been endorsed by scientific and professional organizations around the world.[55]

On February 21, 2010, while I was deeply immersed in writing this book and might have said I now knew quite a bit about the realities of war, I attended an exhibit of Goya's Disasters of War series of aquatint pictures at the Art Gallery of Alberta. Looking at his black-and-white images, I was struck by how many aspects of war I had never thought of. I wondered how much of that was because I am a woman and never played with toy soldiers as a child, never served in the military. But then I remembered that I have never spoken with a veteran who failed to say that the realities of war had stunned him, even those who had had hundreds of toy soldiers or even World War II memorabilia collections. Like Goya's illustrations, the veterans' stories begin to teach us the specifics of war, and through these exposures we experience countless moments of shock at the *inhumanities* of war that stun because they do not match what all but the most violent and sadistic among us have imagined. For us to explore the ultimate question of whether war is inevitable, more an essential part of human nature than seeking peace, one place to begin is not just to learn the names of generals and their battles and strategies but to seek intimate knowledge of everything that is war.

At a somewhat more mundane level, what feeds the separation of veterans from other Americans is the high rate of geographic mobility in the United States, because it has meant a loss of the kind of small-town or neighborhood cohesiveness and of extended families living near each other that were more common decades ago. Thus, as veterans advocate Barry Romo has said, people may be as likely to fear their neighbors as to ask them for help or offer help to them, and that includes vets asking that their stories be heard and nonvets offering to listen.[56] Further, Romo points out that since veterans are expected to return to functioning like their prewar selves, when they try to do so and put up a good front, they *look* just fine and attract no helpful attention; if they do not function well, then family and friends are often quick to say, "Get over it. Put it behind you. Just move on."

Other factors in the realms of individual psychology and social trends impede our vision and comprehension of the emotional consequences of war. These include:

1. a discomfort with intense feelings that is prevalent in much of American culture;

2. a lack of confidence in the ability of ordinary citizens to help people who are in emotional pain; and

3. contemporary American work and family life pressures, such as the dramatic increases in single parenthood, in standards all parents are expected to meet, and in the numbers of hours the average American works,[57] which make the prospect of taking responsibility for listening to veterans' stories feel overwhelming.

The Good News: Starting to Think about How to Help

You have opened this book, so you care about the veterans from the wars in Iraq and Afghanistan and other wars and are willing to think about what they need. What I have to say about America's war veterans strikes me as simple, even obvious, and rather middle-of-the-road, but I know from long experience that many will call it wrong, insensitive, even heretical. I ask you, as you read, to keep firmly in mind that this book comes from deep concern about the ways veterans are suffering and is an attempt to break the bonds of conventional thinking by mental health professionals and the public in order to look at what will help alleviate that misery. In a nutshell, this book is not only about the good news of how every one of us can help the vets but also about what makes it hard to see what they really need.

What makes it even harder, for those who have not gone to war, to recognize veterans' problems is that in significant ways, veterans are truly different in important ways and are wrongly assumed to be different in other, important ways from people who have not been to war. Very briefly, the actual differences include the obvious ones, such as that, unlike most other people, veterans have been exposed to mortal danger and have lived for years in highly regimented environments with extremely hierarchically based functions and standards of conduct focused primarily on building team-based forces whose purposes are to defeat, capture, and kill. Actual differences also include abrupt (and, for many, unpredicted and undesired) departure from a job (even, for some, a career), family, friends, and surroundings that, whatever their drawbacks might be, are at least familiar. Soldiers' departures from home and their returns are often fraught with difficulties, including those of:

• switching first to and then away from a mindset focused on violence, in which violence is considered to be necessary and even good, whereas tenderness and compassion, even the capacity to see shades of gray, are considered signs of weakness and even of danger;

• first entering and later breaking out of the hierarchical systems and authoritarian approaches of the military;
• focusing intensely on avoiding mortal danger and later trying to focus on something other than avoiding mortal danger;
• learning to think constantly from within a dichotomized framework of winning/losing and friend/foe and later needing to switch out of that framework; and
• leaving important people and jobs and the fears and risks associated with these separations and the possibility of losing them altogether, and later the difficulties of trying to reconnect with those people, reenter one's original community, and get one's job back or find a new one.

What nonveterans share with veterans is everything involved in our fundamental, common humanity, including an understanding of the importance of connection, empathy, support, mutual education, and making a better world.

There is so much that ordinary citizens can do to help. No special training or expertise is needed. It is ironic that in our highly psychiatrized society, the pervasive belief is that all negative feelings and behavior stem from brain or chemical problems and require professional treatment. Researchers have shown over and over again that what helps not only vets but most people experiencing emotional pain has been remarkably and beautifully ordinary: a listening ear from a person who can show respect, concern, understanding, and patience, as well as the community's offering of acceptance, support, and reintegration.[58] Furthermore, when laypeople provide this, whether to vets or to others in pain, those who are suffering are often spared the additional heavy burden of being classified as mentally ill. And, as with veterans from previous wars, many of their problems, such as unemployment and homelessness, simply are not the sorts of problems that can be fully addressed by drugs, good therapy, or even a listening ear and community acceptance, although the latter two are necessary. For these kinds of needs, diagnosing vets as mentally ill can take the focus off the practical needs that anyone can have and that make employers, rental property owners, and loan officers likely to shy away from them.

We can feel encouraged and energized to know there are steps that every citizen can take to get us out of the powerless funk into which so many have sunk as a result of the miasma of these bewildering wars. This is the case no matter what one's position about the wars might be. It is good to know that all of us can provide at least some effective caring and assistance, that we need no special training or expertise but only the most touching elements of humanity, which have too often been lost in our technologically oriented society. And until we reach out to help, the suffering of the vets is the elephant in our living room, casting a huge and haunting shadow as we try to go about our busy lives as though the elephant were not there.

Precisely because our society is so psychiatrized, many laypeople mistakenly believe there is little they can do to help, because they wrongly assume that specialized training and high-level knowledge are required. But often that is not the case. In fact, the more we confine the emotional effects of war to the province of professionals, the more unjustifiably mystified the enterprise of helping veterans becomes, simply because there are fewer stories to share about someone's friend or family member having been helpful. The focus on individual therapy also cultivates a culture of silence and mystery that furthers the alienation and disempowerment of everyone. It may also tend to promote certain kinds of privileged relationships that can get in the way of reconnection with and reintegration into a community. And it promotes blindness to the limitations of therapists' expertise and power to bring about change. Of course, there are times when some special information or powers (such as the authority to physically confine people who are clearly dangerous to themselves or others) may be important, but this book is not about those times. In fact, a cardinal rule of a preventive approach is that early intervention, support, and understanding can keep problems from escalating to the point at which physical and legal restraints must be called into play. This book is about nothing less than transforming the cultural landscape in ways that are likely to reduce veterans' suffering and thus the frequency with which extreme measures may be needed.

It is helpful to start by assuming that we can find ways to understand what veterans experience, that a great deal of that understanding requires no special training or powers. For instance, any college student returning from a junior year in another country can explain that being suddenly immersed in a culture and community with very different rules, standards, and practices than one's own, followed by rapid reimmersion in one's original culture and community, can make one feel isolated, alienated, disoriented, and profoundly confused.[59] A brilliant, resourceful college senior who had always been able to go with the flow, adapt to changes in her environment, and who had easily made the transition from high school to a high-powered university told me that when she returned from her junior year in South America, she experienced emotional vertigo from the changes in culture: She was profoundly disoriented, thrown by the pressures on her to act and feel as she had before she left, despite having adapted well to the increased freedom and cultural variety she found in her travels and wanting to hold on to what she had gained. So shaken was she that she began to question who she really was—the person she had felt like before going away or the changed person into whom she had grown while away—and this led her to question her abilities every time she had to complete even the slightest task. As a result, she became despondent and extremely anxious and came close to dropping out of school. Of course, vastly more disorienting, terrifying, and mortally dangerous than a junior year abroad or most civilian life in the United States are the communities and cultures of the military, contemporary Iraq and Afghanistan, and war itself. Let us consider the added effect of the horrors of war on veterans' tasks of the immersion in those different communities—the military community itself and, to a greater or lesser degree for different soldiers, the local community in Iraq or Afghanistan—but for many, an environment of danger, unpredictability, and violence. Add to this the burdens of rapid reimmersion in their home communities, and the combination is clearly more than enough to make returning soldiers feel isolated, disoriented, and profoundly confused. It should come as no surprise that vets feel alone, bewildered, and despondent, but it takes no expertise for anyone to hear a vet describe these differences between home and war and the suddenness of their uprooting and return home and to understand these feelings. A woman like the college student described above—and in fact, anyone who has ever started a new job or moved to a very different place—will have some idea of at least part of what the vets are going through, and this can be one example of a base from which connection and help can begin.

I want to emphasize here that it would be a mistake to conclude from anything I say in this book that I am opposed to psychotherapy, that I think it never does anyone any good, or that I am opposed across the board to psychiatric medication, for veterans or anyone else. In a quarter century of writing about mental health and emotional problems, I have always taken a middle-ground position—that all people who suffer have the right to all available information about the possible causes of their suffering, the entire array of potentially helpful approaches, and the pros and cons of each. People who are totally opposed to traditional mental health approaches have often mistakenly assumed that I support traditional approaches across the board, and some in the mental health establishment have mistakenly said that I oppose across the board everything they do.

No matter how many times or how forcefully I explain that neither is the case, that my concern is with full disclosure to everyone so that the individual can make *informed* decisions by learning to *think critically* rather than accepting claims from those who hold either extreme position, my own position is assailed from both sides.[60] I say this here in the fervent hope that readers of this book will understand its most fundamental underpinnings.

A crucial caveat: Nothing that I have said means that no veterans had serious problems before they joined the military. Nor do I mean to say that war trauma cannot precipitate something beyond what could be called a normal, understandable response to the horrors of war. But we need to think long and hard about where to draw the line between a normal, understandable response to war and one that is otherwise. Since war itself is made up of extreme events, how shall we choose which responses to those extremes should be categorized as mental disorders? It is an exceedingly difficult task, and I can offer no easy way to achieve it. In chapter 3 we will see that therapists themselves disagree about how to define the overarching category "mental illness"; it is no simple matter for anyone to decide who is mentally ill. Even if we draw the line at some point between what we do and do not want to label mental illness, there remain serious questions about how to provide help, and ultimately, whether or not a person is called mentally ill. The label has little benefit but can lead to considerable harm.[61] We cannot say that if a therapist is helpful, then the patient must by definition have been mentally ill. To acknowledge that therapy itself sometimes helps is light years away from mistakenly labeling as mental illness the effects of war that should *not* be said to constitute mental illness. And the common response of "If they were at war and are now upset, they have a mental disorder" means we mislabel hordes of vets as mentally ill, leading us far from the best path to helping them heal.

War is hell, no argument there. But are the ways that war's horrors affect those exposed to them mental illnesses? What does it mean if the answer is yes, and what does it mean if the answer is no? What is gained, and what is lost by these different answers? And how do the different answers help or hurt those who are suffering, their families and friends, and indeed society as a whole, America, and the world?

The next chapter is a description of some of the major forms veterans' suffering takes. Chapter 3 is about the psychiatrizing of society and the wizard behind the curtain, revealing the profound flaws in the mental health system that limit our ability to help veterans within that system and make it hard for us to see what will help outside that system. Chapters 4 and 5 are about the military's efforts to help current soldiers and the VA's efforts to help veterans, as well as which initiatives are helpful and which are inadequate, terribly misguided, or harmful. Chapter 6 is a description of what every citizen can do to help, and Chapter 7 affords a brief look at the dangers that await us as individuals and as a nation if we fail to ask new and difficult questions about how to help veterans deal with the emotional consequences of war, as well as the important, potential gains we forgo if we fail to listen to what veterans have to tell us.

2 Being a Veteran

To see what is in front of one's nose needs a constant struggle.
—George Orwell, *In Front of Your Nose*[1]

What you write is never, never good enough. You do your best, but it is always more than you can say. You do your best, but it is incommunicable.
—Martha Gellhorn, World War II journalist[2]

Homelessness, suicides, rages, substance addictions, serious family problems—what is happening to the vets from Iraq and Afghanistan parallels what has happened to vets from previous wars, perhaps most especially Vietnam, in stark and frightening ways. There are lessons we ought to have learned from the vets of earlier wars that could help us help the vets of both past and current ones. I am alarmed by the rush in the United States and other countries to call the effects of war trauma "mental illnesses," because no matter how you want to define mental illness, for many veterans these effects should by no stretch of the imagination be classified that way. That is the main subject of this chapter. Furthermore, it's a common but mistaken belief that only a psychiatrist or psychologist knows how to help someone labeled mentally ill and that the best help consists of psychiatric drugs, psychotherapy, or both. But that approach has been tried with veterans from earlier wars, and as the statistics in chapter 1 reveal, it has miserably failed vast numbers of people who suffer from having been at war. To try to understand what besides mental illness could be plaguing veterans, we need to consider some of the most common and significant problems they report, as we do in most of this chapter. Let us see this chapter as only a beginning, as we stop averting our eyes from war. Many veterans will say they had important, positive experiences in the military, but the focus is on the negative in this chapter because this book is about trying to help veterans who are having a difficult time. Although most of this chapter is about vets who have been in combat, much of the material applies to anyone who has been through military service, even those who did not see combat.

The psychiatrizing of society, which is what I call the casting of all negative emotions and difficult behavior as mental illnesses, has made it hard for the American public to see the nature and scope of veterans' problems and the full array of possible solutions to those problems. It has also masked the experiences of vets who were not helped or were even seriously harmed by well-meaning therapists, friends, and relatives. Veterans who talk with me uniformly tell me that even those family members and friends who will listen to them for a few minutes are quick to say, on realizing they are upset, "You need to see a psychiatrist. I am not trained to deal with a mental illness." Friends and family are not to blame for fearing they are inadequate to the task of providing help the veterans need, but those fears are often unwarranted and are serious barriers to the vets' emergence from their nightmares. Furthermore, through being psychiatrized, vets today are often made to feel even worse than before—both "crazy" and more isolated—so that they become even more anguished and more paralyzed emotionally than before they went into treatment. Later on, we will address the fundamental ethical problem of allowing psychiatrists and psychologists to pathologize healthy, normal responses to the horrors of war, and we will consider the consequences that classifying those reactions as mental illnesses have for the vets and for us as a nation.

Concerns Were Raised

In the spring of 2003, at a conference of the Association for Women in Psychology (AWP), AWP Collective Coordinator Maureen McHugh remarked that we knew that President Bush was about to take the country to war in Iraq. She asked AWP members if there was anything we could do. I was at the conference and was the AWP Spokesperson at the time. Having come of age during the Vietnam War and having known people who suffered the rest of their lives because of what they went through in Vietnam, I pictured waves of new vets coming back from what was already the U.S. war in Afghanistan and the war about to start in Iraq. Suddenly, it struck me: When the new vets came home, many devastated by their war experiences, what would most Americans think? "Oh, yes, we know what that is: It's Posttraumatic Stress Disorder. PTSD. We heard about that after Vietnam." And what would most think should be done? "Send them to therapists, because therapists know how to fix people with PTSD. And they'll probably need to give them psychiatric drugs, too." I could only think how many vets from Vietnam, the Gulf War, and other wars had not been helped by that approach.

As AWP Spokesperson, I wrote a white paper about this misguided approach and what might replace it, then issued a press release on behalf of AWP. Next, based on the white paper, I wrote an opinion piece that was published in the *Washington Post* to intensely positive and appreciative responses from veterans of past and current wars. These vets indicated that I had said what they wanted people to know. My article had two main messages: (1) many veterans' feelings needed to be depathologized, because they are not mental illnesses, and (2) every American should take some responsibility for telling the vets that we want to hear what they saw and heard during their time in the military, we do not think they are crazy, and we want to help them rejoin their old communities or find new ones and help ensure that they have jobs, housing, food, and training or education.

The psychiatric diagnosing of so many troubled veterans is based partly on the bizarre expectation for veterans to come back from war exactly as they were before they went away. Clearly, this is impossible. But since they don't come back the same as before, we rush to conclude that they are mentally ill. Furthermore, to declare that what's really wrong with veterans and their loved ones who suffer from the hell of war is that they are mentally ill takes the discussion away from the realities of war; this, in turn, makes people less likely to challenge the government's war policies or question whether the harm they cause is worth the benefit. Thereby, it diverts attention from the principle that everyone has a responsibility to participate in decisions about going to war and to share each other's burdens. It switches our focus away from such matters and to the realm of psychopathology, the place occupied by Others. These Others are assumed to be somehow different from us, their problems to arise from individual, internally caused emotional disorders best dealt with through drugs and the isolation of treatment behind therapists' closed doors.[3] In that way, the rest of us need not confront their pain or its real causes.

What would we think if someone told us, in the abstract, that "Situation X is causing A amount of homelessness, B suicides, C acts of violence against others, D cases of drug and alcohol abuse, and E instances of relationship breakdown"? We would be horrified and want to stop Situation X immediately. But when we see suffering, we are most likely to turn away when we feel helpless to end it. It appears that few people feel they can do much to end the current wars, despite the apparent connection between protest marches and the cessation of the Vietnam War and despite the wise reminder attributed to Margaret Mead, "Never doubt that a small group of thoughtful, committed citizens can change the world. Indeed, it is the only thing that ever has."[4] To acknowledge what war has done to many veterans would make us feel hopelessly helpless, because we feel we cannot stop war. What many do instead is to attribute veterans' suffering to individual, more personal causes we call mental illnesses, which laypeople assume they are unqualified to deal with and therefore need not think about.

Despite—and in some ways because of—these barriers to discussing vets' troubles, the fundamental aim of this book is to draw attention to those troubles. Perhaps being aware of the barriers will make it a little easier, or make it clear that there is a pressing need, to look at the problems of former servicemembers. Therefore, we look now at some of what makes both war and homecoming so hard for vets. To do full justice to this subject would require many volumes rather than a single book, so in the rest of this chapter I attempt only to describe briefly some of the sources of suffering that vets have most commonly described.

What Makes War and Homecoming So Hard for Veterans?

There are so many of the living who have burned into their brains forever the unnatural sight of cold dead men scattered over the hillsides and in the ditches along the high rows of hedge throughout the world. . . . Dead men in such monstrous infinity that you come almost to hate them. Those are the things that you at home need not even try to understand. To you at home they are columns of figures, or he is a near one who went away and just didn't come back. You didn't see him lying so grotesque and pasty beside the gravel road in France. We saw him. Saw him by the multiple thousands. That's the difference.

—Ernie Pyle, writing about World War II[5]

On some nights the air becomes sick and there is an unspoken contagion of spiritual dread, and you are little boys again, lost in the dark.

—Ernie Pyle[6]

Whether or not we have ever listened to a vet describe what it was like to be at war, we've all seen war movies or clips on TV, so we may think we know. But if we have not been there ourselves, it's a good bet that at some point while watching a video of the wreckage from an improvised explosive device (IED) or suicide bomber, we go numb, tune out, stop watching.

Vets can try to go numb, and some do, but as soldiers they were not free to escape the scene.

Setting the Scene: Learning—and Trying to Unlearn—Hypervigilance and Violence

In principle, we all know that war involves violence, and most people have heard about basic training, weapons practice, and military strategies, but few civilians have much specific or deep understanding of their components and the emotional impact they have on soldiers. How could we? Much of this we would never imagine. The authors of a scholarly journal article describe "the military's requirements to follow rigid orders and procedures for hypervigilance that it ingrains and relies upon for survival of its troops," and note that soldiers "are rewarded in many combat situations" for following them.[7] They are often punished for any failure to follow them as well. The drilling that shapes soldiers to fight and kill is tightly focused on preparation for a constant state of high alert and hair-trigger responses.

Basic training involves not only hard-driving physical exercise but also, as virtually every vet brings up in interviews, the order to take a gun outfitted with a bayonet and run around a field, jabbing the bayonet and screaming, "Kill! Kill! Kill!" Hundreds of thousands of moments and tasks are aimed to train soldiers to commit acts of violence as well as of self-protection and to do so as split-second, automatized responses. Describing his training in the Marines, Nathaniel Fick gives examples of the training for violence:

When the whole platoon stood at attention by its chairs, Olds would roar, "Ready. Seats! . . . Kill!" we shouted in response. It was an early step toward acclimating us to violence. We had one second to drop into our chairs, or else we'd stand and do it again.[8] [. . .] According to Captain Fanning . . . a good plan violently executed now . . . was better than a great plan later.[9]

[A Dr. DiGiovanni, a psychiatrist, is introduced to speak to the men.] He defined "killology" as the study of healthy people's reactions to killing. Its corollaries are the factors that enable killing and the maintenance of psychiatric health during prolonged exposure to mortal danger. DiGiovanni explained that an infantryman's effectiveness is more fundamental than his ability to shoot a rifle or carry a heavy pack.[10]

In World War II, journalist Ernie Pyle described the change he saw as new recruits became soldiers. He heard the transformation in the casual and workshop manner in which they now talk about killing. They have made the psychological transition from the normal belief that taking human life is sinful, over to a new professional outlook where killing is a craft. To them now there is nothing morally wrong about killing. In fact it is an admirable thing.[11]

Once a soldier's service ends—or even when the soldier is on leave—the task of unlearning hypervigilance and violence is daunting. Many have had little or no guidance in how to do this, and many have tried and failed. Martin A. Sweeney, a behavioral health social worker at a VA hospital and a Vietnam veteran, says that in war, "You have to be very aggressive, very vigilant, and you live that way day in and day out for a year, and when you come back here, you can't just turn that off."[12] When one's own life and the lives of others have depended on giving orders, it can be hard to stop giving them, even when one notices that civilians do not respond well to them and may even react negatively.[13] In her *New York Times Magazine* article, "The Permanent Scars of Iraq," Sara Corbett writes that military combat stress teams are supposed to offer counseling and medication to servicemembers returning home, but

It may be impossible . . . to fully counteract the shock of going from a 24-hour state of generalized fear-apprehension-paranoia, sustained for a year through wartime, to evenings at home on the La-Z-Boy, asked to fulfill the requirements of love and tenderness needed to sustain a family.[14]

And as Bryan Bender wrote in a *Boston Globe* article,

Due to the nature of the conflicts in Iraq and Afghanistan—where an innocent-looking bystander can be a suicide bomber or enemy insurgent—service members must be constantly aware of their environment, scanning their surroundings for the smallest sign of a threat. That vigilance can be hard to turn off at home, sometimes leading to the false impression that a family member or other person wants to cause harm.[15]

Here is a description of three vets who had several days of reorientation at Fort Dix after returning from Iraq: "They have spent the past four months trying to retrofit their old lives and step away from their military personas, though after a year of power, aggression, uncertainty and fear, it is not always easy to fold up these feelings like a set of fatigues and store them neatly on a shelf."[16] Indeed, since the stakes for learning hypervigilance and violence are the highest possible, life and death, and since soldiers learn to wage war through seemingly endless repetition of drills and engagement in actual combat over many months and even years, it is hard to think what stakes and what drills or engagements back home could possibly compete with the former. (This issue is addressed further in chapter 4.)

Attempting the Impossible

The movie *Saving Private Ryan* became famous partly because of the realism of its representation of the D-Day landings—the shock, the blood, the vomit, the pieces of bodies blown apart, the fire, the relentlessness of the attacks, the utter vulnerability of hordes of soldiers who died as they hit the shore. That was all about physical carnage and the terror and helplessness that went with it, and it is important to show that reality. But based on what veterans of that and more recent wars say, one feature that warrants special attention is how often soldiers end up in situations where they have to attempt the impossible or nearly impossible, to make excruciating choices when not one is a good one, to endure more than humans are meant to bear. And virtually always, there is the mind-numbing juxtaposition of intensive pressures to kill some people with desperate attempts to save the lives of others. First Lieutenant Dean Allen wrote to his wife from Vietnam:

Why I have to watch a man die or get wounded—why I have to be the one to tell some one to do something that may get him blown away—have I done everything I can do to make sure we can't get hit by surprise—are we really covered from all directions—how many men should I let sleep at a time, ¼. 50% or what.[17]

Daniel, a Vietnam vet, said that in order to survive his time in combat as an infantry sergeant, he had to "become a machine," program himself to do the strategizing and decision making and barking of orders for which the stakes were—relentlessly—nothing less than the lives of his men and others. On one occasion, his platoon was surrounded by the enemy, and he knew that either some or all of his men would be killed. He was supposed to call in the artillery to help, and to do that, he had to give them the coordinates to inform them of the infantry's location and say where he wanted the artillery to fire. The artillery was not supposed to fire at its own infantry, but this sergeant knew that if it did not fire at some of his men where enemy soldiers were also located, then all his men would die. He had to make the horrific, split-second choices and then at the speed of light do the mathematical calculations to lie about his location so the artillery might, by killing some of his infantry soldiers, save some others. As he told me the story forty years after it happened, he seemed to go into a flashback, *reexperiencing* this moment of soul-destroying choice rather than remembering it as from a distance, and his face and voice were transformed from their usual states to reflect the torment he must have felt in the jungles of Vietnam that day. He went back to those moments of having to make unbearable choices between different kinds of losses, each unthinkable, with too many dangers flying at him at once and too many calculations to make on the instant. Still worse, the men in his platoon, at least some of whom would die because of the orders he would give, were not anonymous soldiers but friends he held close to his heart. I call this *Daniel's Choice*. He made a desperate attempt to save some lives at the same time he was unavoidably sacrificing the lives of some of his men and killing some enemy soldiers—risking life, saving life, ending life, all in an instant. It was about love and about death. He had to learn about too many kinds of wounds all at once. Then and at many other times, he confronted unspeakable moral dilemmas, trapped in unthinkable situations in which far more was at risk than should ever be at risk.

Those sent to fight our country's current wars have done and are doing so under some conditions that are even more intense than most of those from previous wars. These have included late cancelations of promised ends of duty and longer and more repeated deployments, as well as the spending of the deployment time in essentially constant combat operations.[18] As Scott Shane has written, what had been planned as a short and clear-cut intervention in Iraq became a lengthy, confusing insurgency,[19] with its ultimate goals unclear. The same thing is now happening in Afghanistan. As General Stanley McChrystal said when he was directing the war in Afghanistan, "You can kill Taliban forever . . . because they are not a finite number,"[20] and journalist James Dao reports that of the 30,000 soldiers constituting the "surge" President Obama ordered for Afghanistan, some were on their fifth combat tour in nine years.[21] Related to this is the devastation many vets have described to me when they have found, in the words of one, that "I wanted to save the world, but it's not happening."

Other factors making current wars still more terrible include that soldiers are regularly sent back into combat even if they have been severely traumatized emotionally and that the vast majority of seriously wounded servicemembers now survive injuries that would have been fatal in previous wars, including frequent amputations of not only limbs but also genitals.[22] Furthermore, since early in the Iraq War, there have been frequent reports of soldiers being sent into combat without proper equipment or protection and without adequate rest.[23] And owing to low recruiting numbers, people who are troubled or who have been in trouble with the law are able to enlist in greater numbers than before. I have heard firsthand stories of judges who have given some men they have convicted of crimes the choice of going to jail or joining the military.[24] These are only some of the features that characterize current wars and make everything more difficult. In addition, there are the physical conditions under which the wars are fought. What does it do to one to try to function in unbearable heat and humidity, as in Vietnam's rainy season, or in unbearable heat and with fierce sandstorms hitting one's eyes and lungs, as in the desert wars? Soldiers in Afghanistan "carry heavy gear and weapons over rocky ledges in scorching heat, stopping only to rehydrate, sometimes with the help of intravenous drips."[25]

The Eight Plagues of Combat

Putting together what vets from various wars have told me with what they have written or spoken about publicly, at least eight sets of feelings and experiences are common consequences of fighting in a war:

- trauma
- grief and sadness
- fear and anxiety
- guilt and shame
- rage
- conflicts of values and crises of meaning
- betrayal and mistrust
- isolation, alienation, and numbing

These are often present in various combinations. As we consider each one, it is helpful to keep in mind the questions, "Does this seem to be a mental illness? If so, why? And what is gained and lost by calling or not calling it a mental illness?" I will come back to these questions later in the chapter, but it is good to carry them along with us. Surely few or none of the effects described below will come as surprises to the reader, but what matters is to have a sense that many veterans deal with many or all of these (and more) all the time. And remember that I do not pretend that what follows is a comprehensive list of all of the causes of anguish vets may feel.

An important part of the context for considering these eight kinds of feelings and dilemmas is the young age at which many people enter the military. Novelist Kurt Vonnegut in his book *Bluebeard* has a character say that "Because of the movies . . . nobody will believe that it was babies who fought the war."[26] Indeed, many people enter the service soon after their prom, not long after discovering the glories of lovemaking, when many people their age have a strong if misplaced belief in their own invulnerability and power and are confronting nothing more dangerous or abhorrent than starting their first jobs, driving across the country, or attending karaoke nights in bars. Although some enlist in the military because they feel that they saw their parent or older sibling "grow as people" from their military experiences or because they see it as a way to serve or protect their country, many are stunned by the specifics of what that turns out to entail.[27] War often shocks them out of their innocence—about the safety of the world, about what human beings are capable of doing, about what they themselves can and cannot do—in ways that can provoke feelings of grief, betrayal, and rage. I am about to describe briefly a variety of experiences of these shocking realizations, and although it may seem that these are unusually horrific assaults on the reader's sensibilities, virtually every veteran tells at least one such story of her or his own:

• A *New York Times Magazine* reporter in 2006 quoted one soldier who said he "never knew bodies could burn on their own like that. . . . It must be from the fat and the oils," and another who warned that if you need to tow a vehicle, "you'd better be prepared to reach through a man's intestines to put it in neutral."[28]

• One Iraq vet I interviewed told me that his unit ran out of the standard opaque body bags, and he and others had to pick up pieces of dead American soldiers and put them into see-through body bags instead. He said,

This one kid was 18 years old [and] was standing on top of [an IED] when it went off. Only thing left was parts of his torso and parts of his leg. And we had to put him in the bag. They make you pick up your own guys.

• Feeling guilty and empathic about the adversary he had killed, Navy hospital corpsman Chanan Suarez-Diaz said, "I don't know how it is to be occupied and have your country devastated by another country."[29]

• In a 2006 *USA Today* article Corporal Seth Judy, age twenty-five, is quoted as saying, "I don't have a free spirit the way I used to" after being in a Marine unit that lost many members in Iraq.[30]

• Many servicemembers as young as eighteen years of age realize they need to write "death letters," messages to be given if they die to their loved ones —something most people that age never feel any urgency to do.

• War reporter Dexter Filkins describes a soldier surveying the dead bodies of Iraqi soldiers killed by Americans and saying that during training, soldiers can't wait for this kind of scene, but once they do see it, they hope never to see it again.[31]

• A close friend of mine asked her neighbor how his flight home for a brief period of R&R between his stints in Iraq and Afghanistan had gone. He replied that before boarding the plane, he had carried into it the coffins of his friends who had died there. These dead friends made up one-third of his unit. The coffins were extremely light, because there were no bodies, not even body parts inside. These people he loved had been blown to dust, and all the coffins held were dogtags.

• A former Army psychologist treated a man whose job in Iraq was to "recover the bodies of soldiers," and the patient was devastated by having had to pick up "this corpse that was so badly burned, it weighed about 20 pounds. . . . For him, it was like picking up his daughter." The psychologist called that "an extreme case," but his next sentence was, "But you get those at least once or twice a week."[32]

There is rarely much preparation for these kinds of shocks. No soldiers I have ever talked with said they joined because they wanted to kill people, not even those who said they wanted to protect Americans they saw being slaughtered on TV, who said they wanted to protect freedom or defeat the enemy. Somehow, they did not make the leap—how could they, before going through it?—to the understanding that "I may see those friends I am going over there to protect blown apart" or "Some of the enemy I aim to kill may strike me as human or innocent" or "I may catch sight of a child whose eyes watched the slaughter I helped commit, and that will haunt me the rest of my days." Servicemembers carry out life-and-death jobs, but there is almost no possibility that, even under optimal conditions—that is, with no one attempting to gloss over or cover up their reality—one can ensure that a person enlisting in the military is giving informed consent, is fully aware to what they are agreeing. Every veteran I have spoken with from any war felt that, no matter how well-prepared and highly-motivated they felt they were for war, they were stunned by what it was really like.

When I asked what the military does to prepare new recruits for the worst of war, servicemember Michelle Dillow gave an answer that was typical of those I interviewed. She said that in the Army, they were told only that if you felt depressed, you should speak to your chaplain, treating upset feelings caused by war as though they were problems coming from within the individual. (In chapter 4 we will see that the military very recently began to take some steps beyond such simple advice, but it is extremely hard to find ways while people are in combat zones to treat the horror and terror they feel as legitimate while keeping them in the jobs they are there to do.) Of all the stories I heard when I asked whether the military provided any warning of what was to come, one of the most negative forms of "preparation" for new recruits came from a soldier from the West Coast, who in response to my question, "Did they prepare you for the kinds of loss and tragedy you were likely to experience?," said:

In basic training we had a drill instructor, part of the Army basketball team, big, tall guy, basically say, "Fuck you, you stupid faggots. . . . You motherfuckers better get your heads on straight, because you're all gonna go to Iraq and get blown up, and you're all gonna die."

It is simply human to bemoan one's loss of innocence, but to do so does not fit with the military's expectations for servicemembers to be emotionally tough and resilient. It can feel unjustified, too, to be upset about losing one's innocence when one has watched others lose their lives. But certainly it seems impossible to avoid losing that innocence in light of what war is: By one report of Marines from combat units that were involved in the early stages of the war in Iraq, nine out of ten had been attacked or ambushed and had been fired upon; more than half had killed an enemy fighter; 86 percent knew someone who had been killed or seriously injured; almost all had seen death; half had handled the dead; most had seen ill or injured women or children they could not help; and 28 percent had killed a civilian.[33] Although the percentages would vary according to type and location of service, these are the kinds of exposures that war brings. Similarly, an Army survey showed that "the most common combat stressors were seeing dead human bodies, being attacked or ambushed, and knowing someone who was seriously injured or killed. The most common operational stressors were uncertain redeployment date, long deployments, being separated from family, and lack of privacy."[34]

Later in the book, when we talk about listening to vets, it will be important to keep in mind that for many, the loss of innocence at war was so painful that they fear robbing civilians of *their* innocence by telling stories of war. But in light of what soldiers go through, it is deeply troubling that no less a personage than Dr. Joyce Brothers advises people that when soldiers come home, they should expect a period of up to eight weeks "to get back to something that approaches normal, both physically and mentally."[35] This kind of counsel can only make both soldiers and their loved ones feel that something is terribly wrong if the former still feel devastated a mere eight weeks after handling the fragments of their dead friends' bodies.

Trauma

Dictionary definitions of trauma are focused on the shock and violence of a physical or psychological injury. The poet and nonfiction writer Annie

Rogers has fixed on its "unbearable" nature, on its being "utterly beyond our capacity to cope."[36] Rogers writes that trauma exerts "a demand on us, which by its nature is an excess of what we can manage or bear."[37] What is unbearable to one person may be bearable to another, and the reasons it is unbearable to two different people will depend partly on their histories, partly on how they have tended to cope with difficulty, partly on the nature of the shock and violence, partly on the expectations and resources of the people and environment where the trauma happens, and partly on the expectations and resources of the people and environment where the traumatized person later goes. In war, one of the many reasons for the inability to cope is the need to concentrate on protecting oneself and others from danger. To do that, one has to focus on the moment-to-moment tasks that help toward that goal: ducking, checking, digging, covering, looking, and listening with utter vigilance. This can mean needing to shut off any emotion, even shut out any perception (a snapshot-type view of another soldier's exploded body) that would switch one's focus away from protection and self-preservation. At those times, coping with the emotional or even physical effects of the violence becomes impossible. But there are other reasons for being unable to cope with what happens in war. These reasons include but are not limited to witnessing destruction and death scenes that are so horrific they would be overwhelming any time, anywhere; suspecting or believing that the government or military in whom you had complete confidence has made major mistakes, whether in starting the war or in the way it prosecutes it[38]; suspecting or learning that your government or someone in the military has lied to you in a way that challenges the beliefs that led you to join up[39]; witnessing or hearing about injury and death from "friendly fire"[40]; and learning that the government or military took steps that definitely or probably put the troops at unnecessary risk.[41] Dave Jones remembers watching the slaughter in Vietnam on television before he was a soldier, seeing "the young soldier's wounds . . . and the heartbreak of parents and family receiving the news of another loved one lost," but says, "None of this really sank in because I was just a spectator." Even when he gave up his student deferment from the draft, he "didn't realize what war was and its lasting impact."[42]

Rogers describes trauma as "unsayable," as too unbearable even to represent. My father described the shock and sadness of seeing during World War II the body of a GI face down, his back exploded. And realizing—as many Vietnam and current war vets describe—that you have killed an innocent, very old person you thought was an enemy can feel beyond human experience, can make you feel less than human. We are not used either to seeing such sights or to committing such acts. Especially when we are powerless to undo the damage, we may feel such horror at witnessing the effects of someone else's power when we see a dead comrade or of our own power when we have killed someone who caused us no harm, that we may have no way to think or speak about it. Even for those of us who have not been to war, it is not hard to understand the impossibility of thinking what to say or do next after such a sight or such an act. Even words like "horror" must seem inadequate. These experiences are often assaults on all of the person's senses at once—the sound of explosions and gunfire, the sight of blood and fragments of bone and flesh, the smells of gunpowder and decomposing bodies, the grit of warfare on one's fingers, the taste in the air of the heat of fire. And with all of that come emotions that shake one to the core. In his poem "Should Have," Dave Jones describes how utterly unprepared he was for what he saw:

I should have known the day I left,
   too young to understand.

That I'd return forever changed,
   full of guilt this man.

I'd seen too much and felt the pain,
   of a thousand screaming tears. . . .[43]

The shock of trauma tends to lead to emotional and mental fragmentation, because the traumatizing event is too much to handle. As a result, the person struggles to deal with one bit at a time on vastly different levels ranging from "Last time I looked at that locker, my buddy was alive" to "Does life have any meaning when it can vanish in an instant?" Further, the fragmentation comes in part from vivid flashbacks. During a flashback, one does not feel as though one is remembering something terrible; there is no observer saying to the person, "This is a memory," but only the experience of its happening all over again, as wrenching as the first time. In a poem that refers to having a flashback, Australian vet Bob Lange describes his meeting in a bar with another vet, who, like himself, had been in Vietnam decades earlier, writing that he told the other man where he had been in country and when. Then,

"When were you there?" I asked him next, as he
   bought us both a beer.
  He didn't give an answer, and I wondered did he
   hear.

I turned my head to face him, and I said, "Are you
   alright?"
He slowly shook his head and said, "Mate—
   I was there last bloody night."[44]

The flashbacks and other consequences of trauma that lead to fragmentation interfere with the vet's ability to cope because they disorient the
sufferer, making it hard to keep a complete and coherent story of events
in mind, to understand the emotions connected with events while avoiding feeling pulled into their undertow, and to create and hold to new ways
of handling traumatic memories when they reappear.

Another facet of a great deal of war trauma is the helplessness and
powerlessness servicepeople have to find ways to live through. Former war
correspondent Chris Hedges has written, "It is impossible to know war if
you do not stand with the mass of the powerless caught in its maw."[45]
Jeffrey Gettleman eloquently describes how the combination of military
training to be supermen and the actual powerlessness of soldiers in much
of war leads to their unbearable feelings of shame and guilt.[46] And in Pat
Barker's World War I trilogy, she describes a compassionate psychiatrist's
theory that what accounts for "the vast number of breakdowns this war
has produced is not the horrors—war's always produced plenty of those—
but the fact that the strain has to be borne in conditions of immobility,
passivity and helplessness."[47]

Consider that when civilians in the United States witness, for instance,
a murder, they are not expected to remain on the spot, helpless and powerless, but are expected to want to flee and then in the future to avoid the
spot where they saw it happen. That is considered healthy behavior. But
soldiers are expected to want to stay in the place where the trauma occurred,
and if they try to stay away, they risk being called cowardly, disloyal to
those with whom they serve, even mentally ill. Based on their direct experiences, vets have told me about some military therapists who consider it
their duty to get traumatized soldiers back into battle as soon as possible.
(More will be said in chapter 4 about the explicit military policies that
mandate this approach.) What is crucial to understand is that, even if one
wishes to remain with close comrades, when that means remaining in
conditions where they feel helpless and powerless and where the stakes are
life and death, those conditions are intolerable for the vast majority of
people, even for short periods of time. Living in a constant state in which
one's fight-or-flight reflexes are activated puts enormous physical and emotional strain on individuals; if they stay in the extreme environment, they

haven't the luxury of coping in ways that go beyond those reflexes, and even if they leave, it can take a long time and a lot of work—with lots of support from others—to go beyond them. Furthermore, once one has in fact been powerless in the presence of danger, one may carry the terror of that feeling for a long time, perhaps forever, and that can lead to intense self-doubt and even shame that get in the way of attempting to better one's world.

Until recent years, a well-hidden but frequent kind of trauma was sexual assault in the military. In 2009 a press release from the Department of Defense referred to sexual assault in the military as "one of the country's most under-reported crimes," and the Defense Department launched a Sexual Assault Awareness Month with a campaign and a Web site aimed at prevention.[48] In spite of these efforts, according to a 2010 report in the *Journal of the American Medical Association*, 23 percent of women using the VA health care system reported having been sexually assaulted in the military, and survivors are frustrated with the processing of their disability claims, especially as they tried to prove that the assaults had occurred.[49] Only about one-tenth of sexual assault charges lead to a court-martial of the perpetrator.[50] Reporting sexual assault is looked down on. And more news came in a *New York Times Magazine* story about many women soldiers being "sent home pregnant," something few people outside the military had heard about before and another source of pain and anguish for some women vets.[51]

Women are more likely to be targets of these assaults than are men, and men are more likely to be perpetrators, but both women and men in the military suffer from sexual assaults. Recent research has revealed that nearly sixty thousand male veterans and slightly fewer female veterans have experienced some sexual trauma during their service. These vets were between two and three times more likely to suffer from serious emotional problems, alcohol abuse, and drug abuse than were other vets.[52] As noted, these effects are likely to lead to their being diagnosed as mentally ill, including with PTSD,[53] rather than recognized as people experiencing understandable human reactions to trauma. Until recently the Pentagon and many politicians claimed these allegations were unfounded or said that the scope of the problem was exaggerated, but under pressure, in 2004 the Department of Defense created a Sexual Assault Prevention Response program that all soldiers are required to take.[54] Even so, an official from the Government Accountability Office (GAO) told lawmakers that "the right questions aren't being asked, and important data are not being collected," so the scope of the problem may actually be greater than formerly believed. For instance, in a GAO survey, 103 servicemembers at fourteen installations had been sexually assaulted in just the past twelve months, but half had not reported the assaults.[55] The reasons they gave for not reporting included the belief that nothing helpful would be done but that their peers would ostracize, harass, or ridicule them; the fear that reporting sexual assault could hurt their careers or the morale in their unit; and the belief that the report would not remain confidential. A 2009 Department of Defense press release included an emphasis on "bystander interventions," calling on people in uniform to prevent their "buddies" from committing such sexual assaults.[56] Although this is a worthy aim, many assaults occur with no witnesses, and sometimes buddies join together to commit them or make them possible.

Like sexual assault by a family member, attacks by members of one's military unit are all the more devastating and confusing because of the intense closeness many people in the military share with each other. That victim and perpetrator live close together while in constant danger of losing their lives can make it especially difficult for the assaulted person to come forward. If it is a superior officer rather than a peer who commits the assault, there is the added, tremendous risk of even worse retribution for speaking about the crime than if the perpetrator is a peer and therefore like "one of the family."[57] The military's emphasis on the sacredness of the team, which in some ways becomes like a family in the degree of sharing and intimacy that characterize it, throws victims into confusion and panic when they are assaulted; if they make a report, they may be seen as betraying the military, as putting their own needs ahead of those of the team, while having to live and work with the perpetrators on whom they depend for safety and for advancement in their work. Twenty-one-year-old Army specialist Suzanne Swift, who had been sexually harassed and abused by three military people, two in Iraq and one on a U.S. base, dealt with her anguish by refusing to report for her second deployment to Iraq and was arrested because of that. Pressures to keep the focus on the work and suppress their own feelings and needs, especially in the dangers of a war zone, often contribute to victims' silence. Furthermore, for both women and men, the shame and fear associated with sexual assault can keep them silent about the sexual abuse, sometimes for decades, to the point that they do not even tell the therapists they have been seeing for years.[58] Of course, if the therapist fails to ask about a history of sexual harassment or assault, or if the therapist asks but the patient denies it because of shame or fear, then to the therapist it could easily seem there is no reason for the patient's serious emotional suffering. This makes it more likely that the therapist will decide that the patient is mentally ill. In fact, the secrecy about sexual assault can compound the problems that the vet might have because of the assault itself.

In addition to sexual assault, many women report being sexually harassed, not, as they say, just "teasing" but in "more vile" forms. This is perhaps unsurprising in a realm that has historically been overwhelmingly male. Valerie Conley, women veterans coordinator for the Oregon Department of Veterans' Affairs, says, "You didn't walk anywhere alone. I got to the point where I wouldn't even walk to the mess hall by myself."[59] And another woman reported that the American soldiers would throw rocks at her breast—and each other's penises—"for fun."[60] Some servicemen actually use sexual harassment and abuse of women as part of acting out the hypermasculine atmosphere the military promotes. But whatever the sources and the intentions of the perpetrators, they traumatize their targets, drain their energy, make them feel unsafe and often ashamed, and generally compromise their capacity to cope with other things. They also make homecoming more difficult, because whether or not the woman victim has a partner, as with any such victimization, the pain of having been physically attacked or emotionally abused and humiliated *because of being a woman* can make it harder for her to relax and relate to someone else emotionally and sexually.[61]

Grief and Sadness

By the time they go to war, many men and women in the military have experienced tremendous losses. Whether or not they joined up with the intention of going to war, the realities of leaving loved ones and one's physical home—whether a farm or apartment building or house, the natural surroundings one is used to seeing, even the corner store or a skateboarding area—understandably lead to sadness for many. For those who have an elderly or sick parent or a child or a pregnant wife, the leave-taking can be especially poignant. For those in the National Guard and Reserves, some of whom never dreamed when they joined that they would end up going to war and who may have difficulty integrating with regular soldiers, the suddenness of being called up can make the losses feel more acute.[62] These people have to leave jobs that they may love or that at least, especially in bad economic times, provide financial security and a work identity that they now lose and cannot be sure they will get back. Furthermore, they are likely to have close family members living far from military bases or resources.[63] And a disproportionately high number of current soldiers and veterans were poor before entering the service.

As noted, a high proportion of military recruits are just ending their teen years, a time when many have an unrealistic but powerful sense of their invulnerability. Being suddenly faced with the reality of going to war—or even boot camp—yanks that rug out from under them, precipitating another loss. The sense of loss can reach the level of grief when what is gone seems permanent, even when it is in a way temporary, such as the unrecoverability of time away from loved ones even if one believes one will return.

Paramount among wartime losses are the deaths of cared-for fellow soldiers. Tom Hanks eloquently portrays the emotions about comrades' deaths in *Saving Private Ryan*, where he sobs over the death of a soldier, his rapidly changing, choppy gestures reflecting the impossibility of finding an adequate way even to *feel* the grief and rage. Other contributors to grief as listed in *The Iraq War Clinician Guide* include:

survivor guilt; feelings of powerlessness in not being able to prevent the death; anger at others who are thought to have caused the death; anger at oneself for committing a self-perceived error resulting in the death; tasks of survival in combat taking precedence over grieving; not being able to show emotional vulnerability; numbing and defending against overwhelming emotions; not having an opportunity in the field to acknowledge the death; and increased sense of vulnerability by seeing someone close killed. Factors important in the Iraq War may include exposure to significant numbers of civilian casualties, exposure to death from friendly fire or accidents resulting from massive and rapid troop movements, and concern about culpability for having caused death or harm to civilians in cities."[64]

Coming home can bring its own kinds of sadness and even grief. A veteran who served early during the war in Afghanistan told me that from the time he landed there, he began counting the months, weeks, days, minutes, and even seconds till he would return home. His images of home during that time had a perfection that was far from the reality of what home had been for him. When he returned to the New England city where he had lived his whole life before shipping out, his loving family's usual jocular rather than openly warm style of interacting caused him immense sadness, to the point that he felt unloved. He repeatedly said to himself, "I know they love me. I wouldn't have acted any differently than they are if it had been my sister who'd gone to war and come home." But after all those months of longing he was more vulnerable than he had ever been, and he sorely needed a little explicit warmth and obvious joy at his return, rather than a slap on the back and "Good to see ya, bro!"

Few people who go to war escape grief. Many will know and care about someone in their unit who will die at war, and many will have a loved one back at home die while they are away. What is less often addressed is the profound despair often felt by the person who *takes* a life, especially that of a civilian.[65]

Grief is often so unbearable that the worst of the memories become unspeakable, may even be forgotten. Michelle Dillow tells about the death of a physically large, warm-hearted soldier she asked me to call SPC Matthews (not his real name). He was much loved by the other soldiers, but when he died, no one mentioned being sad, although she was certain they all were. When she told the story of his death afterward, she would say he had been killed by an IED, but what she became able to say only years later were the words, "He was halfway out of the vehicle, and the IED blew him in half." She said:

I was never able to make it register in my head to make the words come out. Nothing can prepare you for something that tragic, and when it happens, your brain doesn't know how to process it. I guess after awhile I was able to acknowledge what happened instead of just "They got hit by a car bomb." People need to know what happened, fully, because they need to know how tragic it is. People who haven't been to war don't know how horrible it is.

Grief about losses that are inevitable, such as those of grandparents or parents, is devastating for most people. A high-powered male attorney I know described being "in a fog for the whole first year after my mother died." But grieving is more complicated and the fragmentation greater when the loss comes at a time of trauma, which is so often the case in war. The words of Gloria Steinem when asked whether she felt depressed after the death of her husband illuminate how loss and grief feel: she said she was not depressed but sad, because depression is when nothing matters, but sadness is when everything matters. In his poem "Scars of War," Dave Jones describes the grief and unbearable sense of powerlessness and helplessness watching a comrade die:

Through blood-soaked lips, he softly asks,
    Please don't let me die!
    But I can't stop this happening,
    Can't grant his simple needs.
    For he rolls his eyes into his head,
    And I'm the one that bleeds.[66]

For many men especially, being at war is by far the most intense experience of emotional closeness they have ever had with other men, a closeness that is often impeded elsewhere by traditional expectations for men to be reserved and by homophobia. The newness of this intensity can make the loss of dear friends even more difficult than it might otherwise have been. For women, when anger—which is often a normal, healthy part of grief—rises up, they have the added burden of feeling that anger is not feminine and thus should be suppressed.[67] For women, who are more likely to express their feelings fully to other women than to men, it can be even more difficult to grapple with how to grieve, because in the military they may have few or no close women friends, and they may withdraw more, according to Dr. Patricia Resick, director of the Women's Health Sciences Division in part of the VA system.[68]

Anxiety and Fear

Research about change shows that change of any kind, including positive change such as a promotion at work, puts demands on one's energy, time, and resources. For those who go to war, regardless of how they feel about the aim, countless changes create these demands. A civilian may feel anxiety about needing to go to a new doctor or finding out where to buy a good pair of socks, but for soldiers, anxiety about such events is multiplied many times because of their being thrust into a totally different environment. For many, entry into the military means suddenly being and working constantly with a whole group of people who will be responsible for each other's lives. Not everyone will get along swimmingly with everyone else, and this can be a cause for anxiety until (and if) they develop ways to work together. Even for people who have known the others in their unit for some time and have been accustomed to military procedures, it is quite a different situation filled with unknowns when the unit is going to war. Then, too, there is the whole matter of getting used to military rules and procedures, and although some people take to these easily, for some it produces intense anxiety.

Anxiety can also result from the concerns women and men may have about living up to the military's extremely masculine standards. For men, the anxiety can come from feeling they are not manly enough. For women, the anxiety is often more complex, because striving to act in traditionally masculine ways in order to prove they deserve to be in the military can conflict with any wish they have to act in traditionally feminine ways. Thus, women may be anxious about being both insufficiently masculine and overly masculine.

As for fear, unbelievable though it may at first seem, some veterans have told me that, although they had been fascinated by toy soldiers and war stories, even had collected World War II memorabilia, it was not until boot camp, when they were given bayoneted rifles and told to run around a field yelling "Kill! Kill! Kill!," that it struck them: "My God, I am supposed to kill people! And I could get killed!" Once in country, the reasons for fear are plentiful, including the constant reality of the dangers of extreme weather, injury, and death and the hidden nature of so much danger, including uncertainty about who is the enemy[69] and about where mines and other explosive devices are hidden.[70] Career soldier Jenni McKinley was surprised by how much fear she felt: "I thought I was going to do my job, be strong. But three days into it, I broke down crying. The scuds were flying. We were waking up to the sounds of explosions over our heads. It was terrifying." (She hid her fear from the other soldiers, crying only when alone.)[71]

Another cause for fear and anxiety plagues servicepeople who are gay, lesbian, or bisexual. A young man told me that he joined the military while still in high school, immediately after and *because of* the events of 9/11, because he loved his country and felt that joining up was the best way to defend and protect it. He discovered while a soldier what he had begun to suspect in high school: he was attracted to men. During basic training he froze when other men talked about sexual exploits with their girlfriends or wives and even when they just mentioned *having* girlfriends or wives. It pained him to keep silent about his own sexual orientation, but he was terrified about what would happen if the men around him found out. His fears were well-founded, because he had seen another private—who, ironically, was heterosexual—humiliated and beaten because someone claimed he was gay. When this fear combined with the realization that his recruiter had lied by saying that he would only be guarding a harbor on U.S. territory and that instead he was going to be sent into combat, he had heart-pounding panic attacks and fled the service.

A different source of vets' anxiety and fear is the dilemma of deciding whether or not to tell loved ones back home what they went through while at war. They may fear that others will judge them harshly for what they did or failed to do, or they may fear that, because their war experiences were vastly different from the world of those back home, those formerly close relationships will become distant, even rupture. For women veterans who long for understanding and support about what they have been through, being expected as women to give rather than ask for nurturance can make it harder to talk to loved ones. For men, being expected not to need nurturance and support can increase the difficulty of opening up to others. For all vets, it can be tempting to keep knowledge about war experiences from loved ones, so that when the vet looks at them they are not reminders of the trauma: Might it be safer in some sense to keep them associated only with happier, more innocent times in the vet's life, where the vet can go to find some lightness and some joy? Yet keeping that knowledge inside tends also to make the vet constantly on guard, lest signs of the suffering slip out. To suppress this knowledge can also create hurtful distance between the vet and the loved ones. For to be loved well is to be seen for who one is, and when a loved one does not know important, disturbing things about one's life, it is hard not to feel the anxiety and fear that feeling unseen can bring. Related to this dilemma is an increased risk of harming a formerly good relationship because the other person does not know what is causing the vet's new and disturbing behavior. In such a situation, many people (on both sides of the relationship) are quick to assume "My partner no longer loves me" or to become upset by the unexplained distancing. Thus, many vets feel they are in a lose/lose situation—whether to speak or not to speak to loved ones about their experiences—because either way, there is the potential for great loss.

Guilt and Shame

Perhaps the best-known kind of guilt related to war that veterans experience is survivor guilt, which arises from feeling that one has done wrong by surviving when another person has died. As World War II war correspondent Ernie Pyle wrote, "You feel small in the presence of dead men and ashamed of being alive."[72] It has been said that due to the "abiding sense of responsibility" these "bands of brothers and sisters" feel for one another, an "often utterly irrational guilt" takes hold of them when something goes wrong.[73] One soldier said she first had nightmares of a dead comrade calling her selfish and asking why she didn't help save him, and these later became nightmares of his asking her why she had not gone with him.[74]

The intense closeness and sense of mutual loyalty and responsibility for each other's lives[75] that are promoted as part of military training naturally increase the likelihood that soldiers will feel that guilt.[76] Ernie Pyle wrote about this, too:

The ties that grow between men who live savagely together, relentlessly communing with Death, are ties of great strength. There is a sense of fidelity to each other in a little corps of men who have endured so long, and whose hope in the end can be so small.[77]

Thus, said Captain James Key, an Army chaplain who visited wounded soldiers at Walter Reed Army Medical Center in Washington, people with "horrific wounds" and amputations have often focused not on their own problems but on "the buddies they left behind" and "felt guilty that they had survived while others did not."[78] In his poem "The Wall," Dave Jones writes:

Who made the choices? Who drew the names?
　　Why them and why not me?
　And it's haunted me from day to day since then,
　　For reasons I could not see.[79]

And in his "Brothers," these lines reflect the poet's sense that he lives the life his fellow soldiers lost:

They had the same quite lofty goals
　　so young with loved ones there
　Someday to hold a newborn son
　　To kiss a wife with care.
　What they lost is mine today
　　I held the newborn sons.
　I watched them grow in mirrors of me
　　In fields I watched them run.[80]

In listening to veterans who have survivor guilt, finding utterly useless my suggestion that they were not to blame for their comrades' deaths and that if they themselves had died, in most cases that would not have prevented the deaths of their friends, I do not know how to explain the imperviousness of survivor guilt to logic. Of course, some feelings, perhaps especially those involving grief and guilt, are so intense and represent such huge losses and shocks that perhaps it should not be surprising that logic does not help. I also have to wonder whether the very young ages at which so many soldiers first experience survivor guilt plays a role, since they learn how powerless they are to prevent friends' deaths just at a time when, as late adolescents or very young adults, they have been at the peak of their sense of invulnerability and power.

Another kind of guilt veterans have is about leaving responsibilities for family and household when going to war, so that others have to pick up all the slack.[81] This may be intensified for those who feel relief at doing so, no matter how understandable that feeling is. This is another realm in which men's and women's experiences may differ in their specifics: Men may feel guilty about not being home to carry out the responsibilities traditionally expected of a father, and women may feel guilty about not being home to carry out those traditionally expected of a mother, but those are quite different from each other. For instance, a father is more likely to be blamed if his sons are not considered independent or emotionally strong, whereas, as research has shown, a mother is highly likely to be blamed for just about anything that goes wrong with her children, because mothers are still expected to be the primary caretakers.[82] But of course any good parent feels deeply about not being with a child to provide whatever the parent believes is important.

Regardless of the realm to which one is referring, what people call guilt is sometimes more accurately described by some other word, often "shame."[83] Guilt involves a sense of having done something wrong, often morally wrong, whereas shame involves both a sense of having failed to meet some standard and, usually, a sense of having been seen to fail in this way. Some may feel shame because they believe that they were not as brave or as fierce as they should have been, or simply, as with survivor guilt, because they wanted to survive when their friends were dying. Dave Jones describes this shame in "58":

. . . Oh, the horror I quickly felt
   my friends who died in front of me
      legs weak . . . and so I knelt
   and ask an Angel to guide me home
      to see my wife and child

while a thousand men were dying
   it didn't make me proud.[84]

What is called survivor guilt also, for many vets, constitutes a major reason for their fear and anxiety about revealing their war experiences to others; their worry, in effect, is that others will judge them as harshly as they judge themselves.

Many vets have told me that the first question civilians ask upon hearing that they were in Iraq or Afghanistan is, "Did you kill anyone?," and if they did not, the questioners have no interest in continuing the conversation. This makes some vets feel ashamed that they did not end anyone's life. And as another vet said, "When someone asks if I killed anyone over there, I feel so bad, so stupid, because, see, I was in Afghanistan back in 2003, and we were all closed up in this crummy, old building, but we only got shot at once." He felt he had failed to be an adequate soldier, failed to live up to expectations.

Another source of shame may be about the anger that soldiers feel when leaves are canceled or deployments are extended, because they believe they are failing to live up to the standard of a soldier who is fully committed to the war (poignantly, often not knowing that canceled leaves and extended deployments can actually make soldiers' performance worse). And both men and women often feel shame if they feel they have failed to live up to the hypermasculine, John Wayne image (though it seems that John Wayne himself never went to war, except on the silver screen) of the ever-tough, stoic soldier who can endure any physical or psychological pain without a word and without a tear. Dave Jones writes, "I spent my time as any soldier in combat would have done. Survive a day and push your feelings deep inside."[84]

Many vets feel guilt and shame about the extra burdens or other hurtful effects that their military service has on their spouses and children because of the soldiers' physical absence or the emotional turmoil that often accompanies their return from the battlefield. Thousands of people— mostly women—have left their jobs, even careers, to be full-time caretakers of vets who are physically or emotionally wounded. Those who have been exposed at war to toxic substances such as Agent Orange and the burning chemicals from the First Gulf War often torment themselves when their children have problems that might result from those exposures, either because they are passed down physically by the parent or veteran or because the parent's own suffering troubles the child.

Rage

In addition to the sources of "shameful" anger just described, rage is a common feeling for veterans—rage about their own helplessness or pow- erlessness to have made things turn out better, rage about lies they were told by the government or the military[85] (and according to many I spoke with who had gone AWOL or UA, tales recruiters told them, such as that they would never be sent into combat but could learn filmmaking skills, are common), rage about feeling disconnected from loved ones when they come home, rage at how things had changed when they did return home. Men returning home find their wives are often more independent than before, potentially making the men feel they are no longer important or necessary at home. For many vets, regardless of their sex, there is the lonely, isolating rage about feeling that those who were not at war with them cannot possibly comprehend what it was like and how it feels to be back.[86] As discussed, the military's focus on training people to maim and kill promotes in many people a rage that is intended to be directed at enemy soldiers but is hard to limit and hard to turn off, hard not to let fly at the folks back home once the soldier is no longer at war. Journalist Rick Rogers reports a meeting at which veterans discussed their road rage—"speeding, cutting off drivers, throwing things at other motorists or starting fights on the roadside"—and quotes Nico Marcoalongo, "a former Marine major who served two tours in Iraq," as wondering why he does this: "Maybe it's a sense of entitlement because I paid the price (in war). . . . I prepared myself to . . . deal with my death or the loss of a limb, but I never prepared for the mental wound I received."[87] And a 2009 report showed dramatic increases in the previous year of shaken babies, deaths from domestic violence, and calls to domestic violence hotlines, with many of the callers saying that their families' financial situations had recently changed.[88] So for veterans who return to a poor economy, where their previous jobs are no longer available or, if available, involve increased responsibilities and pressures, there is yet another potential source of rage, as well as of shame and fear. This is especially true for those whose sense of identity depends greatly on their work.[89]

Anger and rage are secondary emotions.[90] A person virtually never goes from feeling nothing to feeling anger or rage. What happens is that first, one experiences a feeling that is to that person intolerable—usually helplessness, hopelessness, shame, guilt, or fear—and because it is intolerable, anger or rage kicks in to protect against this intolerable feeling and often to impel action that can reduce the feelings that seem impossible to bear.[91] Because the anger and rage can seem to appear instantaneously, the person who feels them may not have been aware of the underlying feelings that gave rise to them. It does not follow from this that expressions of rage must be allowed even when they hurt others, but it does follow that it can be helpful to understand this principle, to look at what gives rise to the rage, when vets try to help themselves or when others try to help them. An example of a sense of powerlessness, bewilderment, and betrayal leading to rage appeared in a *New York Times* story about a Marine unit in Iraq that had been giving candy to some Iraqi children and helping residents fix their houses; when there was a firefight the next day, the entire unit was "coursing with rage," asking what they were doing there and why the Iraqis were not helping them.[92] Understanding the presence of the feelings underlying the rage can be an initial step toward figuring out what to do besides committing further violence.

The veteran's sex can affect the realm of anger and rage, because women are less likely than men to have been socialized to cope with these feelings and are more likely to feel shocked and disoriented when they appear. But also men who are uncomfortable having such emotions can find them unsettling and even alarming. Women are often the targets of men's rage. Even before the current wars began, researchers found that one out of four women veterans under the age of fifty had been the targets of domestic violence during the year preceding the study, 90 percent reported having been sexually harassed while in the military, and rates of attempted and completed sexual assaults were twenty times higher in the military than in other branches of government.[93] In another study, women Vietnam veterans reported high incidences of having been raped and physically assaulted while in the military, and the effects more than a decade later included more severe health problems and the greater use of medication for emotional problems than for those who were not attacked.[94]

Conflicts of Values and Crises of Meaning

Things you thought or believed in previously, you no longer adhere to. It upsets your world view, your moral guidance or compass, and those are issues that are very difficult to even approach.

—Dr. David Collier, longtime veterans' psychologist[95]

Many parents teach their children that it is important to treat others in caring, respectful ways, that loving, humane values should form their core. When those children grow up and join the military, although they may regard official or unofficial procedures as going against some of those values, as when some sergeants intimidate and humiliate enlisted soldiers, they may hold to the belief that these are necessary in the service of the greater good of being able to go to war to defeat evil forces. But as shown in the brilliant film *The Hurt Locker*, in today's wars, as in the Vietnam War, it is often unclear which individuals are "the enemy," and soldiers may learn with a shock that someone they had demonized as part of that enemy is simply a completely human being. The simplicity of "we are good, they are bad, and we fight the bad so the good can prevail" stops being of use to many people once they are exposed to the complexities of war. As one example, imagine how you would feel about the military's orders to GIs fighting in Vietnam not to kill anyone in certain villages even when the people of those villages had killed your mates. To retaliate in some way is an understandable response which in that circumstance must be suppressed, and this can cause confusion, frustration, and anger at oneself or those giving the order. As a good soldier, you are supposed to follow orders willingly, see that they make sense, believe they are morally right. What, then, do you do with your despair and anger about the killing of your friends, especially if your military is not helping you figure out what to do with the feelings?

Even when it comes to having killed those identified as enemies, Samuel Maoz, director of a film about a war in which he served as a soldier, reflects many veterans' ongoing emotions about the taking of those lives:

[T]he sense of responsibility for killing remains strong. "There is no escape from it," he said softly. "In the end you were there, and your finger pulled the trigger." That there were no choices makes no difference. [he goes on] "I'm trying to explain that war cannot open for you the option to be moral. . . ." If you don't shoot, you die. "But you see the result, and you can't say you're not responsible," he said. "Maybe in court you're not guilty. But you can't cleanse yourself from this guilt."[96]

So common are moral conflicts in war that the Canadian military formally and publicly lists "moral injury"—"when your personal values come in conflict with your experiences overseas"—as a major source of soldiers' suffering.[97] Harvard University president and historian Drew Gilpin Faust has written about war:

Killing produced transformations that were not readily reversible—the living into the dead, most obviously, but the survivors into different men as well, men required to deny, to numb basic human feeling at costs they may have paid for decades after the war ended, as we know twentieth- and twenty-first-century soldiers from Vietnam to Iraq continue to do, men who . . . were never quite the same again after seeing fields of slaughtered bodies destroyed by men just like themselves. . . . Individuals found themselves in a new and different moral universe, one in which unimaginable destruction had become daily experience. Where did God belong in such a world? How could a benevolent deity countenance such cruelty and suffering? . . . Mutilated and nameless corpses challenged notions of the unity and integrity of the human selves they once housed, for, by the tens of thousands these selves had fragmented and disappeared. Death without dignity, without decency, without identity imperiled the meaning of the life that preceded it. . . . The meaning of the war had come to inhere in its cost. . . . We still seek to use our deaths to create meaning where we are not sure any exists."[98]

Faust's comment that the meaning of war had come to inhere in its cost is a reference to the citation of numbers of dead soldiers as an argument that a war has value, that in essence, because some have died, more should die.

Captain Tim Wilson, a chaplain who served outside Mosul, has pointed out that soldiers are usually dealing with "either being shot at and not wanting to get shot at again, or after shooting someone, asking, 'Did I commit murder?' or 'Is God going to forgive me?'"[99] A character in veteran and playwright Sean Huze's play, *The Sand Storm*, says, "Maybe it's all right to do the right thing for the wrong reasons. Or maybe I'm just full of shit." Journalist Aaron Glantz describes numerous recent situations that have provoked other conflicts of morals or values: An American medic was ordered not to treat Iraqi civilians who were about to die because of attacks by American soldiers, and one was threatened with court-martial for giving medicines to Iraqi children. A U.S. interrogator told his Iraqi prisoner that there is "a massive contradiction involved with me doing my job and being a Christian," and he felt there was no justice in the world.[100] And a soldier testified that under the Marine Corps' rules of engagement, "it is permissible to shoot and kill persons running away from a roadside bomb attack, even if they are unarmed and there is no proof that they were involved in the attack."[101] Merrill Cromwell (not his real name), an Iraq War veteran I interviewed, described the one waking nightmare from the war that has haunted him in the three years since he left Iraq, haunting because of the moral conflict it constituted for him. While in Baqubah,

one night a car pulls up after curfew down the street, 300 meters away, a few people get out, start unloading stuff from [the] vehicle and taking it inside a shop. We call it in and get the authorization to shoot them. So I shot. Next thing all I hear is a woman screaming. I froze. I was the only one that pulled the trigger. My Mom and Dad raised us not to hurt women but to protect them and cherish them. I'd have dreams about that scream, sound like it went on forever. But the next day we found out they were unloading explosive components, so it was justified. They were bad persons. Still didn't get that scream out of my head, though.

These kinds of experiences throw soldiers and vets into a maelstrom of questioning and self-questioning: "What are my bedrock beliefs now? Who am I, and what do I believe now? How do I put my beliefs to work if it means going against what the military tells me to do? Does asking these questions make me a bad soldier, a bad American, a bad person?" Grappling with questions of values and identity can be hard enough when we are adolescents living in safe or relatively safe places. But for those who confront such questions—often unexpectedly—in a war zone, where tight focus and black-and-white thinking are required, and questioning is at best a luxury and at worst a dangerous sign that one is un-American, the conflicts can threaten to unhinge them. In a *New York Times Magazine* article, a soldier learns that women to whom he had given shampoo in Iraq had been beaten by their husbands for accepting gifts from Americans. His intended kindness had resulted in violence against those he wanted to help.[102] And Sean Huze says: "It's difficult as a husband and as a father to reconcile who I was over there with some of the things that I saw. I mean, a dead child on the side of the road in Nasiriyah, about the same age as my son right now. And how unfeeling I was at the time about it, with who I am now, how I feel about it now."[103]

Probably the average eighteen-year-old American has not seen the worst acts that people can commit, but few in modern wars escape seeing what they would probably call evil, or at least unbridled violence. Others may commit it, or they may recognize it in themselves. Veterans advocate Ray Parrish says that some former soldiers tell him they "look in the mirror every morning and see a war criminal," because they have killed others, a condition he calls a *spiritual disability*."[104] Furthermore, he says, in training, you are told, "Fear is your enemy," so some soldiers quite literally lock out this aspect of their humanity as well and are left feeling spiritually bereft. In a 2006 *New York Times* article, some American soldiers were said to have come to regard the whole population of Iraq as the enemy and, from frustration at having failed to defeat the insurgency, to have adopted increasingly ruthless methods.[105] In the same article, Northwestern University sociologist and Pentagon consultant Charles Moskos said that soldiers and Marines daily watching close friends die in battle felt so frustrated and powerless that they would often "direct their venom at innocent civilians they assume are aiding the insurgents—and sometimes even at young children. 'If they feel that a local town is covertly involved in the killing of G.I.s,' he said, 'that's when people lose their sense of right and wrong.'"[106]

Related to this:

"Modern combat training conditions soldiers to act reflexively to stimuli," says Lt. Col. Peter Kilner, a professor of philosophy and ethics at West Point, "and this maximizes soldiers' lethality, but it does so by bypassing their moral autonomy. Soldiers are conditioned to act without considering the moral repercussions of their actions; they are enabled to kill without making the conscious decision to do so. If they are unable to justify to themselves the fact that they killed another human being, they will likely—and understandably—suffer enormous guilt."

By military standards, operant conditioning has been highly effective. It's enabled American soldiers to kill more often and more efficiently, and that ability continues to exact a terrible toll on those we have designated as the "enemy." But . . . even when troops struggle honorably with the difference between a protected person and a permissible target (and I believe that the vast majority do so struggle, though the distinction is one I find both ethically and humanely problematic) in war "shit happens." When soldiers are witness to overwhelming horror, or because of a reflexive accident, an illegitimate order, or because multiple deployments have thoroughly distorted their perceptions, or simply because they are in the wrong place at the wrong time— those are the moments that will continue to haunt them, the memories they will not be able to forgive or forget, and the stuff of posttraumatic stress injuries.

And it's not just the inherent conscientious objector our military finds inconvenient: current U.S. military training also *includes a component to desensitize male soldiers* to the sounds of women being raped, so the enemy cannot use the cries of their fellow soldiers to leverage information. I think it not unreasonable to connect such desensitization techniques to the rates of domestic violence in the military, which are, according to the DoD, *five times those in the civilian population.* Is anyone really surprised that men who have been specifically trained to ignore the pain and fear of women have a difficult time coming home to their wives and families?[107]

What do such experiences do to the values one has held and the meaning one has found in life before? As P.J. Riga, who had been a chaplain in the Vietnam War, observed, "What a combat soldier sees and experiences in war can kill his or her soul."[108] And Mark Twain wrote in "The Private History of a Campaign That Failed":

All war must be just the killing of strangers against whom you feel no personal animosity; strangers whom, in other circumstances, you would help if you found them in trouble, and who would help you if you needed it.

When soldiers return home, many are preoccupied by unresolved conflicts about morality or haunted by what they saw in themselves that frightened or appalled them. Believing that they are alone in these torments makes them feel more isolated from their loved ones and can certainly make them feel ashamed. The isolation is sometimes reduced if they can talk to other vets who have shared these dilemmas and feelings or if they can talk to other, trusted people.[109]

Another kind of moral dilemma arises when vets return home, and others expect them to be able to defend completely whatever not only they but also the whole military machine have done. The sense of loyalty the vets feel to their "band of brothers" and sisters still over there, their grief and guilt about comrades who died, and their wish to be respected for the risks they took and the work they did can bring them smack up against their wish to speak openly and fully about their inner conflicts. Many veterans fear that civilians who oppose the war the vets fought in will wonder why, if the vets had questions about what was happening, they did not simply leave. Whether or not vets themselves have questions about their wars, the skyrocketing mistrust of government in the United States in recent years can intensify their need to grapple with what matters to them—how to put together either their own or others' challenging of their wars with the fact that they live in bodies that fought those wars.

The focus in the military and in war es on learning hair-trigger, violent responses as defenses do not apply   ost of civilian life, but they can be hard to turn off. In civilian life, serving others does not usually involve hurting or killing others as it seems to do at war—"We kill the enemy in order to protect our loved ones and American values." So "serving others" needs to be redefined, premilitary modes of operating relearned, and ways of suppressing violence developed. Jonathan Shay has observed that prolonged combat itself can push a veteran toward criminal activity because of remaining in combat mode at home, treating those at home as the enemy.[110]

For men in particular, attempts to resolve moral conflicts are complicated by questions of how a "real man" acts at war and at home; for women soldiers and vets, such conflicts are complicated by the pressure to prove at war that women can be "real men," whereas back at home they are also or instead expected to be traditionally gentle, selfless, and more passive than in the military.

Facing life-and-death situations, and indeed being traumatized in virtually any way, can bring on a crisis of meaning, the loss of one's vision of why life matters, what it's all about, a reason to go on each day, indeed to do anything at all.[111] If it doesn't happen in the war zone, it happens to many vets when they return home and encounter the enormous contrasts between how it was in country and how it is back in the States. It is made much worse the more they feel they are different and apart from, as well as crazier than, the people around them.

A specific sort of crisis of values, identity, and meaning has been provoked by the Don't Ask, Don't Tell policy, which has meant for servicepeople who are gay, lesbian, or bisexual that important parts of their sense of who they are conflict explicitly with the values and rules of military life. The recent repeal of the Don't Ask, Don't Tell legislation will not, of course, do away with homophobia or heterosexism in the military, and it will be important to be aware of the ongoing effects of these forms of bias.

Betrayal and Mistrust

We have already mentioned some of the ways that soldiers and veterans have felt betrayed, including by military recruiters who mislead them or lie outright, by politicians who make distorted or false claims about the reasons for wars and the degree to which they are achieving their aims[112] or by failing to provide the provisions and protections soldiers need to do their work as effectively and safely as possible, by authorities who distort events in the wars,[113] by officers whose conduct clearly crosses the line from military to abusive,[114] and by others who put them at unnecessary risk.[115] My father would shake his head and say with a wry smile that in the lead-up to the Battle of the Bulge, General Dwight D. Eisenhower took a calculated risk with the lives of my father's men and my father by failing to provide adequate protection and support, an admission Eisenhower made after the war. And Dave Jones told me that in Vietnam, for political reasons, the military laid out "no-fire zones," where soldiers fighting for their lives in the jungles were ordered *not* to fire their weapons. In "The Train," Bob Lange describes the constant, exhausting vigilance and suspicion that plague him because of the danger of trusting:

I can feel the tension building,
    As I step into the train.
    I just can't trust the people,
    So I'm watching them again.

There are no free seats at either end,
    So it means I'll have to stand.
    If I use a seat that's empty,
    I'm too close to a dangerous hand.

I put my back against the door,
    My collar tight and damp from sweat.
    And as I quickly look around,
    I watch the eyes for signs of threat.

We pull into the station,
    Now here's a danger time,
    The people just push past me,
    But I'm clear and things are fine.

I quickly make the office,
    Take my seat against the wall.
    Tonight I do it all again,
    Dear God, please hear my call.[116]

Many soldiers and vets have coped with the loss of their comrades in war by ceasing to feel that love is safe, so they have come to expect those who care about them to desert or betray them. Why trust in love when you have felt the pain of seeing loved ones massacred—and have been powerless to help?

Another kind of betrayal hits some soldiers hard as they come home from war. Imagine the feelings of vets from Korea onward who watched World War II newsreels and saw famous photographs of long-separated couples joyously embracing when the soldiers returned from war and who found that, when it came their turn, they were met at the airport by a loved one who, for whatever reason, simply walked slowly toward them. As a vet of whatever sex, to feel met with a less than an eager face and open arms can be devastating. Even if they tell themselves that World War II was clearly considered a "good war," so it was more easily romanticized, a partner's less than total joy at the time of reunion cuts deeply.

Although historians differ over whether some people spat on Vietnam veterans and called them baby-killers when they came home, having myself been a protestor against that war, I can attest that no one I ever heard in the antiwar movement blamed or reviled the soldiers. Rather, those I knew blamed the government and knew it was distorting the truth. However, some vets have told me they were called baby-killers, even though I myself had not heard that happen. And anyone who did not know what the soldiers had gone through in country during the Vietnam war or in any war since then might well have said and done hurtful things, misplacing blame on the vets for decisions politicians made. To have risked one's life and then to be attacked or even simply unappreciated is to feel betrayed.

After betrayal of any kind, mistrust and suspiciousness are natural, self-protective responses. These reactions add to vets' difficulties in trying to connect with others: How long and how well do you have to know a person before you can take the enormous risk of letting your guard down and trusting again?

Isolation, Alienation, and Numbing

In the final stanza of "Reasons?," Dave Jones describes a sense of isolation and alienation:

Then don't scratch my name into a "Wall";
  Don't carve it on a stone.

Just understand, "I tried to live,"
  but never could come home.[117]

And here is the full text of Bob Lange's "I Don't Fit In Here Anymore":

I don't know where I'm going to go,
  When I walk out through that door.
  I know that I am going, though,
  I don't fit in here any more.

I suppose I'm hard to live with,
  But I can't help the way I am.
  I'm living with the legacy,
  Of a place called Viet Nam.

While I was in the Army,
  I kept on going strong.
  I had my mates around me,
  And we helped each other on.

Back then there was no problem,
  'Cause we were all the same.
  There was nothing wrong with us;
  It was the world that wasn't sane.

But now that I'm a civvy,
  I've tried to change my ways.
  But the pressure keeps building up,
  My head just pounds for days.

I've stayed at work, I've changed my job,
  But at night I walk the floor.
  There's just one thing I'm sure about;
  I don't fit in here anymore.[118]

In one study, 42 percent of veterans of the Iraq and Afghanistan wars felt like a guest in their own home, 22 percent said their children were not warm to them or were afraid of them, and 36 were unsure about their role in regular household responsibilities.[119] One veteran said he could not hold his wife, since she looked like an Iraqi woman to him, and he couldn't hold his children, because he had seen children die over there.[120] National Guardsman John Crawford described how, about a week after his return home from Baghdad, he felt "like being at a party and going to the restroom for 15 months and then trying to rejoin the conversation. Everyone and everything had changed without asking me first."[121]

Veterans, as well as soldiers home on leave, often feel icily separate and alienated from the people to whom they were close before going to war. This tends to result from the combination of their having gone through so much that people back home have not been through and the various factors that make it hard to talk to others about what they experienced and what they currently feel. These factors include much of what was just described, among them that the consequences of trauma are, almost by definition, hard to convey in words (at least until one is well on the way to understanding the effects); that few Americans want to think or hear about these wars, and most consider themselves—wrongly—incapable of responding in a helpful way if they do listen; that many vets are ashamed of themselves for any number of things they feel they did wrong or should have done differently; that many vets consider it their responsibility to protect their loved ones from even having to *hear* what war is really like;

that many vets, regardless of their sex, feel it is shameful to speak about their pain or ask for help; and that many vets know they will be considered overly sensitive or even crazy for not being "over it" by now. A loving, well-meaning cousin of a vet from the early part of the war in Afghanistan was struck by her relative's tendency to avoid family gatherings. She asked him why, and when he said he felt weird and out of place, she told him he needed to "Put all that behind you. You're home and safe now, so you've got to shape up and get on with your life." She simply failed to understand that he had no idea what kind of life he could have now, so overwhelmed was he by his experiences at war and his feelings of being different and apart since coming back. Like many men and some women, he had been socialized *not* to think about his feelings, and as though the traumatic times he had been through in Afghanistan had not been enough to make it harder to get a handle on what happened, his belief that "I am not a person who thinks about feelings, and I'm even worried that makes me gay if I *do* think about them," kept him even more isolated. So he could not begin to tell his cousin why it was not possible to get on with his life. Some pain is too intense to convey in words, and sometimes the only way to begin is to begin small, with a statement about a tiny fragment of what happened or what one is feeling. But imagine how impossible it seems to do that when someone you love tells you to get on with your life. How would you even start?

The film *The Hurt Locker* begins with an onscreen quotation that ends, "War is a drug." Many researchers and clinicians have claimed that it is a drug in the sense that, as with an addiction to a medication that makes one feel better, some soldiers and vets somehow have an addiction to war but in what seems a bizarre, almost inhuman way, since war is hell. But Kathryn Bigelow, the film's director, has brilliantly shown why people who have been at war might want to go back, and it is because of the kinds of factors that are positive for most people: Being at war can make one feel important, virtuous, needed, and powerful. And as the film lets us see, even in the hypermasculine world of bomb detonators in the military, the very life-or-death nature of daily experience and the emotional intensity that this creates makes the soldiers dependent on each other and creates a remarkable degree of emotional closeness that few people—and especially men—ever experience. For many American men, who have grown up with emotionally distant or physically absent fathers and whose closeness to other men has been constrained by our homophobic society, these war experiences with other men are especially rare and precious. The intense connections among fellow soldiers that develop in the military often stand in stark and troubling contrast to how alone they feel when they come back home. Small wonder that many long to go back! Safe conditions for men to experience such closeness are rare once they come home, and even for women, who are more likely to be allowed to be emotionally close to other women and to men, only in unusual situations in the United States will the conditions for such emotional intensity be present. After all, although women are expected to be more expressive than men, they are also in danger of being considered *too* emotional, and especially for women soldiers the disparity between what is expected of soldiers at war and what is expected of women back home can be impossible to manage. Instead of saying, "War is a drug, and anyone who *wants* to go back to war is mentally ill or must have damaged brain chemistry," it seems to make more sense to say, "The clarity and intensity of war experiences, as well as the knowledge that others at war understand what it's like for you, can be so positive in contrast to what feel like unbridgeable chasms between yourself and your loved ones back home, that it is not surprising that when these chasms remain unbridged, some of you want to go back to war."

As psychiatrist Samuel Shem and psychologist Janet Surrey beautifully show in their book, *We Have to Talk*,[122] people need connection, men as well as women. That many men have been shaped to avoid showing that need, sometimes even to be unaware they have it, does not extinguish the need. (And Shem and Surrey also show the power inherent in the meeting of that need in their play, *Bill W. and Dr. Bob*, about the origins of Alcoholics Anonymous.) The most extreme form of traditional expectations for men is that they need no one and may be better off toughing everything out alone than in connection with others. Male veterans who fall toward that end of the continuum have the added burden of self-doubt, because they feel they are not *supposed* to need what they nevertheless long for. Thus, men grapple with whether to attempt to connect with other people, in which case they feel ashamed of being unmanly, or whether to remain isolated, in which case they are much less likely to heal from their war trauma. Many female veterans face this complicated situation: Having been in the military, they have had to appear more independent than they perhaps felt, but being women, they are at the same time *expected* to need connection. Thus, women vets grapple with whether to act on their wish to connect to other people, as a result perhaps feeling that they are not worthy to be in the military, or to avoid connection but thereby risk feeling unwomanly. Furthermore, although vets of both sexes may worry about the *danger* of telling the real story of what happened to them at war, women vets carry the additional burden that to tell that awful story will be to hurt their loved ones and thus go against the traditional expectation for women to nurture rather than harm or even ask for understanding from loved ones.

Many practical matters can add to the isolation or alienation of veterans from their loved ones once they are home. For instance, 24 percent of veterans from the current wars had friends or family give up jobs to be with them or act as their caregivers.[123] Since men are far more likely than women to be veterans, and women are far more likely to be caregivers for the wounded and disabled, this means that women may take on the traditional feminine role of nurturer but be troubled about having to give up their previous, paid jobs, and men may find themselves in a role that goes against the prescriptions for them, because they are in a dependent position and thus often frustrated and ashamed. Again, most veterans are men, and women are traditionally expected to help their male partners deal with feelings of loss and rage, as well as with the helplessness and shame the men often feel because of being poor or unemployed. The women are usually expected to do this unpaid work with utter selflessness and while making it possible for the men to maintain their dignity, and they are supposed to guide the children through the changes in their fathers and the households while minimizing their hurt and fear.[124] In general, women are more likely to be targets of their male partners' violence than the reverse, and, as noted in chapter 1, there is a hugely increased incidence of domestic violence in families of veterans.

Often related to isolation and alienation is an emotional numbing that many vets experience. It often begins in country as a way to get through danger and stay focused on survival tasks, but it can recur any time a vet feels incapable of enduring any kind of feeling, even back home. Combat vets are often numb and have trouble showing compassion or caring because of having faced life-or-death situations every day for so long.[125] War correspondent Dexter Filkins describes the numbing he experienced, which began in Iraq and continued when he returned home:

When I was in Iraq, I might as well have been circling the earth from a space capsule, circling in the farthest orbit. . . . For me, the war sort of flattened things out, flattened things out here and flattened them out there too. Toward the end, when I was still there, so many bombs had gone off so many times that they no longer shocked or even roused; the people screamed in silence and in slow motion. And then I got back to the world, and the weddings and the picnics were the same as everything had been in Iraq, silent and slow and heavy and dead.[126]

In the many ways that women veterans, because of their own trauma, grief and sadness, fear and anxiety, guilt and shame, rage, conflicts of values and crises of meaning, and isolation and alienation, may need and long for someone to care for and nurture them, they risk feeling they are wrong to have needs of their own rather than, like "good women," wanting only to meet the needs of others. If they have male partners, those partners may resent that the women are less available to provide nurturance to them than they were before going to war. In general, women are expected to have boundless energy and limitless compassion for men who need to heal.[127] Today, many women with suffering partners are also soldiers or vets themselves and may be trying to provide total, constant nurturance (and often have the primary responsibility for children and aging parents and in-laws as well). As these women try to help, some male veterans are so frustrated or ashamed to need nurturing, tenderness, and understanding that they find it hard to accept and appreciate what the women have to give and may keep their emotional distance. Caught in these various dilemmas, women vets may feel uncared-for and isolated.

Some Groups at Special Risk

In considering the sources of psychological suffering due to war, it is worth noting that Dr. Matthew Friedman, a leading expert on emotional trauma, has written that three groups in the American military are at risk for problems that can increase the emotional effects of being in a war zone. He says that those groups are women, whose experiences may be "complicated by sexual assault and harassment; nonwhite ethnic minority individuals whose premilitary, postmilitary, and military experience is affected by the many manifestations of racism; and those with war-related physical disabilities," for whom emotional trauma and medical problems "often exacerbate each other."[128] As described throughout this chapter, sexism also affects men, though in somewhat different ways than it affects women. Also in this chapter, I have mentioned another group—those affected by economic adversity and thus by classism, and I have addressed some additional problems of gays, lesbians, and bisexuals. With regard to those with war-related physical disabilities, they of course encounter major additional problems, but they are not a primary focus of this book. As part of the context for understanding what being a vet is like, let us look here at some of the additional problems encountered by veterans because of their sex, race, or social class.

Sex and Gender

In addition to some of the sex-based problems already noted in this chapter, the sudden upswing in the current wars of large numbers of women going into combat for the first time has brought special problems.[129] In considering these sources, it is worth keeping in mind that expectations about differences in how men and women are supposed to feel and act can powerfully affect the sources of suffering, the ways a particular vet experiences them, and the ways a particular vet deals with them. Women in greater numbers than ever before in American history are serving as soldiers exposed—though often not assigned—to combat or other serious dangers, such as from IEDs. As of September 30, 2009, nearly 209,000 women were serving on active duty in the U.S. military.[130] For these women, spending time at war brings special complexities and conflicts, because in war, expectations for hypermasculine behavior are more extreme than at any other time.[131] (This is true to some extent whether the soldier is serving in a provisions unit or as a mechanic.) Indeed, the association of the military with hypermasculinity makes it harder for men as well as women to figure out what to do with their tenderness, vulnerability, moral conflicts, and spirituality. It is not possible to say whether it is harder for women to try to live up to the traditional standards of the other sex—because the expectation is that they cannot and perhaps that they should not—or for men to risk failing to meet the traditional standards for their own sex. Although in some ways our society increasingly expands definitions of what can be considered "appropriate" behavior for men and "appropriate" behavior for women, in other ways the dichotomies have become more rigid.[132] What I am saying here, then, will not apply to everyone but is about the many people who remain influenced by traditional sex-role expectations. What is clear is that these expectations and assumptions create additional, somewhat similar and somewhat different problems for each. Thus, some women in the military wonder, *is it possible* both to act in traditionally masculine, tough, unemotional ways in order to prove one deserves to serve in the military and also act in enough nurturing, expressive ways in order to maintain a traditionally feminine identity? What are the consequences of trying to do both or, conversely, of trying to choose one behavioral style or the other, as a soldier and a vet? For women, a typical conflict is between expectations about what a good woman feels and does and expectations about what a good (read:

masculine) soldier feels and does. As a twenty-three-year-old woman who is an Army Specialist said, "It's hard being a combat vet and a woman and figuring out where you fit in."[133]

Related to the common assumption that women are less rational than men, the former's objectivity about military decisions and judgments is sometimes challenged.[134] Some women vets struggle with trying to behave in traditionally feminine ways while having had to act (and perhaps to continue to act) in some traditionally masculine ones: For instance, one woman was "trying to figure out how to be a wife by preparing meals, doing romantic things, and basically being a woman again instead of GI Jane. None of her female friends in Iraq wore makeup," and as a soldier she had been covered with dirt from "sixteen-hour patrols and infrequent showers."[135] And physical injuries can make it hard to give to or receive physical comfort and affection from a partner.[136]

In her *New York Times Magazine* article, "The Women's War," Sara Corbett recounts the care that some servicewomen take to avoid friendships with other women while they are deployed, out of fear of being called lesbian. She quotes Abbie Pickett, a member of the Army National Guard, as saying that in the military, "you are one of three things—a bitch, a whore, or a dyke."[137] Pickett also describes the tension she feels because of constantly being in the minority as a woman.

A whole set of problems arises for women in the military who are mothers, and this includes a huge number of women. More than 100,000 soldiers who have served in the current wars are mothers, nearly half the number of women who have been deployed. The vast majority are primary caregivers, and one-third are single mothers. Twelve percent of the women and 4 percent of the men in the regular Army are single parents.[138] Kirstin Holmstedt describes many problems of these mothers in her book about women in the military. Those who come home physically injured or emotionally limited (detached, overwhelmed, angry) feel guilty and ashamed of being unable to carry out ordinary motherly tasks.[139] A 2006 *Washington Post* story carried the report of the first female combat amputee who is a mother and who could not do easily some of the things a mother is expected to do, such as cooking and helping a child to dress.[140] And in 2009, a mother who had no one with whom to leave her two children was recalled to active duty (but was relieved to be discharged from the Army because of that).[141]

The sheer variety of problems that mothers in the military encounter is mind-numbing. One woman reported desperately missing her five-month-old baby and being put on antidepressants, her motherly feelings treated as psychiatric symptoms that needed to be suppressed.[142] Another "thought that when she was with Iraqi children, she would be able to relate them to her own children, but that wasn't the case. 'I don't look at those children and see my own at all. . . . [A]ll I felt was anger and almost hatred. . . . There were twelve-year-old children threatening us with IEDs and RPGs.'"[143] In general, exposure to so much violence in the military can sap their patience, tenderness, and resilience.[144] Furthermore, for military women who had positions of power and authority when at war, to come home, where mothers' work is unpaid, often not respected, and often invisible, can make them feel "less consequential." And the transition times between military service and home—"where they are expected to immediately resume household responsibilities—can be excruciatingly difficult."[145] In fact, it is hard to imagine whether it is more disruptive to a woman and her family for her to be home for very brief periods of time in between deployments, so that not much readjustment is likely to be possible, or to be home longer periods, which might make readjustment more likely but render the next separation a more difficult rupture.[146] This would also apply to men who take on significant household responsibilities.

For men, common conflicts resulting from sex-role expectations involve concerns about two kinds of disparities: (1) between the military ideal of John Wayne toughness and the extent to which a soldier feels he fails to match that ideal; and (2) between the masculine military ideal and the degree to which a soldier feels he *wants* to match that ideal or *used* to match it before joining the service. In any case, it has been said that the culture of "Army strong" discourages even the appearance of weakness.[147]

Race

Members of racial or ethnic minority groups make up significant portions of the armed forces, ranging from 24 percent of the Air Force to 40 percent of the Army.[148] Although the military was racially integrated more than half a century ago, racism has not vanished from that institution any more than it has disappeared from the larger American scene. Aside from suggestions that racism helps impel the hostilities against Muslim foes,[149] there is a paucity of published reports of racism in the current military. However, the Southern Poverty Law Center has repeatedly reported extremists, such as neo-Nazis, infiltrating the military.[150] In addition, in 2007 a top Army investigator apologized to a unit of Hispanic National Guard members who were strip-searched and inspected for gang tattoos while they were in

Kuwait.[151] In another recent story, many noncitizens now serving in the U.S. military were said to be slated for deportation after their tours of duty ended.[152] And Holmstedt relates the story of a black woman and a biracial Pacific Islander and Irish woman serving in Iraq, where their fellow soldiers repeatedly subjected them to racist slurs and racist treatment.[153] Michelle Wilmot, the latter of these two women, won an Outstanding Woman Veteran Award from the Commonwealth of Massachusetts for her unique understanding of the needs of veterans, especially veterans of color and women veterans. So disturbing were her experiences as a target of racism that she is writing a book about, among other things, having to deal with that kind of injustice while in combat. In 2008–2009, I conducted my own research about racism on U.S. university campuses and found it to be rampant, so I was surprised to find when contacting a variety of organizations that work against racism and doing online searches that I failed to turn up almost any reports of racism directed against black or other racial or ethnic minority servicemembers in the military. It is clear that Muslims and Arabs are demonized as the enemy, but the reason for the invisibility of most other racism among American servicemembers is a mystery to me. However, it appears from inspecting what material is available that the military's strong (on paper) affirmative action policy makes it easy to overlook or deny the ongoing racism within it.[154] This was a pattern we found in our Voices of Diversity research on U.S. campuses: because of changes in legislation and social beliefs, many manifestations of racism are now subtle and hard to challenge (rolling of eyes, looks of surprise when someone black makes an intelligent observation, the tendency only to choose work partners who are white).[155] This may be part of the reason for the scarcity of reports of this kind of treatment in the military. But as I say, the scarcity is so extreme that I remain mystified.

Class

Because of the all-volunteer nature of the current military, the poor are disproportionately likely to be in the armed services.[156] In fact, the No Child Left Behind Act explicitly allows military recruiters access to high school students on the same basis as college recruiters.[157] As a result, as recent Harvard University graduate Lucerito Ortiz informs me, recruiters came to her California high school, whose student body was largely composed of students of color and the poor, but did not go to the schools that were largely white or middle class. She observed them targeting the black and Hispanic students, knowing they were less likely to be able to afford many options other than joining the military, but not the white or Asian ones.[158] And the *New York Times* carried a report that because of Vermont's rural poverty, young people have been seeking a better life through the National Guard, with the result that, a few years later, disproportionate numbers of the poor are coming home in flag-draped caskets.[159]

Are These Problems Mental Illnesses?

The scope of suffering that many vets live with is vast, and its forms are varied. But does it make sense, and is it helpful, to rush to call such suffering mental illness? Once we know what a vet has gone through, it is an excellent bet that we will recognize the feelings and conflicts discussed in this chapter as deeply human reactions to the monstrosities of war. Most of the behavior and responses that have been described in this chapter seem understandable, human reactions to war, not mental disorders. But even beyond that, surely we would not deny comfort and assistance to any veterans experiencing such reactions, whether we call them human reactions or "moral disorders,"[160] or whether we call them mental illnesses. Some veterans had serious emotional problems before going to war, some did not. Some are now more intensely troubled than others. But all deserve respect and help, and surely no one has the right to declare that the more troubled ones are therefore simply weak or sick. This has not stopped some people from suggesting that those soldiers and veterans who "break," whose functioning as warriors or, later, as family members, friends, community members, and employees is impaired, were probably mentally ill to begin with. One official example that is discussed in chapter 4 is the attempt by some Army personnel to claim that soldiers whose suffering was caused by combat trauma instead had personality disorders before enlisting.[161]

Much help for suffering veterans can come from genuine, caring, respectful connection with others, and much can come from a variety of other healing sources, but all too often the sufferers are simply labeled "mentally ill" and sent behind the closed doors of therapists' offices, where too many fail to receive the help they need, no matter how good the therapists' intentions, and where they are pathologized, isolated, and too often medicated to no beneficial effect or to harmful effect. In chapter 3 we look at what explains the very common impression that what vets need are psychiatric drugs and psychotherapy, and then at what we know about why these interventions often fail to help. But those who wish to go directly into action may wish to proceed to chapter 6. In any case, as we move on, let us carry with us the plea for us to understand and go with vets on their journey that Dave Jones writes about:

Where is the voice of understanding, this Soldier needs to hear.
  Who'll take this place beside me when I'm choking back the fear?

Can you walk beside the man when the ground is shaking still?
  Have you sight of intangibles, to know you always will.
  Or will the load of a pain filled heart with its pleading, screaming way,
  For the word upon your lips, "I'm sorry," all to say.[162]

3 There's Only So Much Emotional Carnage of War That Therapists Can Fix

Believe nothing merely because you have been told it. . . . Do not believe what your teacher tells you merely out of respect for the teacher. But whatsoever, after due examination and analysis, you find to be kind, conducive to the good, the benefit, the welfare of all beings—that doctrine believe and cling to, and take it as your guide.
—Buddha (about 623–543 BC)

Now that we have considered some of the burdens of returning vets and have suggested that it is not appropriate or helpful to call them all mentally ill, in this chapter we look at the widespread overestimate of clinicians' abilities and at what clinicians actually can and cannot do. First we will consider what explains the common belief that *only* therapists can help veterans recover from war's carnage but that no one else can. Then we will take a detailed look at some of what scientists and clinicians have learned about the limitations of what therapists have to offer, as well as some of the problems in the research about their approaches. I am sure that the vast majority of people who do research about what might help traumatized people have the best of intentions. But so many approach the subject as though there were well-established, scientifically grounded, technically based cures. For some, professional or scientific approaches may help. But ordinary and unimpressive though it may seem, we all know people whose suffering was lightened, whose thoughts were transformed, by a warm, understanding friend who was willing to listen, or by lines of poetry or a novel.[1]

Murphy (not his real name) is an extremely intelligent, perceptive veteran not only of war but also of decades of psychotherapy. Desperate for help to end at least some of the anguish he had felt since his time at war, he tried decades of individual and group therapy, as well as psychiatric drugs his many therapists prescribed, to no avail. He writes what he learned about the limitations of traditional approaches:

Most if not all therapists go by one learned procedure whether it is Freud or whatever and everything is pigeonholed into that category. You must be this way because of your mother and your upbringing. Or Bowen. You must be this way because somewhere in your family or upbringing past you were treated in such a manner that it all ties together by history. And still many more theories of many varieties and thinking that each therapist wants to match you with. All the while you in your heart know that none of these apply to you, but you walk out of that office with another label and a new supply of pharmaceutical wonder drug handouts and sample packs.

Why Do We Believe That Therapists Can Help and That No One Else Can?

There are two primary reasons for the common belief that psychiatrists and psychologists are *the* people to fix veterans' pain: (1) psychiatrists' and psychologists' training often blinds them to our own limitations and the limitations of our fields, and (2) authors of a wealth of medical, scholarly, and popular media articles call most war-related suffering "mental disorder," and many people want to believe that therapists are the best people to cure mental disorders.

The Limitations of Psychiatrists' and Psychologists' Training
Based on my own four years as a graduate student in psychology, my subsequent years as director of two clinically related graduate programs in psychology, and discussions with past and current graduate students and instructors, I can tell you this: Psychiatrists' and psychologists' training too often leaves us with, or even creates, blind spots about our limitations. As a result, it is hard to avoid what William James called the *psychologist's fallacy*, the tendency for psychologists to confuse our own mental states with those of the people we study.[2] It is the rare program in which faculty train therapists to acknowledge their own limitations and especially those of their training and their discipline. After all, people who go into the "helping professions" want to believe they will be able to help, whether for altruistic reasons or for reasons otherwise related to their sense of identity. If the truth were told, trainees would learn as their programs begin that mental health treatment is as much art and humanity as science, that such things as the therapist's—or a friend's—compassion, empathy, warmth, acceptance, and respect for the person who is suffering and the ability to think critically and questioningly about dogma in the field are

more likely to help than drugs and most of the psychotherapy techniques in use today.[3] Most trainees, speaking from the heart, will tell you that it is daunting to realize that they might not know how to help, but such thoughts are rarely discussed in training programs or even by fully credentialed therapists decades into their careers. To deal with these fears, therapist trainees often retreat into two beliefs: (1) "My trainers know what to do" and (2) "What I am learning here is science." The need to believe that what we do is scientifically grounded is all the more important for those who want to be considered to hold high-status positions: Saying "I care about my patients and try to help them, but I know that there is little science in what I do" seems to pale in comparison to saying "I use technique X and drug Y, because a study published in Z medical journal shows that it works." (Elsewhere in this chapter we consider some of the flaws in research related to psychiatric diagnosis and to treatment.) The trainees I have worked with have invariably asked why so few therapists talk about the unscientific nature of what they do. Many have a deep and genuine wish to be of help but operate in a whirlwind of uncertainty, guilt, and fear, trying to help suffering people while knowing the work has little scientific basis. I have learned that both therapists and trainees often believe they are alone in feeling unsettled and insecure about the lack of a scientific basis to their work.

The failure to question the work we do and the way we do it may become even more problematic in the future, for UCLA psychology professor Patricia Greenfield's research shows that technology's increasing role in our lives is causing a decline in people's critical thinking.[4] Thus, when people need to believe that science is useful in this context, they are apparently becoming less likely to challenge the claims its practitioners make. The holding up of science as the be-all and end-all in the mental health field contributes to the creation of a hierarchy within the field: those who are more detached and removed from people's real-life problems and ways of coping are more highly regarded, whereas those who say that they work with suffering people through compassion, respect, listening, and careful thinking are regarded as the "fuzzy, touchy-feely" ones and assumed to be less effective.[5] Included with this latter group are community psychologists, those who work with people in their local environments, ask them to identify the problems they want help with, and tell them straightforwardly what ideas and tools psychologists can offer, but who make it clear that the professionals do not consider themselves more expert overall than the people they try to help.

Some Dilemmas Therapists Confront   Imagine a therapist reading a report showing that the greatest risk factor for developing what is labeled post-traumatic stress disorder (PTSD) is exposure to combat (which it actually is).[6] Anyone who is not a therapist might read such a study and think, "That's a good reason to end these wars. Imagine how many hundreds of thousands of people we could save from suffering if we did that." If that makes sense to you, consider that most traditional psychotherapists believe their work should not involve social or political action (though some therapists may engage in either outside the office). In fact, many therapists—as I have heard many of my own colleagues say—consider it their job to help people adjust to the status quo. Even most therapists who might oppose the wars feel, like most people, that they are helpless to stop them. Thus, most therapists comfortably operate primarily within their consulting rooms, doing what they were trained to do, trying to help veterans one at a time or maybe in groups, sometimes succeeding, but not leaving their comfort zone to think how much more good they might do by advocating for peace or even by helping the vet in less therapy-bound ways.[7] It is interesting that the choice *not* to be involved in social and political action is rarely recognized as a politically- and possibly financially-based decision, and some professionals are quick to call involvement in such action inappropriate for therapists. As a result, most therapists are unlikely to become involved in what might seem the most direct way to prevent suffering for vets in the future. Staying out of the arena of antiwar activism makes it easier for them to keep their focus on traditional approaches, treating current veterans as though the problems came from within them and could be cured through therapy and medications.

Another limitation that affects many therapists and maintains their narrow vision of what can help suffering vets is that the mental health field is heavily laden with jargon. Psychologists Ken Pope and Melba Vazquez express concern in their classic book, *Ethics in Psychotherapy and Counseling: A Practical Guide*, about ways that words are used to cover what people in the mental health field do, calling them "word blankets." They note that "even when used with the best of intentions, careless or bloated language makes it hard to think clearly. . . . Too often we lose sight of ethical issues as they disappear in clouds of cliches, jargon, dogma, deceptive words, and careless language."[8]

The use of opaque jargon (such as the terms for various "mental illnesses," discussed later in the chapter) saves therapists and researchers from having to think clearly about what they do, because it makes non-professionals feel they cannot possibly comprehend what therapists and researchers do, so the former do not challenge the latter. In addition to these limitations of the field of therapy, various kinds of published reports add to the impression that therapy and drugs are what vets need.

How Medical, Scholarly, and Media Reports Persuade Us That Therapists Can Provide What Veterans Need

Three aspects of many reports promote this belief: (1) the authors' mistaken treatment of psychiatric diagnosis as a science, (2) their claims about what is helpful, and (3) the frequent failure to mention anything helpful other than professional therapists and drugs. In combination, these factors make it seem that what veterans need can come only from therapists. Veterans who talk with me tell me uniformly that even those family members and friends who will listen to them for a few minutes are quick to say, "You need to see a psychiatrist, because I am not trained to deal with a mental illness."

Let us look at some examples of the way in which authors of both scholarly and popular media reports purvey the notion that therapists, and only therapists, can fix war's emotional damage. What all of these examples have in common is that they present the effects of war trauma as though they were indisputably mental illnesses, or they present psychotherapy or psychiatric drugs as the indisputably right treatments. The National Institute of Mental Health's Web site states baldly that PTSD is an *illness*,[9] not an understandable response to trauma, and the Society for Women's Health Research has issued a press release instructing that if you think a loved one has PTSD, "The first step is to talk to your doctor or mental health professional."[10] Advice columnist Dear Abby makes the claim that "a large number of vets returning from Iraq and Afghanistan will need professional help to overcome their trauma."[11] A reporter for *American Medical News* quoted Daniel Potenza, a Department of Veterans Affairs psychiatrist, telling an American Medical Association symposium that "Promising therapies for PTSD exist, including medications and psychological treatments."[12] And in a *USA Today* article, the chief of the traumatic stress program at the National Institute of Mental Health is quoted as claiming, "Treatment gives most people [with PTSD] relief from symptoms."[13] Authors of major medical journal articles write widely disseminated articles about treatments for psychological problems in which the only treatments even studied are drugs and therapy.[14] And a journalist, no doubt intending to be helpful and indeed providing useful information about a variety of resources, including nonprofessional, nontherapy, nondrug assistance such as mentoring, outings for vets and their families, and care packages, repeatedly includes these in the category of "mental health services" and says they are aimed not at vets who are suffering but rather at vets who have "mental disorders."[15] In that article, veterans who are suffering but who might not appropriately be called mentally ill are invisible. In the same article, the journalist describes a clearly well-intended, massive undertaking by psychologist Barbara Van Dahlen Romberg, who created the Give an Hour program, which involved at that time three thousand "licensed mental health professionals" to provide at least one hour per week of free counseling to "military personnel, veterans and their family members who are experiencing the psychological effects of the wars in Afghanistan and Iraq." To be sure, to see that thousands of professionals are willing to offer some free care to suffering people warms the heart.[16] The problem is the unquestioned implication that dealing with the "psychological effects" of war requires licensed professionals, added to the journalist's earlier presentation of war-related suffering solely as constituting mental illness. Is getting some help for those who are suffering better than getting them no help? Of course. But some forms of help carry dangers that others do not, and that is true of the labeling of all suffering vets as mentally ill and putting them on drugs and in psychotherapy. Once again, although some may benefit from either or both of these approaches, we must not lose sight of the fact that they carry dangers for at least some people, whereas other approaches are available that do not involve making people feel they are "crazy" and do not involve the risks that sometimes accompany drug therapy and even psychotherapy. Some of these other approaches are described in chapter 6.

How to Decide What Is a Mental Illness?

At the foundation of everything that happens to everyone in the mental health system is the psychiatric diagnosis. In principle, no one may be treated for psychological problems without receiving such a label, regardless of the nature of the treatment. Thus, veterans who are told they need psychotherapy or psychiatric drugs have nearly always been given such a diagnosis. And historically, the number of categories of alleged mental illnesses in the successive editions of the *Diagnostic and Statistical Manual of Mental Disorders*, or *DSM*, has grown by leaps and bounds.[17] Molly Hogan has written, "When I returned to psych nursing in 1989 [after being out of the field since 1972], I discovered that all the psych labels . . . that I was familiar with, which had never made much sense to begin with, had been replaced with new labels. I noted that it was now much easier to get a psych label."[18]

The way we decide what a mental illness is and who has it is important, because getting a psychiatric label is far from risk-free. Even some of the mildest of diagnoses can carry the following dangers:

• the damage done to the vet, who therefore feels "I must be crazy" and "I should have been over this by now, or else I wouldn't get this label"— something that virtually every vet I have talked with has felt;
• the failure to be regarded by oneself and others (including one's therapist) as consisting of more than one's problems;
• difficulty obtaining or keeping a job (discrimination on the basis of mental disability is illegal, but in the real world there is an enormous burden of proof on people with psychiatric labels to prove that they were not hired or were mistreated at work or fired because of the diagnosis rather than, as management often claims, because the employees were not "team players" or were "hard to work with");
• increased health insurance premiums or denial of coverage on the grounds that the individual has a preexisting condition;
• loss of the right to make decisions about one's medical and legal affairs;
• loss of custody of one's children; and
• the danger that overemphasis on mental illness will lead doctors to overlook traumatic brain injury (or other problems of physical origin) because of jumping to the conclusion that some of its symptoms, such as memory loss, irritability, and sleep problems, are signs of psychiatric disorder.[19]

With regard to learning to consider themselves broken and "sick," which often increasingly becomes the primary part of their identity as a result of receiving a diagnosis,[20] every therapist I know has had new patients come to them after being seen elsewhere and introduce themselves by saying, "I'm Mary. I'm bipolar," believing that this tells much of what the therapist needs to know. The very traditionally oriented psychoanalytic magazine *The Menninger Perspective* has included a concern that "Patients commonly come to identify themselves as their diagnosis, viewing all of their behaviors, emotions and thoughts as aspects of their pathology or diagnosis."[21] Yet the same article ends with the unfounded statement, "A diagnosis, then, is . . . to offer a clear and definitive direction that will guide patients to recovery and to healthier lives."[22]

Were it simply that psychiatric diagnosis does not help, that would be one thing, but it is far worse because of the damage it often does. The other important fact to keep in mind is that *DSM* authors conducted their own studies to see whether two therapists would agree about which *DSM* label a person should receive, and they obtained poor results.[23] To get two professionals to give a person the same label would be the bedrock, the essential first step toward developing a true science of diagnosis, but we have not yet reached even that point. The latest in a long line of attempts to see whether therapists can distinguish people with psychiatric diagnoses from those declared to be normal was broadcast on a British television show: Mental health experts (a psychiatrist, a psychologist, and a psychiatric nurse) who spent hours observing five people who had been labeled seriously mentally ill and five who had not were unable to tell reliably who belonged in which group.[24] Perhaps most important is the way that psychiatric labels impoverish our understanding of the fullness of a suffering person's humanity. As Athar Yawar writes,

A patient's story is a symphony of suffering, longing, meaning, understanding, hope, fear, loss, wit, and wisdom. Not to accompany the person afflicted on his journey is inhumane. . . . Experiences are matched to labels of descriptive poverty. "Depression" implies a low level of something, presumably mood, rather than the rich and complex turmoil felt by the patient.[25]

Every time a servicemember gets a diagnosis, some professional has decided that the person's feelings have crossed the line from a normal response to a "diseased" one. Yet even contributors to the VA's *Iraq War Clinician Guide* note that "the boundary line between 'normal' and 'pathological' response to the extreme demands of battle is fuzzy at best."[26] These authors say, for instance, that when soldiers are about to be deployed, "It is often difficult . . . to determine the difference between reasonable anxiety and an excessive reaction or the development or recurrence of psychiatric illness, [and during deployment] the novelty of the situation may contribute to symptoms of dissociation."[27] The authors go on to describe the difficulty of telling friend from foe and other dangers as creating "chronic strain," "particularly when split second decisions may undergo retrospective analyses to determine their appropriateness,"[28] and the terrible living conditions, physical demands, alternation of intense violence with times of inactivity, separation from loved ones, physical injury, disruption of the environment, and "fear, rage, or helplessness produced by combat"[29] as precipitating various kinds of emotional distress. It can be hard to distinguish these kinds of distress from mental illness, they say. Elsewhere in the same guide, one finds the warning that

diagnostic labels used to identify transient distress or impairment may be unnecessarily pathologizing and stigmatizing and inappropriate because they are confounded by ongoing exposure to war-zone demands and ongoing *immediate* stress reactions.[30] . . . To avoid legitimate concerns about possible pathologization of common traumatic stress reactions, clinicians may wish to consider avoiding, where possible, the assignment of diagnostic labels such as ASD [Acute Stress Disorder] or PTSD.[31]

The editors of the *Iraq War Clinician Guide* further point out that research about the intensity of grief in war veterans, one of vets' major sources of emotional pain, is limited, making it virtually impossible to know how to define even grief that is normal for vets.[32] And when so many veterans I have interviewed have said that just having someone—especially a non-professional—listen to their stories without judging and with compassion has reduced or resolved their sleep problems, it seems to make no sense to say the sleep problems were signs of their mental illnesses.

How, then, should we decide what to call a mental illness, keeping in mind that ideally, we would do so only if it is helpful and not harmful? This is a subject I have been thinking about since I taught an honors seminar as a first-year graduate student in 1969. Few people, even therapists, are aware that even the psychiatrists who literally write the book of psychiatric diagnostic categories have acknowledged that they have failed to reach a consensus about a good definition of mental disorder.[33] The difficulty of deciding on a definition is thrown into greater relief when we realize that different cultures have very different ways of making that decision.[34] In courses I have taught, I have devoted an entire lecture to delineating problems that many people have identified in the very definition of mental disorder, and in *They Say You're Crazy: How the World's Most Powerful Psychiatrists Decide Who's Normal*, I devote to it an entire chapter, "Whose Normality Is It, Anyway?," showing that there are major problems with every kind of definition.[35] I won't repeat here all of these problems, but one that has great relevance in thinking about veterans is this: If huge percentages of people are suffering psychologically from having been at war, then we need to think carefully about what we choose what to call "normal" and what to call "pathological." How many of us, seeing a buddy blown to bits, would not be devastated, would not be plagued with nightmares, would not wonder if there was something we could have done to have saved the person? How many, realizing we had killed an innocent person, would not feel shame and guilt, would not wonder what kind of person we were, would not worry about our own power to destroy, would not feel enraged at having been put in a position (even been ordered) to do such a thing? And as we saw in chapter 1, huge percentages of people *are* suffering psychologically from having been at war.

Putting aside for the moment the question of how to define not only mental disorder but also such categories as PTSD, consider these indications of the magnitude of reported anguish:

A 2007 study by the Pentagon found that 38 percent of soldiers, 31 percent of Marines, 49 percent of Army National Guard members and 43 percent of Marine reservists reported symptoms of post-traumatic stress disorder, anxiety, depression or other mental problems.[36]

And:

The Department of Veterans Affairs reported about a 70% jump in veterans seeking treatment for PTSD in the 12 months before June 2007 and an additional 50% rise in the next nine months.[37]

It does not seem appropriate to sweep all of these sufferers into the overarching category of "the mentally ill" or into individual categories of mental illness such as "Posttraumatic Stress Disorder," "Depressive Disorder," and "Anxiety Disorder." If even this soon after being at war, between one-third and nearly half of servicepeople are *reporting* severe emotional problems—and if we remember that they commonly *avoid* reporting such problems for fear of mistreatment, denial of promotions, and other forms of retaliation—then it makes no sense to call these very common reactions to war mental illnesses.

In chapter 1 we looked at some reasons that in our society, although we rush to call suffering vets mentally ill, we do not take what would seem to be the obvious next step of saying, "If we call all these suffering vets mentally ill, then that means war is causing mental illness on a massive scale" and of looking at the implications of that. We might want to look at these implications especially given the research showing that the Department of Defense itself acknowledges that more signs of emotional trauma appear in units whose members have served deployments of twelve months or more and had more exposure to combat.[38]

Since we do not look at these implications, each veteran is left to feel, "The problem comes from within me. I need to be fixed." Instead of calling war-traumatized people mentally ill, we lose nothing but grant them greater humanity and respect if instead we call them deeply troubled.

The Example of PTSD

[PTSD] has been easier to diagnose than it has been to understand or to treat.

—Erica Goode, "When Minds Snap"[39]

Of course, the best primary prevention for war-related PTSD is the prevention of war.

—Psychiatrists M. J. Friedman, P. P. Schnurr, and A. McDonagh-Coyle[40]

There is remarkably little reason to think that suffering because of having been in combat is proof that one is mentally ill. Looking at what has been done with the category of PTSD adds to our understanding of why that belief is nevertheless so common. PTSD is the most important category to examine because it is the one most commonly applied to soldiers and veterans in official reports from the military and the VA and because lay-people are quick to say that those suffering from the effects of war probably have PTSD. The term has come into wide usage. As Meadow Linder describes in her illuminating history of the label and its problems, some veterans whose suffering had been ignored or treated dismissively came together with some caring mental health professionals and proposed that a new category be added to what was then the upcoming edition of the *DSM*.[41] The category was ultimately called Posttraumatic Stress Disorder. The intention was to persuade professionals and others to take the vets' suffering seriously, and for many, it would mean that they could get insurance coverage for professionals' efforts to help them.

One of the best features of the way PTSD was initially defined (in the *DSM–III*) was that it was described as a normal reaction to abnormal situations, a response to something so terrible that it would "evoke significant symptoms of distress in almost everyone," something "generally outside the range of usual human experience."[42] Even with the inclusion of that statement, however, PTSD appeared in a manual *of mental disorders*, and "mental disorder" is not a term that tends to spring to the minds of therapists or laypeople when someone mentions a "normal reaction." Thus, from its first appearance in the *DSM*, PTSD carried the mixed message, "You are normal. You are mentally disordered." The *DSM* is periodically revised, and as a result of serving for awhile on two committees for one edition, I was stunned and troubled to discover that decisions about how to define "mental disorder," what categories to put in the *DSM*, how to title each category, and what symptoms to list for each category are vastly more likely to be marked by misuses of science and poor-quality science than by responsible, straightforward use of well-done scientific research.[43] As time has passed, and new editions of the *DSM* were produced in 1987 and then 1994, the *DSM* authors decided to specify that, in order to receive the PTSD label, the person must have "experienced, witnessed, or been confronted with an event or events that involved actual or threatened death or serious injury, or a threat to the physical integrity of self or others," and to have responded to the event with intense fear, helplessness, or horror.[44] By that definition, couldn't we say that virtually everyone heading for Iraq or Afghanistan was likely to come back with PTSD? And if that is the case, what benefit is there—other than getting insurance coverage for therapy (not an unimportant benefit)—from giving so many people this label? If it helped therapists predict what kind of treatment would be most likely to work, that would be different, but that is not the case. In fact, it has been said that there is currently no known cure for PTSD.[45]

Some veterans have told me that in a way, it was a relief to be told they had PTSD, because getting a label made them feel that their suffering was taken seriously. However, it is easy enough to let people know that we take their suffering seriously without making it a condition that they allow themselves to be labeled mentally ill. Furthermore, there are the major risks of psychiatric labeling that were described earlier in this chapter; the risks do not affect everyone with a diagnosis but can affect anyone.

According to the VA's *Iraq War Clinician Guide*,[46] perceived threat, low-magnitude stressors, exposure to suffering civilians, and exposure to death and destruction each have been found to contribute to what is called PTSD. It is hard to imagine how these experiences could fail to be deeply disturbing, even traumatizing, so it is puzzling to think of calling these responses proof that one has a mental illness.

Two recent developments warrant concern about the consequences of the presence of PTSD in the *DSM*. One is that the Army has put pressure on its medical staff to avoid diagnosing soldiers with PTSD, and "the Army and Senate have ignored the implications" of this.[47] Because the symptoms listed for PTSD are so blatantly connected with exposure to the horrors of war, perhaps the Army worries about the financial drain on the military and the VA if they were expected to pay to help everyone who goes to war and ends up traumatized. This is an example of the Army playing fast and loose with psychiatric diagnosis, still more evidence that diagnosis is not a scientific enterprise. Furthermore, its focus on anything other than how best to help soldiers is disturbing. As we will see in chapter 4, the military has been quick to report high rates of PTSD in its servicepeople, but when convenient, it tries to avoid using the label. The other recent cause for concern about the military's dealings with PTSD, according to the military newspaper *Stars and Stripes*, arose when a military psychologist suggested awarding a Purple Heart for people with PTSD as a way to reduce the stigma that the label carries in the military. Defense Department officials rejected that idea, conveying the notion that PTSD is not a legitimate wound of war because "it is not intentionally caused by the enemy," even though it is caused by "witnessing or experiencing a traumatic event."[48] So PTSD carries a new, negative meaning, deprived of legitimacy, deprived of respect.

A benefit of the PTSD label is that it is a shorthand way of saying, "We believe that you are suffering. You are not making this up." But with this message comes the burden of believing that one is mentally ill. It is not enough to be suffering the effects of war; now vets too often feel that the effects are lasting "too long," that they should have been over it by now. The good news is that instead of saying "You have PTSD," we *can* say "We believe that you are suffering. You are not making this up," and leave out the part about mental illness. This has the added benefit of opening us all up to considering a wider array of ways to try to alleviate the suffering.

A look at the current *DSM* description of PTSD helps us see other problems with the label:

309.81 DSM-IV Criteria for Posttraumatic Stress Disorder[49]

A. The person has been exposed to a traumatic event in which both of the following have been present:
    (1) the person experienced, witnessed, or was confronted with an event or events that involved actual or threatened death or serious injury, or a threat to the physical integrity of self or others
    (2) the person's response involved intense fear, helplessness, or horror. *Note:* In children, this may be expressed instead by disorganized or agitated behavior.

B. The traumatic event is persistently reexperienced in one (or more) of the following ways:
    (1) recurrent and intrusive distressing recollections of the event, including images, thoughts, or perceptions. *Note:* In young children, repetitive play may occur in which themes or aspects of the trauma are expressed.
    (2) recurrent distressing dreams of the event. *Note:* In children, there may be frightening dreams without recognizable content.
    (3) acting or feeling as if the traumatic event were recurring (includes a sense of reliving the experience, illusions, hallucinations, and dissociative flashback episodes, including those that occur upon awakening or when intoxicated). *Note:* In young children, trauma-specific reenactment may occur.
    (4) intense psychological distress at exposure to internal or external cues that symbolize or resemble an aspect of the traumatic event.

(5) physiological reactivity on exposure to internal or external cues that symbolize or resemble an aspect of the traumatic event.

C. Persistent avoidance of stimuli associated with the trauma and numbing of general responsiveness (not present before the trauma), as indicated by three (or more) of the following:

(1) efforts to avoid thoughts, feelings, or conversations associated with the trauma

(2) efforts to avoid activities, places, or people that arouse recollections of the trauma

(3) inability to recall an important aspect of the trauma

(4) markedly diminished interest or participation in significant activities

(5) feeling of detachment or estrangement from others

(6) restricted range of affect (e.g., unable to have loving feelings)

(7) sense of a foreshortened future (e.g., does not expect to have a career, marriage, children, or a normal life span)

D. Persistent symptoms of increased arousal (not present before the trauma), as indicated by two (or more) of the following:

(1) difficulty falling or staying asleep

(2) irritability or outbursts of anger

(3) difficulty concentrating

(4) hypervigilance

(5) exaggerated startle response

E. Duration of the disturbance (symptoms in Criteria B, C, and D) is more than one month.

F. The disturbance causes clinically significant distress or impairment in social, occupational, or other important areas of functioning.

Specify if:

Acute: if duration of symptoms is less than 3 months

Chronic: if duration of symptoms is 3 months or more

Specify if:

With Delayed Onset: if onset of symptoms is at least 6 months after the stressor

Note that according to Criterion B, a person must have one of the symptoms listed for reexperiencing of the trauma, such as nightmares; according to Criterion C, a person must have three or more of the symptoms of avoidance and numbing; and according to Criterion D, a person must have two or more symptoms of increased arousal. This sounds impressively scientific, but it is not. How, after all, might one choose the numbers of symptoms the person needs to have? For PTSD, as for most categories in the *DSM*, there has been no scientific basis for choosing, and the choices have often depended on political considerations, including which person on what *DSM* committee has how much power.[50] The subdivision of the category into Acute, Chronic, and With Delayed Onset, depending on the number of months after the stressor the problems arise, might seem to make sense but is without scientific basis or use at this point. Possibly, people whose symptoms arise between three and six months after the exposure suffer differently from those whose problems arise before three months or after six months, and perhaps different approaches will turn out to help the people thus slotted into different groups; however, it is not yet known whether this is the case. One might wonder, then, why these subdivisions are listed at all. The only clear answer is that it increases the *aura* of scientific precision surrounding the enterprise of psychiatric diagnosis.

Former *DSM* head Robert Spitzer and his colleagues have documented many problems with the PTSD category,[51] including its sharing of many criteria with other categories, such as phobias, anxiety, and depression, and the potential for meeting the PTSD diagnostic criteria simply by having some symptoms of phobia and major depression. Most revealing is their point that there is a very high rate of overlap between people diagnosed with PTSD and people diagnosed with other serious emotional problems. Thus, when we talk about "PTSD," we are not talking about something that is cleanly different and distinguishable from other kinds or expressions of mental pain. Use of the label gives the false impression of clinical uniformity and precision, but the effects of war trauma are variable and messy. With regard to the overlap between PTSD criteria and the criteria listed for other categories,[52] too often, time and effort are spent trying to figure out ways to differentiate PTSD from other categories. What gets forgotten is that humans invented these categories, connected dots among particular symptoms, and squished them into constellations that have not been proven to be helpful.[53] There is no reason for surprise that a veteran who meets some or all of the PTSD criteria also meets criteria for some other manifestation of suffering. All of this should have us paying close attention to individual veterans, their problems, their resources, their sense of what does and does not matter in their lives, and to finding ways to help them. So far, psychiatric diagnosis is not helping. What would make more sense would be the kind of approach that Spaulding, Sullivan, and Poland use in the tradition of rehabilitation rather than pathologizing: They pay close attention to individuals, their problems and resources, and their perspective on what matters.[54]

The PTSD Label Masks Real Problems and Introduces New Ones   The very choice of words in the category title, Posttraumatic Stress Disorder, should raise concern. Let us think about the word "stress." If you ask five people who are not veterans what comes to mind when they think of the word "stress," you get answers like "distracted" and "worried," with examples of stress-causing situations such as "losing my credit card," "being stuck in a traffic jam," and "worrying that I won't finish a report for work on time." Words do matter, and to use the word "stress" in a label, even just after a form of the word "trauma," encourages us in some way to take less seriously the unspeakable consequences of war trauma that so many vets live with every day. How different it would be if instead of "stress," words like "horror" or "despair" appeared in that title! Furthermore, as noted, in terms used in earlier wars, such as "shell shock," "battle fatigue," and "war trauma," the language of war is used, is crystal-clear. "Posttraumatic Stress Disorder" helps with the cover-up of the fact that it is *war* that is causing this suffering.

A different and helpful perspective on the concept of PTSD comes from a look at other cultures. In a *New York Times Magazine* article, journalist Ethan Watters describes the way American psychotherapists rushed to the site of the 2004 tsunami in Asia, aiming to stave off what they were sure would be a wave of PTSD cases resulting from the natural disaster.[55] Referring to the "remarkable ascendancy" of PTSD in American psychiatry and public consciousness during the past quarter of a century, and noting that "PTSD, many Americans assume, describes the way that all humans react to trauma," Watters reports that this is not the case. For instance, "the deepest psychological wounds" for Sri Lankans were not on the symptom checklist for PTSD but rather were "the loss of or the disturbance of one's role in the group." He describes different symptom pictures in various countries and cultures around the world and quotes McGill University anthropologist Alan Young as saying that PTSD "can be real for a particular place and time and yet not be true for all places and times." Related to this, Derek Summerfield points out that the PTSD category was a "sociopolitical" response to a group's needs rather than a real medical or disease category, but the mental health field treated it as scientific truth.[56] The claim, he notes, was that it was caused not by traumatic events but rather by the *incomplete processing* of those events; according to the latter explanation, the cause of PTSD was within the individual, and it was the individual's responsibility to deal with it. Writes Summerfield, "The notion that war collapses down in the head of an individual survivor to a discrete mental entity, the 'trauma' that can be meaningfully addressed by Western counseling or other talk therapy is absurdly simplistic."[57] He also notes that despite the absence of objective evidence that "psychological debriefing," talking with a professional about the horrific events, is helpful, Western professionals and organizations put tremendous effort into using this approach. According to Summerfield, this happens even when people in different cultures make it clear that the central problem is the need to fix the social world that war has broken rather than to provide counseling.

Even in the United States, individuals grow up in different cultural contexts, in families with varying ways of expressing (or not expressing) feelings and of coping with problems, so it should not be surprising that American veterans' reactions to experiences at war vary. It can interfere with our efforts to help veterans if we try to force their reactions into the symptom clusters that happen to have been constructed for the *DSM*. That individuals have different backgrounds and cultures casts further doubt on the idea of antecedent mental illness or even "vulnerability," if this means a weakness of some kind in the individual. Understanding a person's background can help us understand their responding to trauma in a particular way, without insisting that there had to have been something wrong with that person prior to the traumatic event.

One problem with the list of PTSD criteria is that these symptoms do not always go together in real life: Not every vet who has been in combat has nightmares or flashbacks *and* numbing *and* hypervigilance. What do we do with that information? We can decide that, because they do not meet the PTSD criteria, we will not take their suffering seriously and offer them help, whether professional or otherwise, or we can acknowledge that individuals suffer differently from each other and that their failure to fit an unscientific but predetermined matrix should not exclude them from our compassion. Surely it is better to recognize the uniquely individual aspects of suffering and to offer respect, compassion, and help to those who need it. How sad to waste resources trying to find just the right label for someone when our attention should be on the whole person, the nature of that person's suffering, and the imperative to provide help. Indeed, the *DSM* criteria for PTSD poorly capture the disturbing array of problems and burdens outlined in chapter 2. The diagnostic criteria pale in comparison to the rich but devastating details of individuals' war experiences described in that chapter, illuminating how much understanding we sacrifice when we retreat behind psychiatric labels.

There are problems not only with the description of PTSD but also with the way the label is used. Linder's original research shows that even caring therapists who work intensively with traumatized people vary greatly in what they do with the *DSM* description of PTSD.[58] What insurance companies (and researchers) expect them to do is assign the label of PTSD only to patients who fully meet the manual's criteria. However, being compassionate souls, as the therapists Linder interviewed sit facing people who are in pain, they often throw the *DSM* and insurance companies' rules to the winds; they decide that if someone has been traumatized and is suffering, they will assign the PTSD label, because it is, after all, about trauma. What often happens, then, is what I have elsewhere called shifting sands on shifting sands: The unscientific nature of official psychiatric diagnostic categories is compounded by the variable use and ignoring of them.[59] As one research team has noted, rarely is a distinction made between someone who has some of the features on the PTSD criteria list and someone who supposedly has an illness.[60] They point out that, for instance, hyperarousal in the form of hypervigilance certainly indicates distress, but not all distress should be considered evidence of mental disorder. That the latter happens as part of an effort to be of real help is wonderful. But it makes it even harder for researchers and clinicians to achieve or maintain clarity in the effort to understand whether people with the PTSD label have anything in common other than that they have been traumatized and feel miserable as a result. Even when we consider individually the symptoms listed in the PTSD category, surely hypervigilance, numbing, and problems with concentration should not automatically be considered signs of mental illness when they arise in reaction to experiences of war.

Not only do the PTSD requirements lack scientific basis, but applying them in clinical settings presents practical difficulties. What happens when a therapist who strictly follows them sees someone who is suffering but who, for instance, has only the two symptoms of avoidance and numbing? Does that mean the therapist will not be able to help? It certainly means that the patient's insurance will not cover the treatment if the patient does not receive a label. Since some therapists can be helpful to some veterans, it is important to be aware of this. It reveals a major problem in our system of delivering mental health care, which is that it depends so heavily on fitting perfectly into one of the *DSM* categories. Those who do not fit but who encounter therapists who want insurance to cover their fees may be slotted into another category as the therapist goes label-hunting to try to find one that fits. How much better it would be if insurance companies allowed truly caring therapists to offer help to those who are suffering without having to jump through the hoops of assigning labels that are unscientific and carry risks of harm. (It could be argued that diagnostic categories are useful in deciding whose care will be covered by insurance, but there is little or no evidence that assignment to these categories helps with treatment or prognosis.)[61]

Problems with Other Psychiatric Categories

Many of the problems that characterize the PTSD category also apply to categories such as Major Depressive Disorder and Generalized Anxiety Disorder. This is important because, besides PTSD, depression and anxiety are the terms most often mentioned in reports of Americans' war trauma. Psychologists David Jacobs and David Cohen[62] studied the use of the term "depression," which is employed so freely that most people believe they know exactly what it is and that it is a clearly defined condition. Jacobs and Cohen learned that the term is applied to an enormous range of feelings and states, from ordinary sadness through hopelessness, helplessness, and the inability to get out of bed, accompanied by serious loss of appetite and suicidal thoughts or attempts. So varied was the range that, the authors concluded, the term is virtually useless for purposes of research. Why? Because, as with PTSD, many therapists apply the term loosely. As a result, if, for instance, we want to study the effect of a drug or other treatment on depression, we are likely studying people characterized by such a mixed bag of feelings and states that we cannot know how to interpret the outcome. As for anxiety disorders, when does ordinary anxiety become a psychiatric disorder, and does it make any difference what has caused the anxiety? For every category in the *DSM*, decisions about who fits the label depend heavily on the therapist's judgment, often based on the patient's report of feelings. When, for instance, does anxiety become "marked" anxiety? When does one diagnose Hypoactive Sexual Desire Disorder, which is defined as a low level of sexual feelings and activity? Who decides what is too little sexual desire? Subjectivity, bias, and matters of interpretation enter into the assignment of labels of mental disorder. As Jacobs and Cohen note, the *DSM* authors themselves state that the categories in the manual often overlap with each other, and patients given the same diagnosis are not alike even in the most important ways that are used to assign the diagnosis.[63]

How Psychiatric Categories Are Constructed In addition to problems with how categories and symptoms are applied, it is important to consider problems with how psychiatric categories are constructed. Unlike physical problems, such as broken bones or high cholesterol levels, there are no clear, reliable, and valid tests for almost anything that is called a mental illness. Clinicians and researchers—some of them smart, some of them caring, some both, some neither—see people who are suffering and try to divide the manifestations of that suffering into categories. This is an effort I have compared to looking at the night sky and deciding how to divide the stars into constellations.[64] It is extremely rare that one finds two patients with identical symptoms, and in fact there are 12,870 different combinations of symptoms of PTSD that one can have and still meet the *DSM* criteria for it.[65] It is hard to find well-done studies that truly provide information about how to help an individual who sits before us. At least in theory, researchers have to decide how to find as homogeneous a group of people as possible before they set out to determine what will help them (and what will hurt them). Some researchers are more careful than others about looking for homogeneity, but there is little homogeneity to be found. Human behavior is complex, and a person's strengths and resources, as well as problems, help determine the outcome of any treatment. Trying to find the money and staff to conduct studies that include all of these factors is nearly impossible, and even if one had unlimited resources, the task of trying to cover even all of the factors *most likely* to be relevant— including styles of coping, strengths and inner resources, social supports, financial situation, goal-setting abilities, etc., etc., etc.—is impossible.

What happens, then, when therapists read research about the kinds of problems their patients have? Some clinicians care about thoughtfully evaluating reports about various treatments and the claims by makers of drugs, and some do not care so much. Some have learned enough about research methods to be able to evaluate the quality of a piece of research, and some have not.[66] (Interestingly, psychiatrists are far less likely than psychologists to have been trained in research methodology, as even one prominent *DSM* psychiatrist has pointed out.[67]) If you have an idea for creating a new psychiatric category, ideally you should have to prove that there are some people who have important kinds of suffering in common with each other *and* that they do not fit better within some other category. Because 12,870 symptom pictures can fit within the PTSD specifications, those who get the PTSD label can differ tremendously from each other. And, as noted, the symptoms listed for PTSD overlap a great deal with those in other categories, such as depression and anxiety. There are similar problems with symptom pictures and overlap for virtually all other psychiatric categories. Even there, if someone exposed to war trauma feels anxious or sad or depressed, we should not have to worry about what category to slot them into or just choose one or two.

If the creation and use of labels led to more knowledge about how to help, this would be a different conversation. However, at this stage of the evolution of psychiatric categories, there is little or no evidence that choosing a label helps much in deciding on treatment or predicting eventual outcome.[68] An enormous amount of ado about nothing fills the psychiatric and psychological journals, which bulge with well-funded but largely uninformative studies about psychiatric labels and treatments. (In chapter 6 we make suggestions based on what *has* been shown to work.)

Again, we will use PTSD as an example, this time to illustrate the difficulties of doing research about all kinds of psychiatric categories. Like most studies of human behavior and emotional pain, those about PTSD are plagued by a wealth of problems in the ways they are conceived, designed, carried out, and interpreted. Some begin with "people who have been diagnosed with PTSD," and surprisingly often, no one checks to see if all of these people even meet the (unscientifically derived) PTSD criteria. When you interpret the results of such studies, it is hard to know where to begin, since you cannot be sure of much about whom you have studied, and you almost never know anything about their individual and social strengths and resources, which certainly affect treatment outcome.[69] Similar problems apply to studies involving virtually any category of mental illness.

Where the Brain Fits In

Research about the brain and its possible relationships to emotions and behavior has burgeoned in recent years, and many people believe that much more is known about brain/behavior relationships than actually has been documented. One reason many have the impression that therapists can fix veterans' emotional suffering is that their suffering has been prematurely portrayed as explained by brain research. If only, we think, it were possible to do a brain scan, pinpoint the location of the problem, and give a pill or excise a bit of the brain to make the suffering stop. But the state of the science is such that, for the vast majority of (and perhaps all) veterans, this is far from possible.[70] In fact, it may never be possible. In the meantime, without such solutions, in an article in the medical journal *Lancet*, Athar Yawar expresses concern that "instead of the art of expert companionship, psychiatry has become the discipline of brain mechanics"; and Yawar laments, "In our fervour to understand mental illness, we have applied grossly oversimplified biochemical models to the brain, with usually unhelpful results."[71] Of course, if "expert companionship" were not helpful, and brain science were helpful, it might not matter so much. But it is too easy to believe that if any study includes research about the brain, it must yield some important and useful truth. As Jeremy B. Caplan and I have written:

> When the popular media report neuroimaging studies, they often give the impression that if you see brain activity associated with a kind of behavior, the brain activity measured somehow tells us something more important or true than would the behavior itself. . . . [However,] just because you observe a brain-activity *correlate* of behavior does not on its own mean that you have come any closer to understanding the behavior or what causes it.[72]

This does not mean that studies of the brain are useless. They can be extremely important, especially for veterans who have suffered actual damage to their brains, with traumatic brain injury (TBI) being one of the signal injuries of the current wars. For people with TBIs, brain scans are sometimes useful but may be of only limited help, especially in telling us what kind of treatment is most likely to be effective. And many people with TBIs also either suffer emotionally as a result of upset, frustration, and despair about their new physical problems or even apart from their brain injuries have had terrible experiences that also caused them emotional pain. In fact, the common emotional concomitants of TBI make it all the more important that we not too quickly diagnose veterans with emotional upset as having PTSD, because in so doing, we may miss actual, known injuries to the brain.[73]

In general, when it comes to exploring connections between emotions and the brain, there are serious, real-life limitations to brain research. These include the following:

• "Neuroimaging is expensive," so "the numbers of people included in the vast majority of studies are usually quite small"[74]—and not many studies have been done with veterans unless they have probably suffered brain damage, so those will tell us little about vets whose suffering is primarily emotional.

• The small numbers make it risky to draw conclusions about differences between groups, such as between veterans and nonveterans.

• Researchers usually discuss average findings when they report their research, but treatment decisions have to be made about one individual at a time.

• Different people's brains differ in shape and in location of specific functions, making it hard to know the meaning of which parts of the brain "light up" on different brain tests.

• Related to the above, it is often unknown whether more or less activity in a particular part of the brain is better for a particular purpose (such as reducing hypervigilance).

• "The brain is composed of 100 billion cells, each connected to multiple and often unknown numbers of other cells, each affected by other neurons and by what the person eats, does, feels, and thinks and has done to them," and "brain function comes not just from a particular location but also from the complexity and strength of many neural connections acting at once."[75] It is currently impossible to measure every chemical or electrical change in every part of the brain at every level of functioning simultaneously, so even if individual differences are found on brain scans or EEGs, we do not know whether we have identified all of the differences relevant to the suffering of veterans.

• Rarely is presuffering brain-study information available for veterans, so it is impossible to know how and whether the war experiences changed the brain chemistry or electrical activity in ways that might help us understand the nature of the suffering and what to do about it.

• Even if we could determine with certainty that a particular kind of suffering corresponds to activity in a particular part of the brain, we rarely know which is cause and which is effect, or whether there is a feedback loop between an experience or emotion and changes in the brain.

• Rarely do we know how (1) to change that part of the brain in a way that will stop the suffering, (2) whether there is or ever will be such a way, and (3) whether there is a way to experiment with such changes (especially if through surgery or drugs) without risking greater harm.

• The nature of any one individual's suffering cannot be described or measured with accuracy, especially not compared to the suffering of another (at this point, this is more helpfully done by poets and novelists than by brain researchers). Thus, it is hard to know what to make of differences we might find in the brain chemistry and electrical activity of different suffering people.[76]

William Uttal has written about the "enchantment of 'looking into' the brain."[77] In a fascinating study, researchers showed a report of a scientific study to two groups of people. One group saw just the report, and the other group saw the report accompanied by an illustration of a brain scan.[78] Those who read the report with the illustration were significantly more likely to find the research believable than those who saw the version without the picture. The very presence of *some* kind of brain scan illustration persuaded people that the research report somehow carried more truth than did the identical article without the brain scan. This is not far beyond the tendency of some schoolchildren to say that anyone intelligent *"is* a brain," and it fits with the contemporary emphasis on technology as holding answers to whatever we want to know.

In a recent lecture I attended, a prominent psychologist claimed that researchers have found where depression is in the brain. Even if that were true (and ignoring for now the problems described above with defining depression), does that tell us anything about cause and effect, since behavior and emotions can lead to changes in the brain, as well as vice versa? Not at this time. Does it tell us what can be done to help people who are suffering? Not really. Maybe someday sticking a needle in just the right spot will make terrible feelings stop, but we are far from being there yet. The main point here is that we must guard against a tendency to believe that any research connected with the brain is more illuminating than other research or other ways of thinking. Let us consider an example of the pitfalls.

Suppose someone does a study of people given the PTSD label and finds that something about their brains differs from those of people not diagnosed with PTSD. What does that tell us? For starters, we might say that we must be careful not to assume that it tells us much of anything,[79] because (1) PTSD is not a scientifically grounded category, and its symptoms were not scientifically selected, and (2) those who assigned the label to the people in this study might or might not have scrupulously followed even the unscientific *DSM* criteria. Thus, we cannot be sure who was studied. Furthermore, in few studies do we learn anything about participants' coping mechanisms, their strengths and resources, or much else other than diagnosis, age, sex, and maybe race and social class. But even putting these problems aside for the moment, and even if the study reveals a correlation between some aspect of a brain scan and whether or not someone has received the PTSD label, we are highly unlikely to know whether something related to the PTSD was a cause or an effect of a change in the brain. Which came first? That there is a *correlation* with brain imaging findings does not tell us what is cause and what is effect.

Experience can change the brain (for instance, parts of the brain related to spatial relationships are different in taxi drivers than in others[80]), but that does not mean that finding brain differences is useful for war veterans. It does not help us know how to help them, and it can do harm: To focus on brain differences of traumatized people tends to make us think of them as more different from ourselves than they probably are, and it certainly inclines at least some people to consider vets as stranger, even less human, than others. At least as worrying is that focusing on the brains of people who have been emotionally traumatized by war takes our focus away from the most obvious cause of the trauma: war! It is not clear what part of that is so hard to understand, but it can be less painful to think about vets in a clinical way, picturing bits of their brain lighting up differently from ours, than to picture what they went through in Tikrit or Kabul. Furthermore, focusing on the brain diverts clinicians' and researchers' attention away from the real problems vets face as a consequence of their experiences, roles, relationships, and expectations, as described in chapter 2.

If we hear some researcher suggest that an aspect of the brains of people diagnosed with PTSD may differ from that aspect in the brains of others, we should not jump to the conclusion that we should call reactions to trauma mental illnesses. Experiences and feelings affect our brains, so it would not be surprising if we found differences between the brains of some who have gone to war and the brains of some who have not. But surely there should be some guidelines other than "it changes the brain, and it is a terribly negative experience" for deciding what to call a mental illness. Surely we would not want to call someone's deep sorrow after the death of a loved one a mental illness because it might lead to a change on a brain scan. (Note, however, that the authors of the psychiatric diagnosis manual pathologize just about everything and have indeed declared officially that someone grieving just two months after the loss of a loved one has the mental disorder of Major Depressive Disorder.)

Other Biological Factors?
Sometimes the emphasis on a physical basis for PTSD or other emotional problems is focused not on the brain but on something else in human physiology. When widely regarded experts make blanket assertions, such as that PTSD is "a biologically based condition . . . with the body's stress-response system in overdrive,"[81] we may be tempted to think, "Even if not much that is known about the brain can shed light on veterans' pain, surely here is something that can!" We all can think of times when we felt our own stress-response system go into overdrive, as a Mack truck nearly hit us, and we swerved away just in time, or we grabbed our toddler as she flew from the swing, just before she hit the concrete. Servicemembers experience these kinds of physical reactions constantly in combat. It is common for people to assume that if there is any biological cause, then there must be a known cure. It is important to look at such assumptions. As with correlations between the brain and emotions, correlations between emotions and the functions of other parts of the body, such as those that go into action in the presence of danger (heart pounding, adrenals

pumping), do not necessarily tell us much that is currently useful. Some people claim that those who have been in combat develop an "addiction" to the symptoms of physiological overdrive, such as a pounding heart, and then seek danger in order to repeat it. But that kind of thinking is both simplistic and likely to make us think of veterans as grotesque and quite different from the rest of us. As we see in *The Hurt Locker*, the main character knows when at war that his value to others is tremendous, his importance phenomenal, and he develops deeply caring connections with the people who are with him and going through the same dangerous, bizarre, but suddenly common experiences as he. When he returns home to a caring woman and their young child, despite their mutual affection, the differences between the world they live in and the one in which he lived in Iraq create a chasm that seems unbridgeable, and shopping for cereal in a grocery store fails to provide him the sense of being valued and important. As the audience hopes that he and the woman will talk and try to find some way to live in the same world, that he will find meaning and feel valued back at home, the couple fails to connect, and he returns to Iraq. This feels tragic for the couple and their son and frightening because the soldier is heading back into daily danger, but it is not hard to comprehend, and it certainly feels different from "nearly dying feels so great that I can't stay away from it."

Perhaps there is a somewhat helpful parallel with the way that victims of abuse may stay with their abusers because being alone is too scary or leaving the abusers is too dangerous, rather than that the victims somehow "love being beaten." We can search for common humanity with others, or we can "explain" their motives in ways that create further distance, alienation, and isolation. We have a choice. Furthermore, focusing on correlations between emotions and the brain or emotions and other bodily reactions do not actually clarify the nature of the problems vets have and do not lead in directions that are helpful for patients. Rather, this kind of focus creates an aura of scientific precision that promotes certain beliefs about the problems, the therapists, and the therapies, and such beliefs divert attention away from vets' real problems and away from the best ways to help them (as shown in the next sections).

Why Is It Wrong to Diagnose Veterans as Mentally Ill and Put Them on Drugs and Psychotherapy?

While reading a report of a major study from the National Institute of Mental Health about the question, "Which helps depressed teenagers: Drugs, psychotherapy, or both?," I felt uneasy, and only at the end did I realize why. It was that these were the only options mentioned, despite the well-known fact that they often fail to help and that other options, including (but not limited to) talking with friends and family, meditation, exercise, involvement in creative pursuits, volunteer work, dealing with existential or spiritual issues, and having adequate food, housing, and employment, can be effective.[82] Although some people are helped by therapy, drugs, or both, these interventions often fail to help and may do harm. Many veterans who are currently homeless, violent, addicted to drugs or alcohol, sad, or isolated have taken psychiatric drugs and seen psychotherapists, often numerous ones of each, but have been helped little or not at all, while increasingly suffering from the negative effects of the drugs and blaming themselves because even with psychotherapy, no matter how helpful or unhelpful the therapists, they have not been "cured." As I have said, I would never want anyone to feel that they should not avail themselves of drugs, therapy, or both; however, (1) they need—and have the right—to be fully informed about everything known about the potentially positive and potentially negative effects of *anything* that is recommended (some clinicians are actually told in their training *not* to disclose harmful effects, on the infantilizing theory that the patients will then believe that all these terrible things are happening to them even when they are not), and (2) they need to be fully informed about the full range of things that have helped at least some people. Unfortunately, this information is too rarely given, and suffering people are rarely in any condition to know that they need to ask for it. Even if they do ask, some professionals have not bothered to learn about the limitations and problems with either drugs or psychotherapy (some of which I discuss here), and some of those who have bothered are not inclined to share that information with their patients. The whole medical model of giving people psychiatric labels is far more likely to lead to what professional therapists recommend, drugs and therapy, than to less scientific-seeming approaches such as support and understanding from nonprofessionals, finding community, participation in the arts and sports, doing volunteer work and outreach, and meditation, to name just a few.[33]

We now look at some of the many problems with psychotherapy, and then at problems with psychiatric drugs. It is important to be aware that the ones addressed here represent only a fraction of those that exist, and that entire books have been written on these subjects.

Limitations of Psychotherapy and Drugs

In our highly technologically oriented society where people lucky enough to have paid jobs spend far more time than ever at work[84] and where standards for good parenting move steadily upward, people under tremendous pressure on all fronts often want, even need, to believe that quick fixes are available: Get someone to diagnose you, then get a pill (despite the absence of a solid, useful definition of "mental disorder," the use of psychiatric drugs has skyrocketed in recent years[85]) or see a therapist fifty minutes a week. The psychiatrizing of society has persuaded many people that if only a professional can find the right diagnostic label for them, they will know what pill to give and what to say in therapy that will speedily make things better so that the patient can get back to family and work. How much more might veterans long for this? The longing is furthered by the human need to believe that the world is safe, so that if someone is suffering, help must surely be close at hand. Since nontherapists often fear that they are unqualified to help with the suffering of others, it becomes even more important to believe that therapists can do what is needed. All of these factors contribute to the widespread belief in the curative powers of therapists and drugs.

It is not so simple, however. We see this, for instance, in the television advertisements that have recently begun to appear: the speakers in voice-overs note that alarmingly high percentages of people diagnosed with depression are still depressed after taking one psychiatric drug or another, and they encourage viewers to add another one. Other signs of the clay feet of the traditional therapy-and-drugs approach are:

• the many people who have been taking psychiatric drugs or have been in psychotherapy for years and still say they are not sure if it's really helping or not;
• revelations of the limitations and even sometimes the ineffectiveness of psychotherapy[86];
• the major roles that political and financial considerations play in the medical and mental health professionals' associations creation of "professional practice guidelines," which are their instructions about what treatments to use with patients[87];
• the number, large and growing, of discoveries about drug companies' malfeasance of various kinds,[88] including concealment of the ineffectiveness and even dangers of some of their drugs;
• drug companies' intimate connections with vast numbers of people who write the manual of psychiatric diagnosis,[89] the *DSM*[90] and even with the American Psychiatric Association (APA), which publishes the *DSM*, and the APA's current president[91];
• drug companies' payments of huge sums to doctors who give lectures or teach courses in which the companies' drugs are heavily and dispropor-

tionately (compared to other companies' drugs and to nondrug therapies) promoted, and their negative effects glossed over[92];

• drug companies' use of ghostwriters to write reports about their drugs, reports that are published under M.D.s' names[93];

• the greater likelihood that studies showing positive effects of clinical trials of drugs will be published in medical journals than will studies showing negative or no effects[94];

• the discrepancies between reports that some drug companies send to the Food and Drug Administration (FDA) when trying to get new drugs approved and the reports the companies publish[95];

• the enormous amount of work revealing the unscientific nature of the vast majority of psychiatric diagnosis[96]; and

• conflicts of interest and other serious problems in the operation of the FDA.[97]

This is not to say that no one should have access to psychiatric drugs or to psychotherapy or that they never help or always do harm, for some people have been helped and not harmed. It is to say, however, that in our society, we leap immediately to classifying suffering as mental illness[98] and to assuming only two kinds of help are possible. What may be the most important principle to keep in mind is that missing from both psychotherapy and drug therapy are the veteran's reconnection with the wider community and access to support from those in that community. When we focus too much on psychotherapy and drugs, we ignore the fundamentally important, wider social context of suffering and the alleviation of suffering. The real-life consequences of this ignoring are tremendous, because the individualistic approach to helping those with severe emotional pain and inability to function has not been shown to be very helpful, and an absence of social supports tends to intensify suffering.[99]

Problems with Psychotherapy

A flood of press releases from the Department of Defense (see chapter 4), the VA (see chapter 5), and various therapists' organizations has created the impression that more and more therapists using various techniques are what vets need. Some therapists help reduce the suffering of veterans and other people. (I hope you will remember that I said that, and not assume that I think no therapist ever does any good.) But, like everyone else, veterans and those who care about them deserve to know the truth about the limitations and problems of psychotherapy so that they do not enter a therapist's office assuming that therapy is a science, that virtually any therapist is an expert on that vet's particular problems, and that therapist and patient will work well together. After all, the stakes for many vets are extremely high: In a recent Department of Defense report, an Army general reported that "about half of the soldiers who committed suicide last year sought treatment from mental-health care providers."[100] And in a newspaper report of a veteran's suicide, we learn that the vet had completed a program aimed at teaching vets diagnosed with PTSD "coping skills" two days before he made a call, talking of suicide, to a VA therapist.[101] The reasons these people did not receive enough help to prevent their suicides are undoubtedly many and varied. However, no therapist is capable of preventing all suicides, so for despondent vets, we must not assume that therapists know what to do and have the resources to do it. Furthermore, as for the vet in the story that began this chapter, and as shown in recent research, some suicides and other acts of violence actually result from the introduction or changes in dosage of drugs that therapists provide.[102] Furthermore, as Yawar has said in *The Lancet*, "We rarely have the time, or encouragement, to treat patients according to their story, rather than our diagnosis; outcome measures are too coarse to consider whether the patient has been allowed to preserve and fulfill his or her humanity."[103] This is not to say that no therapists work in caring, humane, and helpful ways with traumatized people, and many chapters in the book edited by Christine Courtois and Julian Ford exemplify this kind of work.[104] But as psychologist and longtime veterans' therapist David Collier has said, whatever the technique or approach, "it is the relationship that helps, that provides the safety, the trust which are important for doing exploration or behavior change."[105]

I referred above to the pressure many therapists and mental health researchers feel to do, and appear to do, scientifically grounded work. But there is a huge difference between doing work that involves a little scientifically based information and work that is as scientifically solid as using an X-ray to identify a broken bone and then applying a cast to speed its proper healing. Psychotherapy bears almost no resemblance to the latter. In recent years, some therapists have begun to use the term "evidence-based practice," which in principle means tailoring therapy as much as possible to the known science, in the hope of helping people as much as possible. It is a worthy aim, and if there were enough well-done research to provide a solid foundation, perhaps it would work. However, for a host of reasons, the foundation is poor. Furthermore, what is too often ignored is knowledge of the nontechnical, inexpert factors that have been proven to help, such as the therapist's respect and compassion for the patient.[106]

Also ignored are factors that make a piece of research inapplicable to real-life situations, such as studying "normal" college students in a laboratory when the research is supposed to be about helping people who come to clinics seeking help.[107]

Alan Kazdin, past president of the American Psychological Association, has written a penetrating critique of evidence-based practice, referring primarily to psychotherapy but also to some extent to other treatments, including drugs.[108] It takes no expertise to understand the problems he describes with evidence-based practice. These include the following:

• Researchers virtually never study treatments under the same conditions or with just the same patients or kinds of patients as those who come to the clinics and offices where these treatments are administered.

• "[M]any critical clinical issues and concerns are not heavily researched," or else little is definitely known about them, such as how to prevent suicide[109] or about the effects of "psychological debriefing," a technique therapists often use with traumatized vets.[110]

• Clinicians constantly make judgments about combining treatment approaches, quite appropriately intending to tailor treatment to fit the individual, but it is not yet well established that different clinicians would select the same or a similar individualized treatment plan (i.e., reliability) when presented with the same case. Even if the treatment selected were the same, we do not know that it would make a difference or achieve palpable change in this patient's life (i.e., validity). How to individualize therapy for each person and how to show that doing so makes a difference are topics researchers have still not helped elaborate sufficiently and are difficult to defend.[111]

• "Given the uniqueness of the client in front of me who is about to begin treatment, it is not clear on what basis I can generalize from a prior client or several prior clients."[112]

• Little research exists about whether a particular factor is a predictor of how a particular patient will respond to a particular treatment or combination of treatments.[113]

Kazdin concludes that "individualized therapy based on my judgment of what is needed will not necessarily help this patient."[114] In a 2010 paper, Kazdin points to the importance of integrating "evidence, clinical expertise, and the individual needs, values, and preferences of the patient" but notes that "it is not clear that we know how to do this integration, that we can do so consistently (reliability), and that doing it makes a difference (validity) in patient care."[115]

The concerns of psychologist Alan Kazdin are echoed in a recent paper by psychiatrist Jerold Kreisman,[116] who says that evidence-based practice is a good jumping-off point but that it is wrong to hold it in "reverence." He points out that it is derived mostly from published studies, most of which come from academia. He beautifully describes the following problem: Human behavior is extremely complex, and it is not possible to study all of the variables that might, for instance, contribute to the suffering of veterans. Researchers have to make choices about what to study, and they inevitably leave out some of what in real life matters a great deal. Simplifying research makes it easier to carry out but less useful in the real world. One simply cannot study everything relevant to veterans in the real world. There are too many complexities and their interactions to study very well, including the specifics of each person's war experiences, their history, whether they had major problems in coping before going to war, what kinds of therapies they were offered afterward, the relevant features of the specific therapists who tried to help, and what individual and social strengths and resources they have.

Kreisman points out that it is difficult to know what to make of researchers who claim their studies show particular treatments to be successful, because ways to measure that success are flawed. What looks on a researcher's rating scale like improvement in the patient may not carry over to the patient's functioning outside the therapist's office. And there are what psychologists call "demand characteristics"—in this case, an appearance of improvement because veterans who like their therapists may either feel better while actually in the office filling out the rating scale or want to please the therapist and will seem to be doing better by checking the "right" answers on the scale.

Another problem Kreisman identifies is that scientific articles are often published a year or more after they are submitted, so evidence-based practice is always behind the times. The same applies to what therapists' associations call practice guidelines, which are intended to advise clinicians, "For patients with problem or diagnosis X, you should do Y." Insurance companies similarly use outdated information to make decisions about whose therapy will be paid for, what diagnostic labels qualify patients for coverage, and how many sessions of what kind of treatment will be covered. Referring specifically to studies involving the *DSM*, he notes that even after a new edition of the *DSM* is published (and we have seen that the *DSM* is unscientific anyway), research reports for many years continue to be based on the categories and criteria from the previous edition.

Summarizing his concerns, Kreisman says that evidence-based recommendations may be useful to the average patient but that most practitioners want to provide above-average care. For the individual patient in the professional's office, he feels, an individualized approach may be more useful than one based on invariably limited and often deeply flawed studies of groups of people.

Apart from questions about the usefulness of science for helping veterans, there is a very different kind of reason that psychotherapy may not be useful for them. As discussed in chapter 2, much of war-created suffering involves spiritual, existential, or moral matters because of failure to find meaning in one's life or because of conflicts of values, not because of mental illness. Psychotherapists are primarily trained to focus on conflicts that arise within the individual (often these days assumed, without proof, to be caused by chemical imbalances), on the theory that something within the individual needs to be changed. They are rarely trained to recognize crises of meaning or to say that that is what they are. Further, traditional therapy techniques—talking about one's childhood, expressing feelings, cognitive-behavioral therapy, looking at conflicts between wishes and fears, analyzing dreams, taking psychiatric drugs—rarely help people who feel that life has no meaning or who are grappling with how to reconcile their premilitary values of kindness, creativity, and the affirmation of life with the exposure to (and in some cases even the valuing of) violence and destruction.

Some therapists recognize when the problems of people who come to them seeking aid are beyond their capacity to help or even beyond their field of interest, but some do not. In addition to these limitations of training and knowledge, some therapists have personal problems that get in the way of their effectiveness. As with every other group of people, some therapists are deeply troubled in ways that lead to significant blind spots that impede their attempts to understand and help others. Although some therapists are truly wonderful and effective, others have serious problems that go well beyond blind spots. Some of the most emotionally constricted, most detached, and angriest people I have ever known have hung out their shingles as psychotherapists. Does that mean that these people cannot possibly be good therapists, that they cannot ever help anyone? Certainly not. But it is essential for us all to understand that the category "therapists" includes many people (such as control freaks or people uncomfortable with their own emotions who hope to live vicariously through patients) with severe problems of their own. And how is the prospective patient to know when entering a particular therapist's office? Supervision, which some therapists seek from other therapists, is supposed to help but is often inadequate. And when a patient says that what the therapist is doing is not helpful, some therapists have been trained to dismiss these legitimate concerns too easily as signs that the patient is uncooperative, has problems with authority figures, or "doesn't want to get well."

Another problem with psychotherapy relates to that part of veterans' suffering that comes from their isolation from others, the disconnections that result from having been ripped from their usual lives, sent into dangerous situations, trained to act in violent ways within a rigidly hierarchical military system, and then returned home to a totally different culture, from which they now feel hopelessly isolated. For some vets, developing a connection with a therapist can be a first step toward breaking down this isolation and reducing their vertiginous disorientation. However, to do this with a therapist carries the price of being labeled mentally ill—reducing one burden while adding another. Another common problem is that for veterans used to the reality of intensely close relationships with other servicepeople, the strict limits of psychotherapy—in an office, for fifty minutes, usually with the therapist saying little and disclosing nothing about their own life or feelings, and the therapist being paid to have this relationship—can make it hard to transfer benefits from that connection into the world outside the therapist's office. Knowing that the therapist is paid to connect with the vet can leave the vet feeling that the relationship is not real and add to the vet's feeling of not deserving care for the sake of care.

In summary, the problems that psychotherapy can involve for veterans include the near certainty that anyone seeing a therapist will be diagnosed as mentally ill; that psychotherapy is often paired with medications that might help or might cause harm; that many therapists are simply not very good at listening with respect and compassion; that many therapists have personal problems; that many therapists' training for working with vets has been severely limited; the paucity of evidence that psychotherapy is helpful with many vets; the major problems with research that might otherwise have helped therapists know how to help vets; the awkwardness for the vet of knowing that the therapist is being paid to listen; the fact that the therapist is not part of the community in which the vet must live and function; and the therapist's limited ability to help with the kinds of moral, existential, and spiritual crises that plague so many vets.

Problems with Psychiatric Drugs

Massive marketing campaigns by drug companies have helped create and reinforce the belief that people diagnosed with PTSD, depression or other mood problems, or anxiety disorders have defective brains that can be fixed fairly easily with prescription drugs. This is especially relevant in light of recent research showing that psychiatrists are far less likely to use psychotherapy than before,[117] and the use of psychiatric drugs has thus become disproportionately common compared to other forms of treatment. But according to Greg Miller's recent report in *Science* magazine, major drug companies are cutting back dramatically on research into drugs for a wide variety of emotional troubles, including depression, anxiety, and what have been classified as schizophrenia and bipolar disorder.[118] Why? As Miller disclosed in a companion article, the reason an AstraZeneca representative gave for "pulling out of the psychiatry space" was that "Our understanding of disease pathophysiology is still relatively in its infancy. These are complex and heterogeneous disorders." That is a stunning confession, given the billions of dollars of profits that AstraZeneca and other major drug companies have made from vigorous and often irresponsible marketing about the alleged effectiveness of a wide variety of drugs.[119]

Belief in the effectiveness of these drugs persists despite the striking lack of research proving that irregular brain chemistry causes the symptoms of PTSD, depression or other mood changes, or anxiety. Yet many therapists and laypeople alike irresponsibly assume that drugs will normalize the brains of suffering soldiers and veterans. The assumption has been resilient even in the face of reports like these:

• Most of the women Iraq veterans a *New York Times* journalist interviewed were on antidepressants and receiving counseling, "but few had a sense that their symptoms were going away."[120]
• Shad Meshad, president of the National Veterans Foundation, who has counseled soldiers and veterans for the last three decades, says that antidepressants and psychologists can do only so much for a hurting soul.[121]
• Some veterans say antidepressants cause them to sleep all the time, but more say they sit up "half the night in a drugged daze, waiting for sleep to come."[122]
• Glantz quotes a veteran as saying that "the pain of losing loved ones on the battlefield, the pain of not being there for my children, of not knowing how to live in this civilian society after so many years in the military—I stuffed these things down deep inside because I considered myself a hardcore guy. But after the effects of the methamphetamine went away, I still felt the same. . . . It was the insanity of it all."[123]
• A soldier who became extremely withdrawn decided it might be due to the new antidepressant he had been given, so he quit cold turkey (which can be dangerous for some people) and almost instantly felt much better.[124]

• A woman reported that her boyfriend, a vet, was given lithium to control his mood swings, which turned out probably to have been caused by a TBI that the VA overlooked in its haste to put him on psychiatric drugs instead.[125]

• A male vet wrote this to me: "I have taken nearly every top-drawer medication that is a fix all at one time or another. None of them are lasting because . . . my body becomes accustomed to the effects or lack thereof and some Doc will open his top drawer once again. The hurtful part comes in when you seem to be on someone's conveyer belt and they prop your mouth open, shove in a prescription and send you on your way all the while watching the Prozac commercial on t.v. and relishing the idea that they have a hand and vice-versa of making someone's pockets a little greener."

• A woman vet was sexually assaulted and had also experienced combat trauma, but instead of receiving treatment focused on helping her cope with and work through her feelings, she was put on Depakote for her moods swings and anger, Celexa for anxiety and depression, Topamax for severe migraines, and Trazodone to help her sleep.[126]

• Some of the top trauma research experts have written, "We are at a preliminary stage in research on acute pharmacotherapy as an early intervention for acutely traumatized individuals, with very little scientific information to guide us."[127]

The belief that psychiatric drugs are spectacularly effective also persists despite the sobering statistics cited in chapter 1 about the many kinds of ongoing problems that veterans have, even with the wide use of these medications with vets. And as Yawar writes in *The Lancet*:

Some would argue that even if drugs work, they do not work. The margin over placebo is not large; . . . prognosis may be worse than with the "moral treatment" (rest, respect, good food, work, prayer) of 200 years ago; . . . drug treatment attends to the symptoms, but not to the human being who has the symptoms.[128]

Indeed, in 2002, award-winning investigative journalist Robert Whitaker revealed in his book, *Mad in America*, that beginning decades ago, drug companies corrupted psychiatry and related professions by often exaggerating the benefits and concealing the ill effects of their products.[129] Much of his book is about drugs that in the United States are called antipsychotic medications (elsewhere called neuroleptics, to reflect the way they generally suppress the functioning of the nervous system). Whitaker's work is increasingly relevant for Americans in general because of the skyrocketing frequency with which these kinds of drugs are prescribed for problems that never used to be considered to warrant such strong medication. His work is particularly relevant for veterans, because the intensity of their suffering and the vividness with which many of them reexperience the sights, sounds, smells, and feel of war makes it easy to misclassify them as out of touch with reality, as psychotic, when in fact they are, if anything, well in touch with the foul realities of war.

Some psychiatric drugs help some people for some periods of time, and some even help certain people over the long term. But so much work has shown their limitations and dangers that it could fill many books. Let us focus on some of the most fundamental and general problems. One is that the same drug given to the same person can have one effect at one time and the opposite effect at another time. And as noted earlier, the drugs often simply do not help, and they often cause serious problems when the person tries to stop taking them.[130] Another problem is that these drugs— for sadness, rage, depression, anxiety, hallucinations, or delusions—work on the central nervous system and therefore are parts of feedback loops. That is, a drug can, for instance, raise the level of a chemical that affects the brain,[131] but the brain often responds by signaling the body to lower its production of that chemical (because the person is now ingesting some of it). As a result, some drugs that alleviate symptoms for an individual in the beginning may become ineffective or have adverse effects later on. In fact, all psychotropic drugs can have the *opposite* effect to that for which they are prescribed; thus, what the drug companies sell as "antidepressants" can alleviate depression but also cause it, the drugs they sell to *suppress* hallucinations and delusions can *produce* hallucinations and delusions, and so on. It was sadly unsurprising to hear vets describe making the most terrifying suicide attempts I have ever heard of and then say such things as, "That was right after they started me on that new antidepressant."

In his 2010 book, *Anatomy of an Epidemic,*[132] Robert Whitaker presents a tightly argued case that before the drugs that are marketed as antipsychotics, antidepressants, and anti-anxiety medications came out, the rates at which people recovered without drug treatment were far higher than they are now. He shows further that since each of these kinds of drugs became available, the frequency of symptoms of psychosis, depression, and anxiety has geometrically *increased*, and he describes in detail the neurological basis[133] for this pattern of drug effects. That is, he shows the drugs themselves change the brain in ways that increase the symptoms. He takes care to say that some individuals do well, even over long periods of time, on each type of drug, but that when one looks at the whole populations of people who take each category of medication, the pattern is alarming.

Another fundamental concern about drugs is that often, the companies that produce them have primarily studied the effect they hope the drug will have, neglecting to study (or sometimes to report openly) its negative effects.[134] Sometimes they even fail to discover positive effects other than the one they aim to achieve. Later on, when faced with imminent expiration of the patent on the first use for which the FDA approves the drug, they may look for other beneficial effects.

Psychologist Roger P. Greenberg is an expert on antidepressant drugs, which are the most prescribed class of drugs in the United States and are widely prescribed for vets. In summarizing the research about these medications, he notes that they produce a "very modest effect at best" when compared to placebos and are even less effective in real life than in the controlled trials that are the basis for FDA approval.[135] Why has this only recently become widely known? Because, he says, those selected studies that get published do not accurately reflect what all trials of the drug show about effectiveness. As Erick Turner and his colleagues reported in the *New England Journal of Medicine*,[136] when they compared all studies of antidepressants that the FDA approved for use between 1987 and 2004, in only about half the studies was the drug more effective than a placebo. However, reading only those studies that were *published*, which included only 8 percent of the studies that produced negative results, one can easily get the wrong impression that almost all of the results were beneficial. Such selective reports have also made it seem that the beneficial effects are greater than they actually are. Finally, although many people assume that the government, through the FDA, makes sure that no false claims are made in drug advertisements aimed at both professionals and the public, a *New England Journal of Medicine* article shows that research fails to support many of these claims, and government overseers often fail to examine or monitor them well.[137]

Although antidepressant drugs as a group are of questionable efficacy for many people, one class among them warrants particular mention. The drugs called selective serotonin reuptake inhibitors (SSRIs), which are most likely to be the first ones prescribed when PTSD has been diagnosed, have the dubious honor of rarely producing positive response rates over 60 percent, and fewer than 20–30 percent of people who take them achieve full remission of symptoms.[138] These less than stellar performance numbers, in combination with the psychopharmaceutical emphasis of many current treatment models, often lead doctors to prescribe a second, even a third, or still more psychiatric drugs. This combining of psychoactive substances may (sometimes, we hope) be done with the best of intentions, but we mustn't forget that the already significant risks are very likely to increase as well.

It would be lovely to believe that giving a pill can take away a veteran's pain, but often it does not. Army Sergeant Christopher LeJeune described how troubled he was to go into Iraqis' homes, expecting to find terrorists, only to see "little bitty tiny shoes and toys on the floor," as well as some wounded but still alive bodies of Iraqis he and his buddies had shot. When he went to see a military doctor because of his anguish about such experiences, the doctor put him on an antidepressant and an anti-anxiety drug and sent him back to war. LeJeune was disturbed that the only "solution" offered was to take pills.[139] These, of course, did not resolve his moral dilemmas or take away from how they affected him. The authors of the medical book *Combat Stress Injury* say that "No magic pill can erase the image of a best friend's shattered body or assuage the guilt from having traded duty with him that day."[140] In spite of this, the medicating of the U.S. military has increased during the current wars; as of 2008, about 12 percent of combat troops in Iraq and 17 percent in Afghanistan were taking antidepressants or sleeping pills, but the Pentagon was not maintaining a central clearinghouse for information about such medications, and "the Army hasn't consistently asked about prescription drug use."[141] In spite of the heavy drug use, nearly 40 percent of the Army's suicide victims in 2006 and 2007 were taking psychotropic drugs, usually SSRIs such as Prozac and Zoloft.[142] What is particularly disturbing is that two major studies (one from RAND and one from the Institute of Medicine) led to the conclusion that there was inadequate evidence even to determine whether SSRIs help in treating PTSD. And as one soldier said, "PTSD isn't fixed by taking pills—it's just numbed. . . . And I felt like I was drugged all the time."[143]

Drugs that act on the brain can certainly affect how people feel and act, but as any forthcoming physician will acknowledge, prescribing of drugs for emotions and behavior is virtually always a matter of trial-and-error. In fact, in the magazine published by the famous Menninger Clinic, Dr. Florence Kim is quoted as saying that patients may spend months or even years "trying to find the best medication with the fewest side effects."[144] There are at least two main reasons for this: (1) individuals respond in vastly different ways to a given drug, and even the same person can react in different, even completely opposite ways, to the same drug at two different times, and (2) those who make decisions about research and marketing for most pharmaceutical companies focus resources on the question, "How can we show that this drug does what we want to say in marketing that it does?" This means that many of its effects—certainly negative ones, but sometimes even positive ones—are unstudied or barely explored when a drug goes on the market.

It is heartbreaking to hear about the consequences for veterans (and others) of the cumulative effects of these and other problems with research about drugs and the way the FDA goes about approving them.[145] The following story from a Vietnam vet may sound extreme but is the kind I often hear. I choose this one because, as a veteran of a war that ended decades ago, he has had far longer to seek help from the mental health system than have the veterans from Iraq and Afghanistan, yet still he suffers horribly. Understandably, he does not wish me to use his name with his story, so I will call him Guy:

My sister said that there must be something wrong with me since I did not seem quite "normal." Dr. [A] was her M.D., delivered her children and supplied some medication for postpartum depression. He can "fix" you. Short discussion and a prescription for Zoloft and Trazadone and an agreement not to commit suicide. Just call him first. Seemed to work for a while with various side effects including some sexual, which most men at that age do not enjoy. Medication [benefit] didn't last long. Only follow-up was more medication. New method, try Lithium. I couldn't stand that. Made me worse than none at all. Empty, hurting, more nightmares, suicidal thoughts, and some action with a rifle. Solution: admittance to a psych ward, more medication. Can't remember all [the medications]. . . . Ten days, new doctor [Dr. B], new medication. Can't remember this one doctor, but "cure" was Prozac. Never worked. New medication: Paxil. New doctor [Dr. C] and not a lot of new discussion. Next patient, please.

Things just seemed to stay the same or get worse and heading nowhere fast. New medication, Divalproex, still I was "crazy." Referred to a new doctor [Dr. D] . . . . New medication, this time Buspirone. Can't remember this doctor's name, but he also oversaw another psych wing twice a week. . . . Felt well enough to go home after 12 days. New medications: Effexor and Depakote. This actually worked for a while but didn't keep me from ducking at the slightest sound. . . . But that [beneficial effect] didn't last long, new medication—Buproprion which I think has something to do with Welbutrin. One doctor [Dr. E] actually said there is nothing more that he could do [and asked,] Did I read the Bible? Maybe I should find Jesus. . . .

Was asked to try different strengths of Divalproex some straight, some time-release. Things were really starting to get nuts by now. I was fishing . . . during a good run crowded by eager fisherman. Some guy next to me landed a foul hooked fish (which you are supposed to release), and I informed him to do so. He made some off-handed remark and told me to go "find" myself. I knew things were going to go terribly bad. I knew if I boiled over, it would be ugly. If I ever lose it, I won't bloody your nose and quit. Instead you'd be looking at me with blank eyes, and I'd be in jail. Similar to all the animal trainer tales you hear that go bad. . . .

That's when I went to see [Dr. F]. He finally talked with me. . . . Now I had some understanding but still kept tabs with various other doctors through the veterans. Most of them were medication pushers. They all had plaques but little knowledge of . . . what patience and understanding were all about.

I was referred to a veterans' facility. His name was [Dr. G]. . . . He had his plaque of service medals in the center of his diplomas. He was a good man, a good listener, and non-judgmental. I don't even remember if he mentioned medication other than Clonazepam. . . . He left finally, and I went through more medications than I can even remember, and that's been a few.

The veteran who told me this story is in touch with at least a thousand other veterans of various wars. A primary reason for their ongoing connection is that neither the drugs nor the therapies they have been offered have been of much help, and their pain remains intense.

In summary, for veterans as for people in general, then, drugs are less effective than most people think, they often have terrible negative effects in the short term and the long term, and they can mask real problems such as moral conflicts and crises of meaning, and even make it harder to grapple with such problems.

Moving toward What Helps

Murphy, the veteran described at the beginning of this chapter, finally did receive some help. But although it came from a therapist, what worked for him was nothing unique to therapists. When he walked into Dr. David Collier's office in the Vet Center, he saw immediately that Dr. Collier had displayed his own war medals on his wall. Murphy felt that here was a therapist who would be more likely to understand what he had been through than the long line of doctrinaire, theory-bound ones he had seen over the years. Murphy says that what Dr. Collier did that actually helped was to ask him to tell the stories of his time at war, staying with him attentively and compassionately as he did so, and, each time the pain became unbearable, reminding him to stop, breathe, and remember that Dr. Collier was with him on his journey. Dr. Collier says that what he does can be done by laypeople as well,[146] and this makes it less alarming to recognize the limitations of both traditional professional therapy approaches and psychiatric drugs. Before looking in chapter 6 at what every citizen can do to help, we look first in chapters 4 and 5 at what the military and the VA are doing about emotional suffering caused by war.

4 The Wrong Responses Begin: What the Military Is Doing while Johnny and Jane Are Over There . . . and Why It's Not Enough

Although he had been strongly drawn to the study of animals and plants, Nelson Jamison (not his real name) joined the Army because his father and his father's father had served in the armed forces. Even so, he took well to the orderliness of the military, though not to the verbal abuse that his sergeant commonly directed at the lowest-ranking soldiers. In Iraq, he saw his closest friend from his unit assigned to a convoy that was ordered to travel a road regularly planted with improvised explosive devices (IEDs). During that mission, his friend died a horrible death in one of those common explosions. Nelson saw what he was told was his friend's body, the face unrecognizable. Plagued with guilt because of feeling that he should have insisted on taking his friend's place in the mission, Nelson tried prayer, but that did not help. He spoke with the chaplain, whose assurance that everything that happens is God's will brought him no comfort. Deeply ashamed that he had not found a way on his own to "get over" his guilt and his grief, and seeing soldiers around him apparently unfazed by the deaths of their friends, he thought he did not deserve help or support. But as the weeks passed and his guilt kept him awake night after night, he felt increasingly desperate. He knew that a psychiatrist was attached to his unit—but also that his buddies were likely to find out and mock him if he sought the therapist's help. (The mental health services that the military offers are not used very often, because of the stigma attached, as well as because of stories servicemembers tell each other about upsetting experiences some of them have had when they do use them.) Nelson waited a long time before finally "breaking down," as he called it, and making an appointment to see the psychiatrist. When he did, the therapist accused him of cowardice, saying he suspected that Nelson was exaggerating the trauma of his friend's death in an effort to be sent back to the United States. He told Nelson that in the history of war, millions of soldiers had coped with such events with no trouble, and he was sure that Nelson could do the same.

Nelson's story is typical of one kind of experience I heard repeatedly in speaking with vets. Naturally, some people have had better experiences with military psychiatrists and psychologists. This chapter is about what the military is doing to try to help servicemembers while they are "in country" and afterward. Though some of these therapists may have the best of intentions (not Nelson's therapist, of course) much of what the military is doing is inadequate, unproven, untested, misguided, or even harmful. The tendency to think of emotions other than happiness and tranquility as signs of mental illness pervades the military just as it does civilian society, and this sometimes translates into wrongheaded if well-motivated efforts to help. The added factor in the military is that emotional toughness is considered essential for training warriors; as a result, ruptures of soldiers' tough facades are often considered alarming and in need of repair—including through accusations of cowardice—rather than as expressions of natural human emotions that need to be respected, aired, and shared. One consequence is the military's all too frequent use of approaches that are usually aimed at treating mental illness, some problems of which were detailed in chapter 3.

Since the war in Iraq began, and military recruitment numbers began to plummet and AWOL numbers to increase,[1] military therapists have felt increasingly pressured to think of ways to keep troops in the military and in combat zones. Sometimes this means giving anguished soldiers a brief rest or throwing emotion-numbing drugs at them, courses of action that, servicemembers tell me, too often do not help. Knowing about these approaches keeps some from seeking help. A different kind of impediment to helpseeking is the justifiable fear that reporting overwhelming emotions will lead to unwanted discharge from the service or, at the least, impede military career advancement. Through the stories that some veterans have told me, I have learned that even when members of the military take the huge step of contacting military therapists to seek help, some therapists fly into rages and call them cowards (as did Nelson's psychologist), accusing them of faking terror and despair as a way to avoid going into combat.

These combined factors—an emphasis on pathology, the military's desire to keep soldiers in war zones, and comrades' and military therapists' stigmatizing of upset and helpseeking—have led the military to neglect what most of their members need most. They need someone to listen respectfully, to assure them that their intensely negative feelings are not only *not* signs of insanity or cowardice but are extremely common among soldiers (even though rarely talked about), and to help them grapple with the emotional, moral, spiritual, and existential burdens of being a soldier at war. Today, soldiers get the message that they are not supposed to need or want any of that. One common way that the message is conveyed is through what is not said, including the stunning absence of discussion of feelings about war trauma among the forces. Michelle Dillow says that in the Army, soldiers who indicated they were depressed or upset were instructed to speak to the chaplain, so that, as she says, "It was made an individual thing," treated as though being upset made the soldiers unique. Other ways the message to keep silent about mental anguish is communicated include the shaming responses of some military therapists, officers, and peers, and the superficiality of the lick-and-a-promise debriefings that most soldiers receive on their way home.

Not long after the war in Iraq began, Army Sergeant Georg Andreas Pogany was on his second night in country when he saw an Iraqi cut in half by a machine gun.[2] He vomited and shook for hours afterward; his head pounded, and his chest hurt. He was unable to function and was faced with an "overwhelming" sense of his own mortality, knowing that that could be him in two seconds. He asked his superior for help and was told to take two sleeping pills and go away. Soon thereafter he was court-martialed for cowardice. Although the Army later dropped the charge,[3] the case had made headlines, and there was no guarantee that the next soldier asking for help would not be court-martialed. Ironically, the Army psychologist had said that Pogany's reaction was "normal" but recommended that he have a rest and then be returned to duty, conveying the notion that a bit of relaxation could—and *should*—have wiped out the images and Pogany's reactions to them. The reason the Army gave for dropping the charge against Pogany, according to an Army spokesman, was that it had learned that the soldier might have a "medical problem" caused by an antimalarial drug, once again covering up the normality of his emotional reaction to the horrific sights he had witnessed. It is interesting that in regard to this case, Col. René Robichaux, chief of the Department of Social Work at Brook Army Medical Center in Texas, had said at the time that Army psychologists are trained to let soldiers know their reactions are normal. He noted that it is appropriate to say, "This is crazy over here. What you are doing and everyone else is doing is bizarre. Being scared is not only normal, it is life-saving. If you are not scared, there is something wrong."[4] In a telephone interview in 2010 he reaffirmed this view, saying that it "had been public military policy going back to World War II."[5] Other reports, however, make it clear that many in the military do not share his view.

During the current wars, the military has issued a flood of press releases, some documenting emotional upset in soldiers and many containing announcements about new programs aimed at helping. A chronological tour provides a sense of the content of these releases and whether their often upbeat claims have been borne out. Work by investigative journalists through this period sheds further light on this material, which has been helpful, because the majority of my efforts to learn further details about the military's programs that were described in these releases and about whether research was carried out on their effectiveness led nowhere. I was able to communicate with only a few of the military mental health people I attempted to contact through what the Department of Defense and related press officers told me were the appropriate channels. Where planned research by the military is mentioned, my attempts to learn about the eventual outcomes of that research were largely fruitless.

As early as May 2003—two months after the war in Iraq began—hoping to prevent soldiers from committing violence when they returned home from combat, the Army announced plans to help soldiers "decompress."[6] The initiatives were to include counseling, a "cooling down period," and anger management training. This approach reflects an ever-present problem with counseling, which is what I call the *privatizing* of the consequences of war, treating them as though they come from within the individual rather than from the war itself.[7] What also matters is whether the Army's approach can work. After soldiers have been carefully trained to function in a hierarchical system designed to produce hair-trigger responses, often acts of violence, what role can counseling play? What role can it play in undoing the fight-or-flight responses that increased soldiers' chances of surviving when they were in actual danger? Anger management programs work best when participants are highly motivated to reduce the ways they lash out at others, but anger is an understandable and often legitimate response to having been constantly in danger of losing one's life or having to make excruciating moral choices. Can the Army that puts soldiers in those situations train them not to feel angry about them? And can this be done by occasional, calm conversations or homework exercises that usually comprise counseling about angry and violent behavior, in contrast to the high-pressure, day-in, day-out drills designed to make violent responses immediate? Researchers talk about one-trial learning, in which an event is so powerful that the person experiencing it has an immediate response that lasts a long time, even forever (for instance, battered women often describe this kind of response after the first time they are attacked).[8] One-trial learning is powerful when the event is, for instance, a car accident or getting stuck in a malfunctioning elevator. Therefore, it is understandable that counteracting daily drills to teach violent behavior, not to mention counteracting months of nonstop exposure to mortal danger, would be even more difficult. Thus, we must await compelling evidence that the Army's approach to helping soldiers unlearn violence actually works. (The same will be true, of course, for the other branches of the armed forces.) And then the Army confronts the following dilemma: What if learning ways to deal with soldiers' anger means raising questions about the military's principles and functions in promoting the hatred and demonizing of the enemy?

In February 2004, a time that in retrospect was early in the Iraq War, a U.S. Joint Task Force that included all five branches of the armed forces had charged a team of psychologists with providing "interventions" such as suicide awareness education, substance abuse evaluations, and therapies for anxiety and coping with "uncertainty."[9] Substance abuse problems were known to be legion during the Vietnam War and subsequent wars, and although it can be useful to evaluate soldiers for them, it does not take much to identify them. What is problematic is when suicide, substance abuse, and anxiety are treated as problems somehow springing solely from within the individual rather than recognized as the consequences of unbearable events and conditions of war. Are therapists hired by the military going to find it easy to use such recognition to help suffering service-members? These questions apply to trying to provide therapy to reduce suicide, substance abuse, anxiety, and uncertainty that result directly from being at war. There are serious ethical and moral problems involved in sending people into battle and then treating the resulting emotions as though their origins were irrelevant, as though they were the *individual's* problem (and perhaps due to a chemical imbalance in the brain, implying that the suffering would have arisen if the person had never enlisted). In treating emotional suffering, as in treating physical problems, if we fail to understand the real causes, at least we waste a lot of time, and at most we cover up those actual origins.

Also in February 2004, journalist Sara Corbett quoted a soldier just back from Iraq who had been traumatized when a rocket-propelled grenade hit his Humvee, one soldier in his unit was killed and five were injured, and their blood covered the road.[10] The soldier she interviewed had been told by a military therapist that he was "messed up in the head." Corbett reports that the military, "[h]aving learned from its failure to treat traumatized Vietnam War soldiers 30 years ago," was dispatching "combat stress teams" to Iraq to offer counseling and in some cases to dispense anti-anxiety drugs to suffering soldiers. She described a soldiers' support group for wounded troops, believed to be the first of its kind for this war. In that group at Fort Campbell, moderated by a military counselor, the main point was to listen to each other's stories. The listening would seem to be an important step. The military, she said, was taking note of soldiers with anxiety, sleeplessness, and what they called depression—perhaps more appropriately called grief—and diagnosing Posttraumatic Stress Disorder only when the symptoms were considered to be "intrusive," interfering with the person's life. As we discussed in chapter 3, with diagnoses, it is always a question of who gets to decide when to label horrible feelings "intrusive" or "interfering," thus qualifying them as signs of mental illness. But feelings can be intrusive even when it makes no sense to call them mental illnesses (think, for instance, of mourning the death of a loved one or the end of a romantic relationship).

In 2004, the VA issued *The Iraq War Clinician Guide*, which included information about providing services to soldiers while they were deployed.[11] The guide included a description of the Combat Stress Control Doctrine, which promoted the PIES principle in managing "battle fatigue": *promixity* of treatment close to the front; *immediacy* of treatment; *expectancy* of return to duty (RTD); and *simplicity* of intervention. The information in the guide was that, using this approach, the military was returning more than 90 percent of traumatized service members in Iraq and Kuwait to duty after applying PIES. However, the authors stated, "Contemporary battlefield realities . . . create an environment in which the validity and feasibility of the PIES concept must be seriously rethought,"[12] and because of needs for troops, commanders might decide that such soldiers should continue their deployment even if therapists recommended that the deployment end. They stated the principle that "Military mental health officers . . . must balance the mission requirements with the best interest of the patient,"[13] but they did not articulate how this should be done. This is cause for worry, because it reflects the need for keeping troop numbers high as the priority, to the too frequent exclusion of considerations for the best interests of the traumatized soldier. Furthermore, it is potentially alarming, because such soldiers can put themselves and others in their unit at risk should they break down again in times of danger. It is hard to imagine that many servicemembers who become so unable to meet standards of military functioning that that inability is officially recognized by their move into the PIES program will be ready for return to combat after getting a bowl of soup, a shower, a bit of sleep, and the assurance that they are expected to do fine. The report's authors did clearly recommend certain drugs that are marketed as antidepressants as "first line medications" for military-related PTSD,[14] and this is worrying, too: These medications tend to dull the emotions, but grief deferred or interrupted does not disappear with no consequences to be paid later on. In addition, these drugs have been shown often to be ineffective in alleviating depression,[15] and they have significant risks of causing, among other problems, suicidal or homicidal impulses or actions, serious sexual problems, insomnia, and weight gain.[16]

In December 2004, the Army had deployed what it called the units aimed at "stress control," to provide treatment for "soldiers suffering from emotional overload" and to do so while keeping them close to their unit, where they could supposedly benefit from its "camaraderie."[17] Again, the word "stress" comes nowhere close to describing the emotional consequences of being in a combat zone. Were those working in "stress control" units aware that the very term was a euphemism? Furthermore, one must consider at least the possibility that the Army's wish to keep in combat even soldiers enduring unimaginable suffering would be motivated by a need to keep troop numbers high. As the current wars have dragged on, recruitment of new people into the military has become a major challenge, so that keeping existing troops in action has become increasingly necessary to continue the waging of the wars. In this new program, what kinds of treatment were used to control the "stress"? According to Thomas Burke, an Army psychiatrist overseeing mental health policy for the Department of Defense, they were "sleep, rest, food, showers and a clean uniform."[18] Although rest, food, and cleanliness can help with exhaustion, hunger, and hygiene, how might these reduce the "stress" of constant danger of dying, grief over loss of friends, nightmarish situations of moral conflict, and a sense of powerlessness and helplessness that being at war creates for so many? And how to overcome the many barriers that keep anguished soldiers from seeking help? In a 2004 *New York Times* article, Scott Shane wrote that when Marine reservist Jeffrey Lucey considered reporting being traumatized by seeing corpses, a supervisor told him that making such a report could delay his return to the U.S., so he "played down his problems." After his return home, haunted by fears that he might have killed innocent Iraqis, he hanged himself with a hose.[19]

By 2005, apparently alarmed by the amount of psychological suffering it was seeing in large numbers of soldiers, the Department of Defense announced that it planned to add to the health questionnaires they were already requiring soldiers to fill out within five days after leaving Iraq a new "mental health assessment" to be filled out several months after their return home.[20] The new assessment was to be offered three to six months after soldiers arrived home, said U.S. Air Force Colonel Joyce Adkins, director of operational stress and deployment mental health. It was a good idea, in that the plan was to ask how they were doing back with their families and in the community rather than solely focusing on psychiatric labels. However, the officer in charge of the program said that they would be reminded of "psychological services in their communities," although it was not clear what else would be offered, and there is never any guarantee that providers of standard mental health services will refrain from pathologizing the soldiers.

Also in 2005, the Army reported that morale was low, indeed at a level that would have been considered alarming in any other workplace, and depression, anxiety, and "acute stress" were common.[21] The Army said that a report showed mental health services to have improved in recent months, but this claim seemed to be based on the fact that they had increased the number of behavioral health service providers. In principle, having more helping professionals *could* mean more actual help was delivered, but if attempts to help are misguided, higher numbers in and of themselves are of little use.

In July 2005 the Defense Department announced it was trying to improve the ways it "prevents, identifies and treats mental illness" among troops serving in Iraq or Afghanistan because of high rates of emotional difficulties in soldiers who had served deployments of twelve months or more and had more exposure to combat.[22] It might seem obvious that direct solutions should include reduction of length of deployments and thus of likely combat exposure, especially because in the same article, Army Lt. Col. Charles Engel, director of the DoD's Deployment Health Clinical Center, described emotional upset as "common and expected reactions to combat."[23] However, what were proposed as solutions included research aimed at identifying symptoms and intervening earlier (but not by avoiding war or reducing deployments), better access to mental health care, evaluation of current treatment programs, more psychological debriefing, more assessments after deployments end, more "stress control services," and increased "training modules" to "educate" soldiers, leaders, and health-care professionals. A word about the term "stress control services": In chapter 3 we considered the way that war has been made to disappear from the language of "PTSD" in contrast to "shell shock" and "battle fatigue" or "combat fatigue." The utter inadequacy of both language and treatment are reflected in Carolyn Gage's brilliant play (and title), "Harriet Tubman Visits a Therapist."[24] In Gage's script, Tubman, after living in constant terror and exhaustion from her work on the Underground

Railroad and from being suspected of planning an escape, goes to speak to a therapist, who offers to teach Tubman stress reduction exercises, as she would have for an overworked, carpooling mother.

In August 2005, Massachusetts officials were considering mandatory mental health screening for returning National Guard members, because, as U.S. Representative Martin Meehan said, "The current system is not paying adequate attention to the mental health of our soldiers."[25] The key concern was with PTSD; at that point grief, rage, panic, anguish, and a sense of alienation were not major topics of concern. Although "screening" sounds like it could only be good, its usefulness really depends on two things: (1) how good the screening device is (that is, what does it involve?) and (2) whether the follow-up is useful or is the primarily psychiatric drug-oriented treatment that I have seen come from many "screening" approaches. Indeed, screening can even do harm when, as often, its main goal is to figure out whom to label mentally ill and when what follows includes methods known to be of limited utility and does not include what has truly been shown to be helpful, such as careful, respectful listening and validation of people's feelings rather than pathologizing of them.[26]

Meehan filed legislation to increase funding to ensure that soldiers would be interviewed by a mental health professional before leaving the battlefield and after coming home. This, too, sounds like a great idea, but the details are what matter: mental health professionals' interviews can be helpful or can carry the same risks as screening instruments. Finally, Meehan urged the government to "fight the stigma of mental illness" among troops, another proposal that sounds good but that—counterintuitive though it may seem—has actually been shown to have negative effects rather than positive ones. It does seem surprising, but antistigma campaigns turn out to increase stigma.[27] In fact, that same year, Nathaniel Fick, who had been a Marine officer leading platoons in Afghanistan and Iraq from 1999 to 2003, wrote in the *Boston Globe* that the postdeployment mental health evaluations for active duty forces and members of the National Guard in some states often involved "little more than filling out forms."[28] He said:

I remember slogging through my own mental health questionnaire after leaving Iraq, answering questions such as "Did you ever feel that your life was in imminent danger?" Yes. Or "Check all that apply: I saw the dead bodies of a) enemy combatants; b) American forces; c) civilians; d) all of the above." D.

Answers like mine should have prompted some sort of follow-up, but none came.[29]

And Fick warned that "Psychological screenings in a vacuum are worse than a waste of time because they give a false sense that someone has been 'cleared,'" whereas "healing only happens in community."[30] What is striking about the questionnaire Fick describes is that these are questions not about mental health but rather about wartime experiences. That the military asks such questions might suggest that it realizes that experiences of loss can affect soldiers in ways that warrant attention. But there is little evidence that its programs are designed to deal with grief.

As the wars continued, and reports of emotional suffering and life problems in servicemembers increased, the Marine Corps announced an initiative they called Operational Stress Control and Readiness (OSCAR), which was aimed at detecting problems and treating them right in combat zones. The treatment included prescribing antidepressant medication in the field.[31] As with the above-described PIES principles, the Marines' view seemed to be that it was best to keep their people in combat, even when they were so upset that psychotropic drugs seemed worth trying. A different view might have been that exposing already traumatized, grief-stricken Marines to further trauma and loss would be placing them way beyond the call of duty and that they should be sent home for at least awhile. The latter would not fit with the hypermasculine Marine ethos, however. Furthermore, an argument for keeping such people in combat has always been that they will feel too guilty and ashamed if they get to leave while others in their unit do not. Of course, that view is itself a part of the military and hypermasculine approach, and it is not surprising that one rarely hears anyone within that system ask whether there might be other options. Also important to consider is that, as reported in a *New York Times* article, no one has shown definitively that on-the-spot group or individual therapy in combat lowers the risk of psychological problems later.[32]

A further concern about the OSCAR program is that there are risks involved in rapidly putting suffering soldiers on psychiatric drugs, including that such drugs always carry some risk of negative effects, even of doing the opposite of what their manufacturers claim (see chapter 3). This violates the "first, do no harm" principle of medical practice, or at the very least the principle of providing help more than causing harm. Other moral problems are involved as well. Some such drugs distance people from their feelings, so that they keep silent about their agonies, and this helps isolate them and limits their personal and social functioning. The distancing also masks from the rest of society the emotional effects of war, making it hard for caring civilians to provide help and support to vets and to ensure that wars are not entered into frivolously.[33] Furthermore, as psychologist and philosopher Jeffrey Poland points out, distancing a person from their feelings can undermine their autonomy, their authenticity, or at least their own sense of the authenticity of their emotions.[34] In addition, feelings that are often suppressed by some of these drugs do not disappear but lie in wait, often later causing more harm.[35] At least some people would do better by talking with family, friends, or therapists, and although for some, a degree of distance from feelings may help them begin to speak, for others the speaking becomes harder, because the feelings aren't as available to be examined, experienced, and perhaps to some extent moved beyond. These days it is far too often assumed that drugs are the *only* way to reduce that intensity, and that is just not true. Thus, we send people into terrifying situations, then when they crack (and it is amazing that more do not), we put them on drugs that may change their brain chemistry in a host of unforeseen and harmful ways. This is exactly the kind of practice about which Aldous Huxley wrote in *Brave New World*. It is a parallel to the very common practice of "treating" abused women by putting them on tranquilizers or antidepressants. It is a huge cash cow for the drug companies, and if the past conduct of these companies is any guide, they will market their drugs intensively and under the guise of compassion for the poor folks who are suffering.

In April 2006, the American Psychological Association's *Monitor on Psychology* carried a description of a three-person team of therapists' attempt to make care available to five thousand soldiers—a daunting task when, according to the military psychologist heading the team, just living at war could be "overwhelming."[36] The acronym BICEPS was described as summarizing their approach, standing for Brevity of treatment, Immediacy of treatment, Centrality of location (away from medical facilities to try to reduce stigma of seeking mental health services), Expectancy (conveying the expectation that the suffering soldier will return to duty), Proximity (treating as close to their units as possible, staying within the area of operations), and Simplicity (a good meal, hot shower, and comfortable place to sleep). This approach shares much with the PIES approach described and critiqued earlier. BICEPS, while possibly successful at keeping personnel numbers up in combat zones, also means that all servicemembers are deceived to the extent that those who may not be "fit for duty" are maintained in the field while that fact is kept as private as possible. There are many values and purposes at work in this sort of situation, and they are often in conflict with each other.

December 2006 brought an NPR broadcast by Daniel Zwerdling about the problem that, even with all the above-described programs—and more—in place in the military, suffering members of the military who sought help were being punished with hazing, mockery, and shaming, even being kicked out of the service.[37] Like Nathaniel Fick, many said that even when they filled out questionnaires "that are supposed to warn officials" that they were having emotional problems, no one followed up to ensure they received help. Furthermore, in at least some cases the Army was choosing to discharge such soldiers not on the grounds that the war had traumatized them but rather for alleged disciplinary infractions. The reason was that soldiers discharged for rulebreaking receive either no benefits or fewer than those discharged for emotional problems.

The year 2007 brought a host of bleak reports about the military's problems with servicemembers' emotional reactions to war. There came the story of Tina Priest, a soldier who killed herself in Iraq after being raped by another soldier and put on antidepressants, an Army psychologist declaring just days before she died that she was stable.[38] Investigative reporters for the *Hartford Courant* found in January that, despite a congressional order that the military conduct assessments of the mental health of all deploying troops, such assessments actually happened for fewer than one in three hundred service members.[39] A *Boston Globe* reporter wrote that, although returning Marines and soldiers were routinely asked to fill out a form in which they evaluated their own mental health, they often denied all problems in order to avoid being kept on base to see therapists when they wanted to get home.[40]

In February 2007, despite the flood of assertions by the military in previous years that it was implementing a wealth of mental health measures, the authors of a report from the American Psychological Association indicted the military's mental health system. They concluded there was no evidence of a "well-coordinated or well-disseminated approach to providing behavioral health care."[41] They even said that the military had few high-quality mental health programs. They cited a 40 percent vacancy rate for active duty psychologists in the Army and Navy, so of course one must wonder whether the APA had a stake in concluding that more psychologists were needed. But the report's credibility was enhanced in some ways because an active military psychologist chaired the task force that wrote it, and other task force members were working for the military or the VA.

In other worrying news, a report in *National Psychologist* in May 2007 carried the information that many active duty military psychologists were becoming exhausted from their service in combat zones and "other difficult situations."[42] The same month, Army Private Nicholas Guess said in an interview that his war experiences as a medic, daily confronting "gore and blood," traumatized him. The Army, however, far from providing help, "pressured" him and others into being diagnosed with personality disorders; because personality disorders are considered to be lifelong, this meant they could leave the military but not receive veterans' benefits, because their problems were not classified as caused by their military experiences.[43] Also in May came the report that women whose spouses were on military deployment during the women's pregnancies were at greater risk for postpartum depression than were other pregnant women.[44] Since what is labeled postpartum depression tends to include feelings of guilt or hopelessness, feelings of inadequacy about motherhood, and worries about the baby's safety, it is not surprising that women whose husbands were at risk of being horribly wounded, traumatized, or killed would be more prone to such upset. Furthermore, the fetus may also be at increased risk because of the secretion of cortisol and other consequences of the stress during the pregnancy.[45]

In June 2007 the Army acknowledged that it was "overwhelmed" by the emotional problems of soldiers returning from war and announced that it would hire at least 25 percent more therapists, spending $33 million to add two hundred such professionals to their rolls.[46] These were to be added to the more than six hundred mental health professionals then working at Army medical centers and hospitals.

Also in June, after reports that officers and senior enlisted soldiers were worried that if they sought help for psychological problems they would have trouble obtaining security clearances, the Pentagon announced that it might stop asking troops to reveal previous mental health treatment when applying for those clearances.[47] Although follow-through about emotional suffering has left much to be desired, removing that question could also help mask such suffering, making it even less likely that those who need it will receive real help.

More trouble for the Army came with the June 2007 exposé by Anne Hull and Dana Priest in the *Washington Post* of the poor care that emotionally traumatized soldiers were receiving at Walter Reed Army Medical Center.[48] Such patients were supposed to receive at least one hour of individual therapy a week and "a full range of classes to help them cope with their symptoms." However, one hour a week of someone listening to you with total attention certainly seems inadequate to the magnitude of suffering of these soldiers. And classes to cope with symptoms may be somewhat helpful but by virtue of focusing on symptoms alone may not get at the source of the problem. They are still more examples of the military's carrying out the pretense that applying Band-Aid solutions rather than reducing or eliminating combat exposure is effective and is all that's needed, for the classes include such things as the repetition of statements of affirmation ("I am a worthy person," for instance) and learning to cook in occupational therapy. Put those exercises next to soldiers' flashbacks about losing one-third of their platoons in IED explosions or indelible memories of the faces of Afghani children whose parents they have just blown away, and the utter inadequacy and misguidedness of the official program of exercises and classes are clear. One patient in the program said that most of the classes felt like "B.S. sessions." The patient learned breathing techniques to reduce his panic, but his anger was as intense as ever, and his relationship with his psychiatrist made that worse: They met once or twice a week, primarily to discuss medication, and the psychiatrist made what seemed insipid comments, such as exhorting him to smile and "think today will be a good day."

By July 2007 the Army had decided to introduce a program aimed at training all soldiers to recognize signs of "PTSD" and seek help, even as it acknowledged that it still lacked resources to treat those who needed it.[49] This program was to be achieved in a one-hour briefing to small groups. Why the Army would think this could do much to overcome taboos against feeling or showing fear and upset is unclear. Nonetheless, in upbeat fashion, the Army claimed that the program would "boost the numbers of soldiers reporting symptoms of stress." At the same time, Army psychiatrist Col. Elspeth Ritchie announced that the Army needed to hire an additional 270 people to treat emotional problems, and she was not sure they could attract that many.

In September 2007 the American Psychological Association announced that it was teaching Special Forces trainees skills "very similar to the entry-level basic counseling skills most psychologists get in training—how to recognize emotions, empathize, asking the right questions to elicit more information and being aware of your own buttons."[50] These, of course, are skills involved in being a good and caring observer, listener, and friend, not just in being a good psychologist. What was not mentioned in the report of this program was that these skills are often considered unmasculine, even feminine, and thus, soldiers trained to believe that they must be hypermasculine are unlikely to want to use them. The trainers might at least want to include a portion of the program aimed at airing that very issue.

Even if in some ways this kind of program works, it must be recognized that it involves psychologists and other mental health professionals in doing what psychologist Navy Lt. Cmdr. Shannon Johnson calls "keeping soldiers functioning in a brutal environment. . . . In some respects, we are just keeping people shored up to get through."[51] These professionals may argue that they participate in that enterprise because they themselves cannot stop the war (and they may or may not all wish to), so they try to help soldiers feel better within that unbearable situation. But Dr. Johnson's words make clear that some psychologists keep suffering soldiers in combat zones, thus greasing the wheels of the war machine. Similarly, Army captain and psychologist Jeffrey Bass would be trying to keep soldiers functioning in a combat zone by offering "brief, solution-focused therapy." Getting devastated soldiers out of the combat zone would seem worthy of the term "partial solution," at least, but it seems unlikely that that is the solution-focused therapy that Dr. Bass has in mind. In a somewhat less stark fashion, Navy psychologist Lt. Justin d'Arienzo works with sailors on achieving "personal growth" by overcoming "adversity."[52] Does not "personal growth" after "adversity" suggest something more along the lines of acquiring skills training for a new job after losing an old one than of reacting to the shock of war? Is "adversity" anything like an adequate word for carrying your dying friend to the Medevac chopper after an IED blew off his arm, and you cradle his wounded side to your chest as you lift him? What kind of "personal growth" might we hope would come from that? What kind and amount of personal growth is worth going through that kind of hell?

In October 2007 came the announcement that there were "stress reduction teams" (think "Harriet Tubman Visits a Therapist") "spread all over Iraq" and that the treatments for stress "can be simple: A much-used therapy is simply regular meals and sleep."[53] This seemed to be more of the PIES approach. It's good to think of hungry, exhausted soldiers getting food and sleep, since hunger and sleep deprivation can aggravate emotional and physical suffering, but they hardly get to the source of the emotional pain.

The Marines announced in December 2007 that their OSCAR teams (see earlier concerns about OSCAR program) would "help [Marines] right off" because of having a clinician "right there with them."[54] Stating that the Marines needed to shift their approach to dealing with the emotional effects of combat, officials said that the new approach should "mirror our warrior culture, with its distinctive ethos emphasizing strength over weakness." If it seems hard to understand how that would represent a change, that is because it makes no sense. A Marine official said, sounding for all the world like a cheerleader, that he knew that "The more we get the message out there, the more people will recover," a claim he did not back up with evidence. Instead, he simply alleged that a few days of rest away from their patrol base and "some counseling" could do a lot to help Marines recover. In September of the same year, the U.S. Department of Defense announced a new initiative to try to convey to soldiers that to ask for help is not to go against the "Army Strong" motto but rather is consistent with it in the sense that resiliency is part of strength, and asking for help is part of resiliency and is courageous.[55]

Penny Coleman is the widow of a Vietnam veteran who took his own life, so she knows well the suffering caused by war. In a piece subtitled "Drug Troops to Numb Them to Horrors of War," in January 2008 she described legislation called the Psychological Kevlar Act, Kevlar being a fiber used in military helmets and bullet-proof vests and said to be "five times stronger than steel."[56] The legislation involved the use of the drug propranolol, a drug marketed for treating anxiety, to try to prevent soldiers in combat from developing emotional upset. The prospect of reducing soldiers' emotional pain sounds wonderful. However, the drug's negative effects can include "abdominal cramps, diarrhea, constipation, fatigue, insomnia, nausea, depression, dreaming, memory loss, fever, impotence, lightheadedness, slow heart rate, low blood pressure, numbness, tingling, cold extremities, sore throat, and shortness of breath or wheezing"[57]—some of the last things needed by those in combat. Importantly, it had not been proven that use of the drug in this way would either prevent war trauma or help more than it would harm. In fact, since grief is such a common part of combat experience, it is noteworthy that an official military document includes the warning that suppressing or delaying grief may postpone problems that will become chronic symptoms later on.[58] Beyond that, Coleman raised the serious moral concern described in chapter 2, that the military trains soldiers to ignore the moral repercussions of their acts of violence, and that chemically reducing their anxiety about war's horrors would be a serious further step, a form of "moral lobotomy." She worried that by softening the memories of traumatic events, the drug could create in soldiers "an indifference to violence that will make them unrecognizable to themselves and to those who love them. They will be alienated and isolated, and finally unable to come home."[59] Coleman quoted Leon Kass, chair of the President's Council on Bioethics, as saying that the drug could "medicate away one's conscience."[60] And Barry Romo, a national coordinator for Vietnam Veterans Against the War, said, "That's the pill that can make men and women do anything and think they can get away with it. Even if it doesn't work, what's scary is that a young soldier could believe it will."[61] Coleman wrote eloquently:

Whatever research projects might be funded by the Psychological Kevlar Act and whatever use is made of propranolol, they will almost certainly involve a diminished range of feelings and memory, without which soldiers and veterans will be different. But in what ways?

I wish I could trust the leadership of our country to prioritize the lives and well-being of our citizens. I don't. The last six years have clearly shown the extent to which this administration is willing to go to use soldiers for its own ends, discarding them when they are damaged. Will efforts be made to fix what has been broken? Return what has been taken? Bring them home? Will citizens be enlightened about what we are condoning in our ignorance, dispassion or indifference? Or will these two solutions simply bring us closer to realizing the bullet-proof mind, devoid of the inconvenient vulnerability of decent human beings to atrocity and horror? And finally, these are all questions about the morality of proposals that are trying to prevent injuries without changing the social circumstances that bring them about, which sidestep the most fundamental moral dilemma: that of sending people to war in the first place.[62]

Soon after Coleman's article appeared, *Time* magazine ran a cover story titled "America's Medicated Army" (June 5, 2008). It was focused on the abundant use of psychotropic drugs to treat soldiers both during service and when they become vets, and included important information about some dangers of these drugs.[63] The article included news about a Pentagon policy for all the services that, in effect, encouraged the use of selective serotonin reuptake inhibitors, or SSRIs, and it included the information that three military psychiatrists had published a statement encouraging military doctors in the current wars to request a "considerable quantity of the SSRI they are most comfortable prescribing" to help "conserve the fighting strength." A soldier was quoted as saying, "In Iraq, you see the doctor only one or twice, but you continue to get [psychotropic] drugs constantly."

September 2008 saw the announcement that patients who spent ten sessions on a Virtual Iraq computer simulation reduced or eliminated the symptoms listed in the *DSM* as criteria for PTSD.[64] In the simulation, patients are prompted to recall vividly the trauma they experienced. What is not clear is whether what helps is something in the computer technique or the recall itself or the retelling and talking about the events with an empathic listener (who perhaps might not need to be a professional). The following month, alarmed that the suicide rate for soldiers had risen from 12.4 per 100,000 in 2003 to 18.1 per 100,000 in 2007, the Army unveiled an interactive video aimed at suicide prevention. Viewing the video would be mandatory throughout the Army.[65] The video would "lead the viewer through a detailed drama" that involved an infantryman being hit by troubles with relationships, finances, and the law and would require the viewer to make a series of choices that could lead or not lead to suicide. Periodically, the viewer is asked whether or not to get help by talking with buddies, the sergeant, or a chaplain, and choices to seek help are shown to lead toward recovery, while choices not to seek help are seen to lead deeper into suicidal thoughts. Although the stated goal, "to make preventive lessons stick," is a worthy one, the Army presented no evidence that this had been proven to be an effective tool, and in fact, "Army experts and the creators of the program acknowledge they have no evidence the video will have the intended impact."[66] Furthermore, some experts warned of the risk of doing further damage without gauging the video's usefulness.

In November 2008 the Army announced that with 15,000 soldiers imminently returning home from Iraq and Afghanistan and one-fifth expected to suffer from "stress-related disorders," Fort Campbell had almost doubled its psychological staff. They were especially concerned about the huge numbers of servicepeople who had served as many as five rotations through combat zones. General Peter Chiarelli, vice chief of staff of the Army, was quoted as saying he did not know what to expect: "I don't think anybody knows."[67] He also expressed concern that they would not be able to find enough therapists to deal with everyone needing help. About 40 percent of soldiers who had gone to war had served more than one deployment, and that figure was continuing to rise. The Army was proposing as a "solution" not a reduction of repeated deployments but the formation of mobile psychological teams to head for bases when they were expecting an increase in returning units. Despite General Chiarelli's candor about the lack of certainty about what to do, the base's deputy commander for managed care, Dr. Bret Logan, asserted that 85 percent of soldiers with symptoms of "stress" would recover "with the help of some treatment or medication."[68] He presented no evidence for his claim.

In December 2008, a group of veterans brought a class action suit against the federal government for illegally denying them disability benefits even though they had been diagnosed with trauma from their war experiences, which should have brought them free care.[69] The five veterans who brought the suit said that starting in 2002, the Army "systematically" ignored rules requiring that all servicemen diagnosed with PTSD receive an automatic 50 percent disability rating. Two months before the suit was filed, the DoD ordered the Army to stop deflating such vets' disability ratings.

Also in December 2008, Army psychiatrist Brigadier General Loree K. Sutton announced a "game plan" for increasing resilience in soldiers and providing better treatment options.[70] This was to be a "totally integrated program for recovery and reintegration," which sounds impressive, but the crucial questions are what specifics the program involved and whether there was any reason to believe that these vague-sounding, positive outcomes would be forthcoming. That some approaches would "almost directly counter traditional military culture and practices" was interesting, especially because General Sutton pointed out that soldiers have to "keep a lid on our feelings while we do our job. But nobody tells us when to take the lid off or how to deal with it when we do." Sutton proposed to do this in part by revealing soldiers' stories, trying to counteract the "lamentable neglect and often superficial understanding of the wounds of war that have proved to be different in different eras." She described the use of "Theater of War," which uses top-ranked actors from the two-year-old, New York–based Philoctetes Project for staged readings about warriors' suffering. These ideas seemed wonderful and important, but no further press releases have appeared with reports of whether they were implemented or how they are working.

Despite all these highly touted programs aimed to help soldiers, by January 2009 the Army had failed to fill one-fourth of its positions for drug counselors,[71] and Rick Rogers wrote in the *San Diego Tribune* that, because of the gaps in services left by the military and the VA locally and across the country, "grass-roots groups and major organizations are launching or expanding mental health services [such as free or inexpensive counseling] for returning combat troops, new veterans and their families."[72] The nonprofit American Combat Veterans of War, run primarily by Vietnam War vets, said it would provide volunteers to do mental health briefings as soldiers returned home from Iraq or Afghanistan and safe-house meetings where vets could talk to each other about "substance abuse, spousal abuse, anger, isolation, sleeplessness, nightmares, and frustration with government bureaucracy.

Also in January 2009, because of killings and increased rates of domestic violence, rape, and other sexual assaults by soldiers returning from Iraq and Afghanistan,[73] an Army task force announced it would review the recruitment, service, and personal histories of those committing the violence to see if the military could have prevented it.[74] This was a change for the military, which had previously tried to deny that a history of combat experience could lead to violent behavior in veterans. The *New*

York Times reporter describing this initiative included the military's claim that "most" soldiers who return from war "adjust with minor difficulties," a statement unsupported by research.[75] However, military leaders did acknowledge that multiple deployments are difficult for soldiers and their families.

At the end of January 2009 the Army announced plans for a one-month program aimed at reducing suicides by training peers to recognize suicide-related behavior and to intervene with their buddies, followed by a three-month teaching program about suicide and a "Comprehensive Soldier Fitness" program intended to make soldiers more "resilient" in "an era of high operational tempo and persistent conflict."[76] At this point, then, the Army was coming closer to acknowledging that combat causes harm but retaining an upbeat focus on its ability to develop "a total fitness program"—somehow—that would counteract the effects of battle. The report from the Department of Defense included a description of the Army's "Battlemind training" that "helps prepare Soldiers and their Families for the stressors of war by increasing resiliency and also assists with the detection of possible mental health issues before and after deployment."[77] Its "Strong Bonds" was described as "a specialized training program" to assist with "communication tactics to improve relationships and build skills that enhance relationships and strengthen resiliency"; Dr. René Robichaux describes it as a marriage enrichment program run by chaplains.[78] The announcement also included the note that the Army and the National Institute of Mental Health had joined to conduct a five-year research project about how to decrease suicides. I was unable to obtain information about the results of this research to date.

In February 2009 the DoD announced that Army Major General David Blackledge was trying to help reduce the stigma attached to seeking treatment for war-related emotional problems by sharing his own story of trauma.[79] He also announced that the Army had a new "Real Warriors" program for service members to hear and discuss the stories of those who had sought help for emotional problems or traumatic brain injury.[80] "Real Warriors" was to be focused on coping strategies after deployment, factors that led soldiers to seek treatment, and ways that treatment had helped them.

That same month, Army secretary Pete Geren acknowledged that the military did not know why suicide numbers kept rising but said the Army was "committed to doing everything we can to address the problem" and had hired many more therapists.[81] Advocacy groups for veterans at that time were saying that the military's data about suicide were underestimates of the magnitude of the problem.[82]

Strangely, despite widely publicized information that emotional suffering was correlated with repeated and lengthy deployments, in March 2009 the DoD announced a plan to try to find out *whether* deployment history was related to suicide.[83] In the same press release, Army General Peter W. Chiarelli made the sweeping but vague assertion that "Suicide is a multidimensional problem and, as such, will take a multi-disciplinary approach to dealing with it." Although a multidisciplinary approach perhaps could not hurt, the general's pronouncement smacked too much of what makes for good publicity and diverted attention away from combat and lengthy and repeated deployments as causes of soldiers' anguish and suicides.

Perhaps chastened by nonmilitary groups' efforts to fill in gaps in services, in March 2009 the DoD came up with the idea of "super coaches"—another term with great public relations cachet—in a Transitional Support Program for service members returning to civilian life.[84] The program would include a twenty-four-hour, toll-free hotline to direct people in crisis to mental health services. As so often, the problems cited in this press release included family difficulties and thoughts of suicide but not experiences or memories of war. The following month the Defense Department issued a press release pointing out that since 2004, it had had a Military and Family Life Consultant Program (MFLCP) to "help servicemembers and their families deal with what comes with military life during times of war" on a short-term basis.[85] People might seek help from this program rather than from other military counselors, because use of the former did not go in their permanent files. The MFLCP program was part of Military One-Source, which "offers counseling face-to-face, by telephone and online." In another statement, an official said that the two programs were tailored to meet individuals' needs.

April 2009 brought the troubling news of a psychologist who claimed that the Army had pressured him not to diagnose PTSD but instead to use "anxiety disorder," which could lead to the labeled soldier receiving wrong treatment and lower disability payments if anxiety was not the only or primary problem.[86] The Senate Armed Services Committee declined to investigate the matter, and a veterans' advocacy group described the Army's vice chief of staff as "dismissive" in their meeting with him. Saying it had conducted an internal investigation of the matter, the Army absolved itself of wrongdoing.[87]

In May 2009 the Defense Department again publicized plans for starting its Comprehensive Soldier Fitness Program, aimed to build soldiers' mental resiliency, exercising their minds as they do their bodies, starting that summer. This came in the wake of the Fort Hood killings by a military psychiatrist.[88] In the press release, a military official who stated that "the vast amount of people have growth experiences" from being in combat neglected to provide evidence that that was the case. It may be true that soldiers learn discipline, perseverance, and intensity of focus and that they form close bonds with other soldiers. But it seems evasive to mention only growth while failing to describe the many soldiers whose nights are sleepless and haunted by memories that wrack their souls.

Journalists like Robert H. Reid persisted in telling the public that the increases in number and length of deployments were creating more "stress" than in previous wars.[89] For instance, in a May 2009 article, Reid contrasted Vietnam with Iraq and Afghanistan: "Most soldiers spent just one or two assignments in Vietnam, but many American soldiers and Marines are on their third or fourth tours in Iraq and Afghanistan."

In June 2009, General Chiarelli said that soldiers' suicides were "not a single problem with a defined set of symptoms or markers. . . . There are no easy answers or solutions. We still haven't found any statistically significant causal linkage that would allow us to effectively predict human behavior."[90] But at the same time, Army Brigadier General Rhonda Cornum, chief of the Comprehensive Soldier Fitness program, made the upbeat statement that "psychological fitness is essential in today's era of persistent conflict." Of course, the essential question is how anyone exposed to persistent conflict, danger, and tragedy can remain psychologically "fit." Cornum voiced the lovely fantasy that "Eventually, more mentally fit soldiers will be able to pass their knowledge on to less-fit soldiers, just as soldiers always have done with physical fitness." As a character in a Hemingway novel says, "It's pretty to think so."

In a June 2009 *USA Today* article, Gregg Zoroya reported that Congress was spending more than $700 million on programs to help families of servicepeople deployed to Iraq and Afghanistan.[91] Included were some helpful, practical measures, such as education and job training for spouses and free YWCA memberships. Undoubtedly well meant were "Elmo videos designed to help children ages 3–5 cope with deployment and family changes" and plans for a future video "addressing the emotional trauma of losing a parent." It's not that such tools cannot be helpful, and it's not that the military fails to offer real-life counselors as well; it's that here again, amid the flurry of announcements about new audiovisual aids and techniques, as well as still more increases in offers of therapy, what is not raised is the possibility of decreasing the number and frequency of deployments or the possibility of exploring ways to avoid engaging in new wars and wind down the current ones. It is as though the latter are up to the politicians, and the military is not allowed to propose such solutions, though the lives that are risked and lost are those of people in the military, not in politics. It is widely acknowledged that politicians decide what wars to wage and provide the resources, while the military conducts the wars. There is, then, some tension when the political decisions affect the well-being of soldiers, which is a concern of the military; clearly, that tension needs to be more intensively examined.

July 2009 brought news that the Army at Landstuhl Regional Medical Center had created "an intensive eight-week therapeutic Post-Traumatic Stress Disorder Day Treatment Program called 'evolution,'" which included "art therapy, yoga and meditation classes, substance abuse groups, anger and grief management, tobacco cessation, pain management and multiple PTSD evidence-based practice protocols." Dr. Daphne Brown, chief of the center's Division of Behavioral Health, called herself a believer in "the kitchen sink," throwing in everything and hoping that "something will stick."[92] For the first part of the program, the goal was to offer patients tools to help them "calm down," and Dr. Sharon Stewart, who works with Dr. Brown, told me in 2010 that about one-third of their patients had experienced a drop on a measure of anxiety from one category (severe, moderate, mild) to another.[93] Perhaps the most interesting program feature was the use of "cognitive processing therapy," an attempt to help trauma-tized soldiers consider that combat has ended their earlier belief that the world is safe. Dr. Brown says that after combat, a soldier may believe the world is now unsafe and consider most of the world to be unsafe. This could be an attempt to get at one of the most profound and shattering changes that result from being at war, this loss of innocence and mistrust of the world. However, it would remain to be seen whether a cognitive processing approach in which the therapist tries to change the soldier's beliefs would be effective. According to Dr. Stewart, this includes having them write out the assumptions they make that are related to their trust in themselves, others, and "the process of living" in a way that accounts for their traumatic experiences but still allows them to have some trust; this can involve their trying to take different perspectives and incorporate new information.[94] Using a mindfulness approach, which includes focus-ing on what is happening in the moment, Dr. Stewart notes, participants are encouraged to observe which of their fundamental needs for autonomy, esteem, intimacy, meaning, safety, belonging, and purpose are being met at that moment and to consider strategies for meeting them.[95] It has not yet been possible to conduct research about whether or not there have been changes in their beliefs about whether the world is safe.[96] Dr. Brown also described the use of "prolonged exposure therapy," exposing the patient to the story of their traumatic event "continually" in the hope that their upset will become less intense. Although Dr. Brown compared this to riding a roller coaster repeatedly in order to overcome fear of roller coasters, roller coasters rarely lead to harm, whereas the kinds of traumatic experiences that shatter soldiers' peace of mind have that effect precisely because of the death and destruction they wrought.

In July 2009, in another *USA Today* article, Gregg Zoroya wrote that Army commanders were failing to monitor troubled soldiers in their barracks when they returned home after deployment and that that was a factor in Army suicides hitting their highest levels since statistics were first kept in 1980.[97] Zoroya quoted an Army official as pointing out that more soldiers than in previous wars were entering the service with preexisting anxiety or depression or had stopped taking their psychiatric medication in order to meet standards for Army admission. These factors were cited as contributing to the high rate of suicides as well. Training classes for more than 7,600 sergeants in how to manage troubled soldiers had often been postponed for as long as 270 days in order to accommodate combat training.[98]

Perhaps one clue to why some of the military's behavioral programs failed to work appears in the Army's July 2009 press release. There we learn that the MFLCP program (mentioned above) provides counselors "who rotate every four to six weeks on military installations." Since death in combat of people with whom they have close relationships is a major source of soldiers' grief, how well can they be expected to work with therapists whom they know from the outset they will never see again after a few, short weeks? But the military loves to trot out impressive-sounding numbers, and the article includes the boast that "in May 2009 alone, for example, we provided problem-solving counseling for over 35,000 individuals." Huge numbers indeed, but quantity of appointments does not inevitably lead to effective delivery of help.

Still working hard to come up with yet more ideas, in July, 2009, the Army announced its pilot project for teaching soldiers techniques "drawn from sports psychology such as visualization and bio-feedback to help deal with . . . mental consequences of combat."[99] They also included goal setting, imagery integration, and energy management. These are aimed at achieving "the relaxation response," an admirable goal but one for which these outside-in techniques may not be helpful: That such tools help reduce irrational responses such as terror of elevators in someone who has never or only once had trouble in an elevator does not mean they can reduce the physiological manifestation of the grief or horror of soldiers who are haunted by what they lived through in combat.

Also in July 2009, the Marines were facing a rise in suicides in their ranks, and they ordered sergeants and corporals to "become more involved and knowledgeable about the intimate details of the lives of their young charges."[100] This, Marine officials acknowledged, necessitated switching away from the usual Marine emphasis on doing "the hard thing" and instead doing "the soft thing." Furthermore, like many techniques the Army had chosen, the Marines' approach also involved having Marines watch a film rather than talk to another person about their traumas. Training for those leading the post-film discussions lasts only three hours, and those trainees then spend only half a day teaching other noncommissioned officers, perhaps enough time to effect the switch from a tough to a compassionate approach, but perhaps not.

The DoD in July 2009 said in testimony on Capitol Hill that it did not know why servicemembers kill themselves.[101] Particularly striking was that those testifying included the second-ranking military officers of each service. As he had noted previously, Army vice chief of staff General Peter W. Chiarelli said, "The most frustrating thing is trying to find a cause," but he speculated that an eventual recommendation would be to increase time the troops spent at home relative to deployment time. Since it had already been established that length and number of deployments were correlated with serious emotional suffering, it is not clear why Chiarelli apparently considered it premature to change deployment patterns at that time.

In an August 2009 DoD press release, the Army's Suicide Prevention Task Force's director, Brigadier General Colleen McGuire, said that they still had not determined which programs were most effective.[102] That same month the Assistant Secretary of Defense for Health Affairs announced the creation of a congressionally directed DoD Task Force on the Prevention of Suicide by Members of the Armed Forces.[103] Note that in February 2004, a U.S. Joint Task Force that included all five branches of the armed forces had, among other things, planned to work on suicide prevention. One wonders if the new DoD initiative came partly in reaction to the failure of the Army's parallel task force to come up with information about program effectiveness. The new task force was charged with addressing the full sweep of matters related to suicide, including "trends and causal factors, methods to update prevention and education programs, suicide assessment by occupation, suicide incident investigations, and protective measures for confidential information." It was to present its report within twelve months. Once again, everything imaginable was included in the plan except a drawdown of forces and a reduction in deployments as ways to reduce suicide.

September 2009 brought yet another DoD press release referring to "alarming numbers" of soldiers' suicides, other forms of violence, reckless behavior, and substance abuse, and announcing another "renewed" emphasis on soldiers' mental well-being. General Chiarelli said at a conference that current troops are "much more stressed" than those in previous wars, struggling with "depression, anxiety and post-traumatic stress disorder," but missing from the article was mention of prolonged and repeated combat exposure as probably the primary reason for all that "stress." Undoubtedly with good intentions, Chiarelli said the Army now planned to intervene *early* in the process and "mitigate issues before they become significant concerns."[104] With that, he had just described in a nutshell the aim of *every* ideal program intended to alleviate suffering. But anyone can say they plan to intervene early and prevent troubles from developing; finding ways to make it happen is much harder than stating that one wants to do it. What is certain is that looking away from the factors that *can* be changed and that have been proven to be crucial to creating emotional carnage—length and number of deployments, length of exposure to violence—is far from the ideal way to proceed.

How ironic that well over six years into the war in Iraq, Chiarelli could say that they realized (only then?) that they needed to "become proactive" in the "challenging environment we find ourselves in."[105] He spoke not a word about attempts to change that environment, though that *would* be true prevention. There is no mention of trying to reduce deployments. One could argue that the military cannot talk about reducing deployments, since deployments are part of the military's mission. But many servicemembers, even high-ranking ones, believe that battles are not their only mission, that sometimes fighting of certain kinds in certain places is unlikely to achieve the desired aims, and that on balance, the damage done to troops outweighs the benefits of at least some deployments. At the very least, the kind of approach Chiarelli described makes it clear that the role of mental health professionals is to help the military pursue its aims regardless of the emotional cost to the troops. This raises serious ethical and professional problems for therapists who recognize that there is only so much carnage they can undo. Some would argue that a therapist who sees a suffering soldier is ethically or professionally obligated to try to help alleviate that pain. But as discussed in chapter 3, therapy is of limited value and carries risks for many soldiers who are in pain. Furthermore, how does a military therapist avoid helping to cloud politicians' and other citizens' thinking about war by contributing to the impression that whatever war does, therapists can fix it?

The closest Chiarelli came to talking about real prevention was to suggest that the amount of time *between* deployments might be increased from, say, sixteen to twenty-six months. But it is not hard to imagine the host of problems that could arise from having the soldier home for a longer period of time, only to leave yet again and go back into danger. What do the repeated separations from loved ones, especially children, do to all parties? Chiarelli reported that the Army planned to add hundreds more behavioral health specialists to "mitigate mental health issues associated with increasing deployments and a growing operations tempo," but again, there is no evidence that therapists are successful at alleviating not just the stress but also the fear, guilt, shock, and horror that result from repeated deployments.

In October 2009 the DoD issued yet another press release, this one containing the bizarre statement that the Army is "making progress in its efforts to prevent suicides despite the increasing number of reports."[106] The Army's 2008 suicide rate had been at an all-time high since such statistics were first recorded in 1980 and represented an increase for the fourth straight year. Suicide rates for 2009 were on track to pass the 2008 figures. On what basis did the Army claim progress? On the basis of the "stories they're hearing from the field."[107]

In November 2009, perhaps increasingly desperate about the lack of proof of the effectiveness of its mental health programs, the Pentagon's "top military official" claimed that *others* needed to help, too, that improving servicemembers' and vets' mental health care required "a coordinated effort beyond health care providers and the military community."[108] The same month, Army Brigadier General Dr. Loree Sutton, director of the Defense Center of Excellence for Psychological Health and Traumatic Brain Injury, said that before the current wars, "there was little research on effective treatments" for war trauma but that her center has been trying to standardize the "hundreds of disjointed programs around the country."[109] Sutton's goal was to produce "event-driven protocols," so that, for instance, if a roadside bomb hit a vehicle, every person in the vehicle would receive certain "standardized" treatment. This is problematic, because it leaves no room for individuals to have different patterns of problems, ways of coping, and resources for dealing with the same event.

In a November 2009 *New York Times* front-page story, Benedict Carey and Damien Cave reported that military therapists were exhausted from

trying to shore up traumatized soldiers.[110] The reporters wrote that "Therapists in Iraq said that they could often do little more than provide a few
coping tips to soldiers, just enough to keep them functioning," and "Few
who are deployed feel prepared" for the work they have to do and the
tragedy with which they are dealing.[111] Added to the sheer magnitude of
that task was the pressure of knowing that commanders who needed soldiers in the field could overrule therapists' recommendations. The article
appeared soon after the shootings at Fort Hood, and psychiatrist Dr.
Stephen Stahl said that Fort Hood's program for soldiers coming back from
Iraq and Afghanistan "simply lacked the staff it needed."[112] A shortage of
therapists did not, however, keep the Pentagon from planning to fly them
(if they could hire enough?) directly into combat zones to treat soldiers on
the spot.[113]

Also in November 2009, a *Washington Post* story carried a description of
a research project aimed at predicting who would end up with PTSD as a
result of going to war.[114] The study involved exposing people to images of
war on a computer screen while tracking the number of eye blinks and the
amount of electrical activity in the skin. The hope was that understanding
"underlying triggers" might help reduce psychological burdens by serving
as signals to provide extra help early on. What they could not control, of
course, was what war horrors any given soldier would encounter in real
life, and eye blinks and levels of carbon dioxide in the blood in response
to seeing *images* of war pale in comparison to what might be expected in
response to actually being in the throes of combat. Furthermore, what
would we do if we knew that someone who had been horribly traumatized
had on pre-war tests blinked more or less than other soldiers? Would we
refrain from sending them into combat? That might be the plan. If so, it
would be the first I have seen that would involve considering actually
keeping some soldiers from going to war.

In November 2009 the Army announced that at Fort Campbell, officers,
doctors, and counselors were holding monthly meetings to try to identify
emotional suffering early, so that they could intervene.[115] They were also
planning to move counselors from hospitals and clinics right into brigades
as a way to "break down barriers and overcome the stigma of seeking help."
This was supposed to increase soldiers' resilience to "stress" after "repeated
deployments over eight years of war."[116] Whether or not the counselors
would actually know how to provide truly helpful services is an empirical
question not addressed in the article about this program.

The authors of a 2009 article in the *Journal of Consulting and Clinical
Psychology* reported that their study of the Army's Battlemind program,

which was aimed at easing postdeployment transitions back at home, had reduced some problems such as sleep difficulties, depression, and other effects of trauma.[117] The Army's own description of Battlemind reflects some careful thought that went into describing experiences and responses that are essential (or at least common) in combat, such as driving fast and unpredictably, but are dangerous at home.[118] One concern about the program is the pat description that for the transition from combat to home, "Professional treatment helps, the earlier the better," because in light of the evidence, that seems a rather sweeping statement. Furthermore, the danger is that people who seek professional assistance and find that they do not feel better will blame themselves if they believe that it was expected to work.

In February 2010 the story broke that the DoD was about to investigate the kind of mental health care that Marines at Camp Lejeune were receiving.[119] What led to the investigation was a series of complaints made by Dr. Kernan Manion, who had reported inadequate care programs, including those for PTSD.

Wondering, as I was finishing this book in the late spring of 2010, whether research results were available to show whether the various mental health questionnaires are helpful, I contacted Dr. Elspeth Ritchie, Medical Director of the Army Medical Department's Office of Strategic Communications, to ask that question. Dr. Ritchie said the Army was doing "an incredible amount of surveys and screenings" and that "Our soldiers are surveyed more than soldiers have ever been surveyed before," but that "It's always difficult to assess the efficacy of questionnaires when you're doing so many."[120]

In late April and May of 2010, several alarming stories appeared. The *New York Times* carried a devastating, front-page, lead story about conditions in special trauma care units the Army had created specifically to help soldiers with physical wounds and severe psychological trauma, where about 7,200 people were being treated in thirty-two locations across the country. Patients told reporters James Dao and Dan Frosch that they felt they were in "warehouses of despair."[121] They described being treated harshly by noncommissioned officers— "often using traditional drill-sergeant toughness"[122] and accusing the patients of being weaklings, fakers, or "crazy." One patient reported being put on twenty-four-hour guard duty repeatedly, although his doctor had issued an order against this. The soldiers described receiving only minimal psychotherapy, and the wife of one said that when she requested additional psychotherapy for her husband, a staff member yelled at her that her husband did not even deserve to wear his uniform. Many described being medicated with psychiatric drugs to no effect or to harmful effect, including addiction (sometimes to heroin), but with no improvement in mood or emotions. One patient said they were all taking medications for sleep, anxiety, and pain, and some were so disoriented they could not recall which pills they were taking. The ways the drugs were used made it difficult for them to exercise, wake up for morning formation, and attend classes, but they would be disciplined for these failures. Some said they spent long hours alone in their rooms, drinking or playing video games, feeling worthless. Senior officers running the units attempted to justify the use of punishment when patients deviated from treatment plans, on the grounds that "these guys are still soldiers, and we want to treat them like soldiers."[123]

In May 2010, Senator Jim Webb told a Senate Armed Services subcommittee that, according to a *Military Times* report, more than one in six servicemembers were taking one or more psychiatric medications and that the use of such medications had increased 76 percent since the start of the current wars.[124] That same month there came the news that, despite all the programs the military had put in place in recent years, more U.S. servicemembers were hospitalized for emotional problems in 2009 than for any other reason.[125] In fact, nearly every new program for emotional suffering described in this chapter had been implemented since 2005, yet according to Lieutenant General Eric Schoomaker, the Army's surgeon general, hospitalizations for mental disorders actually *increased* significantly between that year and the end of 2009, when the number reached 17,538. This is particularly disturbing in light of the recent news just described about the trauma treatment units. Also, in light of the heavy use of psychiatric drugs in the military and some of the documented effects of these medications, it would be important to investigate whether the drugs may, for many servicemembers, increase the likelihood of hospitalization. In fact, Gregg Zoroya reported in *USA Today* that mental health problems were the leading cause of hospitalizations of U.S. servicemembers in 2009, accounting for almost 40 percent of hospital days for the military.[126] According to military officials, this represents a significant increase since 2005 and reflects the effects of multiple deployments and extended exposure to combat. Zoroya wrote that "The Pentagon is learning that mental issues can take months or years to develop,"[127] but this is surely not a new discovery for them. And it was Lieutenant General Schoomaker who made the most clearly, directly relevant observation: The skyrocketing rate of hospitalizations for emotional pain reflects the toll that war takes.

This book went into production May 2010. Between then and the end of August, when my editor sent me the copyedited manuscript, the patterns described so far in this chapter only continued.

In June, 2010, *Air Force Times* carried the story that "cocktails" of drugs prescribed to Marines and Army soldiers had led to at least thirty-two accidental overdoses since 2007.[128] Nearly all of these overdosed while under the care of the Army's or Marines' special treatment units for wounded warriors, and most had been put on combinations of drugs including painkillers, sleeping pills, antidepressants, and anti-anxiety drugs. Included in the article was the report that despite a *Military Times* Freedom of Information Act request submitted two months before, Pentagon officials had not provided information about the military's accidental drug deaths. Also included was the note that during the past decade, with the United States waging two wars, the use of these kinds of drugs in the military has dramatically risen, yet as one expert pointed out, they had not been tested in combination with each other.

Also in June came yet another announcement, this one jointly from the DoD and the VA, that mental health treatment via long distance (telehealth) was being considered;[129] it seemed that the military continued to seek one way after another to help, while apparently continuing to ignore what were known to be the root causes of this suffering.

Late in June, the DoD announced in a news release the opening of a $65 million, 72,000-square-foot center that would use "extraordinarily new and comprehensive approaches" for, among other things, psychological suffering of those who have been at war and, as though this were a terrific, new idea, that it would create individual treatment plans for servicemembers.[130]

In June there also came word of high prevalence rates of emotional troubles from combat, ranging from 9 to 31 percent,[131] and the following month, *USA Today* reporter Zoroya obtained statistics from the Army indicating that "The number of soldiers forced to leave the Army solely because of a mental disorder has increased by 64% from 2005 to 2009 and accounts for one in nine medical discharges," and an Army behavioral health official, Lt. Col. Rebecca Porter, said that the statistics showed "a clear relationship between multiple deployments and increased symptoms of anxiety, depression, and PTSD."[132] Furthermore, Zoroya reported, a Pentagon analysis revealed that in 2009, "for the first time in 15 years, mental health disorders caused more hospitalizations among U.S. troops than any other medical condition, including battle wounds."[133] In the August issue of *Military Psychology*, James Griffith reviewed research studies and described the unsurprising pattern that deployed personnel were more psychologically distressed than nondeployed personnel.[134] Griffith described DoD programs aimed to help with such problems but noted that, "Regrettably, many of these activities are not accompanied by program evaluation study."[135] In spite of these increasing, crystal-clear causes for alarm, neither politicians nor military leaders publicly proposed that they might be good reasons to try to cut back on combat exposures. What a Congressional task force did in late August, however, was—predictably—to announce that it was creating "a new top-level" Pentagon office for suicide prevention.[136] But happily, the task force also produced a report in which, among other things, they recommended increasing the time that servicemembers spend at home between deployments,[137] a long-needed change that one can hope will be implemented soon. Finally, in a late August, McLatchy Newspapers article with the subtitle "Military suicide prevention efforts inadequate," journalist Barbara Barrett reported that, according to a DoD task force mandated to prevent suicide in the military, the military has "nearly 900 suicide prevention programs across 400 military installations worldwide" but their approach is "a safety net riddled with holes."[138]

July 30 brought two newspaper articles, in each of which something besides war itself was blamed for the suicide rates. The headline for the one in the *Wall Street Journal* read "Soldiers' suicide rate tied to access to problems at home," the point being that those who are deployed but stay in close touch with family members are "dragged" into a life at a home where there are problems they cannot fix.[139] The headline for the one in *USA Today* indicated that military leaders were to blame for failing to notice and deal with soldiers' "high-risk behavior."[140] It's not, of course, that servicemembers' worries about troubles back home and military leaders' failure to deal with high-risk behavior might not contribute to the suicide rate but simply that the best-documented, most obvious causes are still ignored.

On September 1, 2010, we heard from the DoD that now the Navy is concerned about its suicide rates, with suicide being its third highest cause of death.[141] The DoD's press release for the proposed solutions was poignantly similar to those from the other branches of the military: The Navy aimed to train people of all ranks to be good friends to sailors who seemed upset, they had developed a training kit including video material and pocket-sized reference cards, and personnel were to be encouraged to "be a friend" to those who were anguished.

It is clear that the military's reports of how they are trying to help servicemembers are marked by continual announcements of new programs, techniques, and approaches, in the absence of announcements of documented progress and interspersed with candid comments by people like General Chiarelli, who acknowledge ongoing bewilderment about how to help. To be sure, some of the military's programs may have helped some people; but it would be good to see some high-quality studies designed to test whether that is the case, and if so, what has made the difference.

Thinking back to the powerful emotions and the moral, spiritual, and existential crises described in chapter 2, the inadequacy if not the utter misguidedness of many of the initiatives is evident. For instance, it seems strange that so much energy would be poured into trying to help soldiers by teaching them to alleviate the intensity of bad memories through eye movements. This is not to say that such techniques might not help some people but just that they do not reach the foundations of the trouble. In addition, when researchers claim that people's symptoms improve somewhat if they hold horrific memories in mind while moving their eyes in prescribed ways,[142] it takes some doing to figure out how much of the improvement might come not from the movements but from revisiting trauma while in the presence of someone supportive, who happens to be telling them how to move their eyes. Veterans' psychologist David Collier believes it is the relationship between the professional and the patient, not the specific technique, that promotes healing,[143] and this is consistent with research discussed earlier.

A fundamental tenet that led me to write this book has been that psychologists and psychiatrists, especially those whose practice is very traditional and dogmatic, are of limited help to servicemembers and can even do them harm. But even if we assume that most are effective in working with those traumatized by war, as Glantz points out, the Pentagon itself shows that the military has fewer mental health professionals currently than when the United States invaded Iraq in 2003.[144] Glantz also notes the pressures on military therapists to assign certain psychiatric diagnoses rather than others (specifically, personality disorders rather than PTSD) in order to get "undesirables" discharged so that they can be replaced with "a fresh body." Glantz describes cases like that of Brian Rand, who reported on a military form that he was having combat-related nightmares and mood swings and feeling down or hopeless, but whom the Army deployed to Iraq a second time instead of providing him any help.

In chapter 1 I asked what we would think if someone told us that, in the abstract "situation X is causing A amount of homelessness, B suicides, C acts of violence against others, D cases of drug and alcohol abuse, and E instances of relationship breakdown"? We would be horrified and want to think how to put a stop to it immediately. In chapter 1 I noted that it seems likely that to acknowledge what war has done to many people would make us feel hopelessly helpless, and perhaps those who run the military feel that way; that would help to account for their introduction of a succession of programs that appear to provide help that is at least only marginally relevant, if not misguided.

It is clear that much of soldiers' suffering is due to grief—grief over loss of people they love, loss of limbs, loss of innocence, loss of close relationships in the military, loss of connection with and understanding from those back home. To grieve the loss of a close one, a person needs either to be able to rely on one's own inner strength or the care and support of others, as well as, ideally, talking with someone else who knew the person. This is what makes the film *Blackhawk Down* so powerful: Through the eyes of his fellow soldiers, we observe the tiny quirks of a person whom we later see killed, and we watch the moments of caring or lighthearted connection between the one who dies and the one who cared about him and watches him go. After such a loss, it is especially important to be able to talk freely with others who knew the person about their quirks and about the interactions the survivors had with the one who is gone. However, as noted in chapter 2, the military does not encourage its members to anticipate devastating losses and does not do much to help them grieve when the losses occur. Furthermore, it appears to avoid looking at how the initial sources of grief—especially war itself—might be preventable. If looking at the initial source sounds like a mindlessly sunny proposal, perhaps that is because our culture is so deeply mired in considering wars inevitable and in avoiding careful, thorough debate and planning before heading into still more wars.

In the next chapter we look at whether the VA does a better job with veterans than those charged with taking care of people while they are still in active service.

5 What the VA Is Doing Once Johnny and Jane Are Home . . . and Why It's Not Enough

The claim went in to Vets' Affairs
  And I went to see some doctors of theirs.
  They accepted the PTSD as a fact,
  Then cancelled the payment for bones in my back.

They never asked me about the pain,
  That's there in the evening and morning again,
  When I get out of bed every day of the week,
  I climb up the door to get to my feet.
—Bob Lange, Australian Vietnam War veteran[1]

Even with the military's seriously flawed treatment of soldiers' emotional burdens, we might breathe easier if we knew that once soldiers become veterans, the VA jumps into the breach and addresses these burdens in helpful ways. Sadly, although many therapists in the VA system are trying hard, the system is riddled with problems. As with the provision of services to active servicemembers, described in chapter 4, many problems described in this chapter relate to obstacles in the VA system that vets encounter in trying to obtain any services at all. And even when the VA does provide services, often they are not helpful. Shortly after the Iraq War began, Barry Romo, National Coordinator of Vietnam Veterans Against the War, told me that many at the VA were saying, "Get over [your emotional upset from the war]. All vets go through this." However, he said, that upset will never go away, "because it is how we survived." Well into 2010, he told me that this concern persisted.[2]

Many veterans do not even get into the VA system: Just as active duty soldiers are reluctant to seek help for emotional problems, so some former servicemembers are afraid to seek help, concerned that having this on their record might interfere with obtaining employment. (Although denial of employment or firing because of psychological problems is illegal, the burden of proof is on the employee to show that that was the reason for failure to hire or for firing, and the standards for meeting the burden of proof are high and difficult to meet.) Others who have returned to civilian life know they may be called back into service, or they may want to return; consequently, they don't want to jeopardize their chances for advancement in the military or risk losing their pensions by being categorized as mentally ill.

Those who do ask to be served in the VA system are often subjected to intolerably long waits to be assessed or offered help. Those who apply to the VA for disability status so that they can receive appropriate compensation often have to wait unconscionably long before decisions are made, and their applications are far too often unjustifiably rejected. Glantz writes that since the start of the Iraq War, according to the VA itself, the backlog of unanswered disability claims has grown from 325,000 to more than 600,000.[3] The entire claims process, he says, is designed to identify veterans who are trying to cheat the system rather than to compensate soldiers whose war service led to their injuries. One of the practical consequences of this aim is that veterans requesting compensation for psychological trauma must submit a twenty-six-page form, including a detailed essay about the specific moments when they experienced one or a series of terrifying events that led to their emotional distress. Commenting on the VA's focus on identifying applicants who do not deserve disability status, Glantz points to a study by Joseph Stiglitz and Linda Bilmes of Harvard University's Kennedy School of Government, who found that almost all veterans tell the truth in their disability claims, with the VA ultimately approving nearly 90 percent of the claims[4]:

Delays in processing claims and deciding appeals are often so long that according to the VA, from October 1, 2007, to March 31, 2008, a total of 1,467 veterans died waiting to learn if their disability claims would be approved by the government. Veterans who appeal the VA's denial of their disability claims wait an average of 1,419 days, or nearly four years, for a response.[5]

Thus, huge numbers of veterans have to jump through the hoops of appealing the rejections and enduring long periods of waiting, while already suffering in the kinds of ways described in chapter 2, as well as, for many, trying to cope with the consequences of physical injury. According to Glantz, a veteran who had taken part in the initial invasion of Iraq later fought for two years to get treatment for his trauma and disability compensation from the VA; unable to endure the continued wait, he shot himself in his head, leaving a note: "We cannot stand the memories and decide death is better."[6]

Once in the VA system, the problems many vets encounter are legion. Consider the story of Merrill Cromwell (pseudonym), who supported and still earnestly supports the war in Iraq, was injured in the fighting there, and would go back in a second, despite 135-degree heat, sandstorms, and constant danger. But he was wounded in service, and he now feels betrayed by the VA system (as he also did by the Army) that is supposed to serve him. He says, "If anything wrong was going to happen with the VA, it's happened to me." A powerfully built man with clear blue eyes, an engaging smile, and impeccable manners, Merrill has struggled with an unthinkable number and array of physical problems and some emotional upset since being injured in Iraq. Some of the emotional upset was due to the injuries and some to the ways he has been treated in the VA system. The son of farmers, he grew up in a small town in the South, was an Eagle Scout, and won awards for his work in music. He had a perfect attendance record all through school and was clearly a high achiever, but he had not wanted to join the military, because he "didn't want to be told what to do all the time." He was thirty when, like many vets of the current wars, he enlisted immediately after the events of 9/11, having felt deeply and personally affected by the attacks on Americans. He said:

I felt like something was taken away from me, a piece of me was stripped, stolen, and it opened up a fire inside me something fierce. I joined, because for the first time in my life I believed in something greater than myself. It's freedom, honor, and duty. It was my duty as an American to serve and make sure that this didn't happen again, and it's everything that goes with it. And that day, even though it wasn't happening to me directly, it did. And a piece of that was taken away. And all those people that it was happening to, it just felt like—I've never done that before watching something like that, crying as if I knew them, because I didn't know any of them, but it felt like I was losing a friend. And the more they talked about it, the angrier I got that they did this. So I wanted some payback. I wanted to go over there and I wanted to help make a better life for them and for us and to make sure not another one of them would strap a bomb onto their chest or climb into a plane and kill thousands of innocent people. Closer to home here . . . you kind of felt let down, too, by the government, that they let this happen.

Although he would later discover that his Army recruiter had lied to him, promising that if he signed on, his student loans would be paid off, Merrill Cromwell thrived once he was in the Army. After about six months in country, he somehow lost consciousness while chasing an insurgent in Iraq: "Something happened, whether it was an explosion or something else, I don't know, but when I came to, I was lying in an orchard about a 12–15-foot drop from the road I was chasing the insurgent on." When he regained consciousness, he was in excruciating pain but nevertheless continued fighting for five days. His neck hurt, his head hurt, his shoulder hurt, his back was "killing [him]," he had trouble breathing, he was dizzy, and he had difficulty controlling his bladder. He tried to explain away each symptom, blaming some of the pains on the heavy packs he had been carrying and assuming he had wet himself because of all the fluid he had been drinking. After those five days of postinjury fighting he woke up on a Humvee, his shoulder frozen. He was taken to a field hospital, where the doctor told him that he had two compressed fractures in his neck and a shattered right shoulder, the bone chips from which had locked his shoulder into its frozen position. He was sent home.

Merrill is the vet described in chapter 2 as having had to pick up pieces of the bodies of his dead fellow soldiers and put them in see-through body bags, and who still has nightmares about the Iraqi woman he killed. The nightmares persist despite the knowledge that the woman was indeed an insurgent who was constructing bombs. In addition, he gets "antsy" when in traffic these days. The reason?

Where I get the most antsy is in traffic, because I drove our Humvee, and all the IEDs, the suicide bombers, those guys would come up behind you, and they'd just keep comin', keep comin', you put that weapon on them, they keep comin', you fire a couple rounds in front of them, they keep comin'. Whenever we got stuck in traffic, they would drop grenades off rooftops, have IEDs planted in areas where [our vehicles would get] congested, and they know it's gonna be slow, so when they click it [to detonate the explosives], it does the most damage. [We were] ordered only to shoot when [we] feel threatened, but you don't know until they get close enough . . . could just be some idiot who's decided to play with you.

He struggles with these emotionally and morally wrenching problems as well as with the emotional consequences of his extreme physical injuries.

Merrill spent two years at Walter Reed Hospital, leaving two weeks before the media broke the story about the horrendous conditions there. Released from the hospital in May 2006, he went home on 20 percent disability from the Army. This is a remarkably low disability rating for someone who, it turns out, had landed on his head in a diving position at the time he was injured, broken off the top part of his sacrum, damaged four discs in his lower back and three in his neck, sustained significant nerve damage (some of which impaired his bladder control), lost hearing in his right ear, suffered damage that causes him to experience vertigo, repeatedly loses consciousness because his blood pressure suddenly drops but his brain is unable to send the signal to correct it, now has angina when going up the stairs, and has constant, extreme pain ("all over") that makes him break out in sweats and interferes with his sleep. He has headaches with no let-up ever, has blackouts, and is "almost completely exhausted all the time." Further, he says:

I only remember 5 to 10 percent of what goes on during the day, and there are times that I can't even remember what I'm supposed to do. For example, last year when I was on campus I stood there on the sidewalk and couldn't remember why I was there or what I was supposed to do until eventually I snapped out of it and I remembered I had to go to class. I have electric shocks that go through my head, my arms and my legs all the time. I have lost some feeling in my extremities to the point where I cut myself without even knowing it and don't even feel it until someone says hey look you're bleeding. . . . I take morphine every eight hours for pain and this does not cure me from the pain but takes it down to about a 6 on a 10 point scale it just makes the pain bearable but still annoying.

Not only is 20 percent disability a paltry amount in light of all of his suffering, but as he says, 30 percent is the "magic number" that allows one to obtain Tricare, which is health insurance provided by the military.

After receiving the 20 percent rating from the Army and being released from Walter Reed, Merrill received the same 20 percent disability rating upon entering the VA system. He says that the VA claimed that some of his injuries were preexisting or that they could not find any evidence from the Army that part of his body was injured in combat. Merrill began at least seven appeals to the VA to have the percentage increased. At each stage, *he* has had to ask repeatedly that they investigate the full range of his symptoms, and at each stage they have run additional tests. Usually these are tests that they should have run when he entered the VA system. He says, "Every time I've gone in there they've found something else due to the injury," something they could have found in the beginning if they had tried. After four years of appeals, his disability rating is now at 80 percent, and the VA acknowledges that he has a traumatic brain injury. He wants his disability rating to reach 100 percent, because at that level in the VA system, one finally gets health insurance that allows one to be seen anywhere for medical care, not just in the VA system.

According to Merrill, although he received $20,000 in severance pay from the Army, now that he is in the VA system and on partial disability, he is required to repay that $20,000 before being allowed to keep his disability payments from the VA.

From day one, Merrill says, he had reported having back pain, and the VA doctors minimized his suffering by saying that it did not look that bad, that he was not hurt. Four times he ended up in emergency rooms with excruciating back pain, the swelling around his spinal cord having increased to the point that he could not move his legs. At his usual VA center, he had been told that if this happened again, he could go to a regular hospital nearby rather than making the long trip to the VA facility nearest to him, and the VA would cover the cost. They said that that would be allowed, because the back problem was a preexisting condition. The next time the problem arose, Merrill took the extra step of checking with the VA to make certain that this was allowed, and when the VA staff person he and his wife spoke with confirmed that it was, they went to the ER of a regular hospital. However, the VA then refused to cover the more than $2,000 cost of the visit, saying that it was not a life-or-death situation, that it was *only* that he could not walk, and saying that what he had been told previously was irrelevant. His account has been turned over to a collection agency.

On a different occasion Merrill went to a VA facility unable to walk and in excruciating pain. They gave him morphine for the pain, and the medication caused him to have horrible spasms. In yet another kind of betrayal by the VA system, his doctor, observing the spasms and his ongoing expressions of his pain, said, "You are doing this to yourself. You are creating the problem. You need to calm down. Just calm down." That physician had worked for the VA for three decades. Merrill asked to be assigned to a different doctor, and this new one, he says, is at last ordering certain tests as the first doctor should have done from the beginning. Despite this doctor's help, Merrill says that he does not want to cause any trouble but finds that sometimes he needs to ask his U.S. Senators or media people to help him get the assistance he needs. He says:

I never thought that if I was ever injured in Iraq or even killed that my loved ones or myself would ever have to worry about getting proper care or help. . . . Less than 1 percent of the U.S. population serves in the military, and I don't understand how they cannot properly take care of us and do what is right. How can they not have the funding to do what is right by us? I know in my case I served my country with honor and dignity, and I asked for nothing in return but just to be properly taken care of if anything should ever happen to me.

I met Merrill on March 29, 2010, a day he told me he celebrates as "My Live Day," the anniversary of the day he was injured in Iraq but did not die. When we met, he spent the first ten minutes showing me photographs of his wife and baby boy, who are the lights of his life and who indeed look beautiful and radiant. Then he told me he had not slept at all in two days because of new medication the VA doctors had put him on three weeks earlier, and that total lack of sleep came on top of his minimal and very disturbed sleep since the injury in Iraq in 2003. During all these years, he goes to bed around 1 or 2 a.m. and gets up between 4 and 5 a.m., in the meantime having gotten up to use the bathroom between six and fourteen times. The new medication was dextroamphetamine, which a doctor told him might "jumpstart my brain." He was taking, as directed, four pills in the morning and two in the afternoon, but no one was monitoring him for the frequent effects of disturbed sleep that this kind of drug causes. In addition, he had completely lost his appetite to the point where he could not force himself to eat at all, another effect of the medication. During our interview, he fought hard to keep from falling asleep and was clearly exhausted. On a number of occasions, he forgot what he was talking about, and that could have been from the medication, his brain injury, his extremely low blood sugar due to lack of food, or some combination of these factors. In any case, his struggle to stay awake and function was clear. He also told me that at the VA he was put on an antidepressant medication that I knew to be highly addictive. He had not been told that it was. Furthermore, he said that he had only been "a little depressed but not enough where I felt I needed medication for it. I was more depressed about dealing with the VA than anything that happened in Iraq." He did not know why he had been told to take this medication and said that it had not helped. Although he had told the VA staff these things, they VA had not taken him off this drug.

Merrill's story is, like every story I chose to include in this book, a typical one. Currently, uncounted but clearly large numbers of veterans (as described throughout this chapter) are going through similar sequences of neglect, betrayal, and victim-blaming in the VA system. The stories of suffering stand in stark contrast to the series of peppy but often insubstantial announcements the VA has issued during the current wars, with some investigative journalists doing excellent work at uncovering the truth behind VA press releases. Furthermore, even some of the VA's own announcements have revealed shocking disrespect for veterans' needs. We shall look chronologically at some of these releases and media stories.

In 2005, the VA was preparing for an increase in veterans seeking help for emotional trauma from war, because some soldiers were then returning from Iraq, according to Dr. Terence Keane, behavioral science division director at the VA's National Center for Post-Traumatic Stress Disorder.[7] Before that, there had only been what the VA called a "trickle" of veterans asking for help, but that trickle consisted of 17,000 vets back from Iraq and Afghanistan. These servicemembers had been described as having PTSD, anxiety, depression, substance abuse, and difficulty adjusting to life at home. But even at that early stage, Keane noted candidly that there could be a huge increase of vets with these problems in the future, because "the most powerful predictor of mental health problems is the intensity of the war, and this is a very intense war." VA leaders were also aware at that time that high-quality surgeries and field hospitals located closer to combat than in previous wars would likely mean that more soldiers than before would survive injuries and then develop emotional problems.

As early as 2005, vets were reporting long delays in getting appointments with VA psychotherapists, and the Government Accountability Office (GAO) had found that officials at six out of seven VA facilities were worried about being able to treat more emotionally traumatized patients.[8] A psychiatric nurse at a VA facility, asking to remain anonymous, said, "We've got our head barely above water" because they could not handle the caseload.[9] The GAO also said that the VA did not have sufficient data for projecting future needs for psychotherapy, but VA officials denied that this was true.[10] At the time, veterans' advocate Paul Rieckhoff, an Iraq veteran who had founded Operation Truth, was warning prophetically and poignantly that "very few people on [Capitol Hill] want to spend money on veterans' issues at this time," and this was when the Bush administration had reduced funding for veterans' services. Rieckhoff opined that those in government were "having a hard time admitting the amount of damage that is being inflicted on the American soldiers and their brains."[11]

In August 2005 came the troubling news that the VA had decided to review the claims of about 72,000 veterans who were receiving disability payments for PTSD to see whether they perhaps did not deserve those benefits because they could not prove they had been exposed to a "stressor."[12] They did not say, however, that they planned to review the opposite kinds of cases: vets who had been wrongly denied benefits. Adding insult to injury, the VA planned to conduct the new, superfluous round of reviews despite already having a backlog of several hundred thousand disability claims, according to Randy Reese, national service director for Disabled American Veterans, who expressed concern about this use of the VA's scarce resources.[13] Around this time, Kayla Williams, wife of a vet, said on National Public Radio that her husband had suffered a serious wound in Iraq, which left him with a TBI and shrapnel still in his brain. The VA, she said, had lost his paperwork and gave him virtually no help in managing his terrible pain.

In the late summer of 2005, the VA was still trying to sell the story that the emotional effects of the current wars would not be so bad.[14] According to a top VA mental health official, Dr. Mark Shelhorse, in contrast to Vietnam vets, most cases of war trauma in vets of the new wars would not become chronic. He said, "We've learned a lot of lessons from Vietnam. . . . If we intervene early, most cases resolve with just a little support and therapy." He did not provide evidence for this claim, however.

In an interview on September 16, 2005, VA psychiatrist Dr. Harold Kudler, who helped write the *Iraq War Clinician Guide*, estimated that only about 15–20 percent of vets would receive a diagnosis of mental illness and said that at the VA, they were "trying very hard to normalize" emotional suffering from war,[15] to make it clear that intense emotional reactions to war were normal. Among other things, he pointed out that trying to adjust to life back home when one is used to living in a war zone is difficult, as the vet struggles with such problems as "jumpiness" that were appropriate in the aforementioned but unwarranted back home.[16] In May 2010, Dr. Kudler said that he and his colleagues had tried to achieve this normalizing by "opening a conversation" about the need for a public health response to deployment stress that they "believed to be universal for war fighters/veterans and their families," and he also said that such problems as anger, impulsivity, and emotional lability are not "always or even mostly due to any mental disorder or PTSD—in fact, very much the opposite."[17] He pointed out in the same interview that he "[sees] those as part of the average expectable problems faced by good Soldiers, Sailors, Marines, Airmen/women, Guard members."

In January 2007, Michelle Dillow had returned from service in the Army in Iraq, where she had been within range of many explosions every single day, had done patdown searches of Iraqis who might be concealing a bomb—and that would have killed her by the time her patdown located the device, had to patch up vehicles that were blown up by IEDs, and had lost close friends to the war.[18] Back at home in Missouri she was plagued by sleeplessness, isolation, and a suppressed rage that was totally different from anything she had experienced before. She described these problems to a service officer from the VA. His reactions, she said, made her "feel like a freak of nature and really made me question if I was crazy." She had also, however, spoken with someone else in an ordinary interview rather than in a therapy context, and that listener had said she thought Michelle's reactions were "normal reactions to abnormal situations." Dillow called this to mind and decided that the VA officer had been "just too naive to understand." After a college student in a class where Dillow lectured about her war experiences reached out to her in a quite simple way that showed that the former did not consider her mentally ill, Dillow's sleeplessness subsided, and she began "finding my way back to the real world." Her experience is the perfect example of one of the main points I am trying to make with this book, mentioned previously and reiterated throughout: Nonprofessional members of the community are uniquely empowered to deliver some of the simplest and most effective "interventions" for the suffering of our returning soldiers and veterans.

In early 2007, a story in the *Boston Globe* highlighted the suicide of an Iraq veteran while he sought care from the VA.[19] Jonathan Schulze, a Marine veteran with two Purple Hearts, drove seventy-five miles to the nearest VA Medical Center, told an intake counselor he was suicidal, and asked to be admitted to a psychiatric ward. That counselor said there was a particular clinician who "prescreened" cases like his but who was not then available and told Jonathan to go home and wait for a phone call the next day. When a clinical social worker called that next day, Jonathan again reported his thoughts of suicide and related symptoms and learned that he was twenty-sixth on the waiting list for one of the twelve beds in that center's PTSD section. Four days later he hanged himself with an extension cord. In light of this, it is particularly disturbing that in May 2008, in an internal email, Dr. Ira Katz, head of mental health services for the VA, was shown to have written "Shh!" about data showing that 12,000 veterans a year make suicide attempts while under departmental treatment.[20]

In April 2007, the *Chicago Tribune* carried the report of a veteran whom the VA had denied 100 percent disability—thus depriving him of the associated extra pay and benefits—because his medical records failed to document that "shrapnel wounds, all over body" were "related to [his] military service."[21] His medical records from Iraq were not available, because like many soldiers, he returned to the United States without them, and then at Walter Reed, staff failed to document the source of his shrapnel. As a result, he was awarded only a 90 percent disability rating, so that he would have to pay property taxes and receive about $1,000 less in income each month than if he had the 100 percent rating. Another veteran who applied for benefits waited "months and months and months" for a decision, so that he felt forgotten. These were just two examples of the backlog of disability claims that had grown to 400,000 and nationwide were taking about two years to process. (Perhaps it would be a good use of stimulus dollars to hire workers to help process these claims; if we can hire workers to conduct the census, why can't we hire workers for this other very important task?)

In June 2007, Anne Hull and Dana Priest, the *Washington Post* reporters who had broken the Walter Reed story, wrote about a veteran who had sought help from a VA medical center when he felt "estranged and alone, struggling with financial collapse and a darkening depression."[22] One psychologist there diagnosed him with PTSD that was "severe and chronic" and said that he was "in need of major help" and had provided "more than enough evidence" to back up his claim to have been disabled by combat trauma. In spite of that, the VA disability evaluators ruled that he deserved no compensation, because, they claimed, his psychological problems existed before he joined the Army. It is nearly always possible to find in someone's history evidence that they had psychological problems, because that term can be so broadly defined, and virtually no one has ever led a completely trouble-free life. The VA also said that this vet had not proven he had ever been in combat. Yet, wrote Hull and Priest, "abundant evidence of his year in combat with the 4th Infantry Division covers his family's living-room wall." Using this case to make larger points about how the VA was functioning, the journalists wrote that the VA was spending $2.8 billion that year on mental health, but all it could offer that vet was group therapy, not a single session of which was held on weekends or late enough at night for him to be able to attend. They wrote further that the VA "chronically loses records" and has absurd standards for determining disability, such as that one major event can be debilitating but that accumulated trauma cannot.

In July 2007, Veterans Affairs Secretary Jim Nicholson pledged to create twenty-three new Vet Centers, which are small, community-based, walk-in clinics. These Vet Centers (there were 232 at the time of the announcement) emphasize peer counseling, group therapy, community involvement, and family treatment and education.[23] This was a promising step, for the vets I have talked with consistently describe the people at these Vet Centers as much more likely to be helpful and respectful than those at other VA services.

August 2008 brought an announcement that, as the military had done previously, the VA had launched an advertising campaign with posters encouraging veterans to consider it a sign of strength to ask for help.[24] But such exhortations might have had little effect, it seems. An internal VA investigation the following month indicated that top mental health officials at the San Diego VA were so busy doing research that they were spending little time treating the huge and growing caseload of anguished veterans.[25] Thus, even if vets had come forward in greater numbers, at least in San Diego it is unlikely they would have been seen promptly. This lack of commitment to patients' care was demonstrated not only by therapists' unavailability for clinical sessions but even by their failure to make follow-up calls or do adequate follow-up for the vast majority of Iraq and Afghanistan vets who missed appointments. Such follow-up is important, because missed appointments can reflect serious upset that interferes with functioning or a sense of helplessness and hopelessness about whether assistance and support will be waiting *if* they get into the VA system. Ideally, of course, high-quality research is a top priority, because it could help reveal what is most helpful. But by this point, new research had not been particularly helpful in that way, and the terrible problems within the VA were making it difficult for many suffering vets to be seen at all. Furthermore, cutting-edge research is useless if the personnel are not putting it into practice. Case workers for vets from current wars were already handling 120 patients each, four times the number set by the VA standard, a caseload that would make it virtually impossible to follow adequately the guidelines that might come from the research. Additionally, the record-keeping system described (in the VA's own report) as chaotic was making it impossible even to *track* the nearly 1,200 cases of Iraq and Afghanistan vets diagnosed with PTSD there since 2003.

Making efforts to help, Dr. Karen S. Guice, executive director of the VA's federal recovery care coordination program, announced in November 2008 that the VA had worked with the Department of Defense and the Department of Labor to create a National Resource Directory, which was a list of "care coordinators, providers and support partners with resources for wounded and ill servicemembers, veterans, their families, and others who support them." It included resources from all branches of government and was organized into the categories of benefits and compensation.[26] (http://www.nationalresourcedirectory.org) The directory was described as offering "more than 10,000 medical and non-medical services and resources" to help veterans "achieve personal and professional goals along their journey from recovery through rehabilitation to community reintegration." Dr. Guice noted, "The community is essential to the successful reintegration of our veterans."[27] This directory is a fine idea, and it seemed especially promising that it included some resources related to practical matters such as education, health, and housing. But the pulling together of these listings would not, in and of itself, do anything to improve the quality of any one, and that includes services intended to alleviate emotional suffering.

November 2008 brought more news of veterans being told that their physical wounds were not considered combat-related and thus did not qualify them for disability status.[28] The previous March, in "a little-noticed regulation change," the military's definition of combat-related disabilities had been narrowed, depriving some injured veterans of huge sums of money in lost benefits and making them feel betrayed and outraged. This was yet another example of emotional consequences not of war itself but rather of the shoddy treatment of soldiers when they came home. The vets' bewilderment and fury were not surprising, given that, for instance, those deprived of combat-related disability status included Marine Corporal James Dixon, wounded once in Iraq by a roadside bomb and once by a land mine, suffering brain and hip injuries and hearing loss and being classified as suffering emotional trauma; and Army Sergeant Lori Meshell, who "shattered a hip and crushed her back and knees while diving for cover during a mortar attack in Iraq" and who has "undergone a hip replacement and knee reconstruction and needs at least three more surgeries." Dixon said, "I was blown up twice in Iraq, and my injuries weren't combat-related? . . . It's the most imbecile thing I've ever seen." According to Meshell, the military had suggested that at least some of her disability was caused by preexisting joint deterioration. "Before I went over there, I was fine—I was perfectly healthy," Meshell said. "This whole thing is causing me a lot of heartache."[29] The changes in guidelines would reduce payments for tens of thousands of veterans, according to Kerry Baker, Associate Legislative Director of Disabled American Veterans. Particularly painful for vets who had risked their lives was that, as Baker testified before Congress, this seemed to be "an intentional effort to conserve monetary resources at the expense of disabled veterans."

As 2008 drew to a close, a shocking report appeared.[30] Despite an order from Congress the *previous* year that the Pentagon should accept appeals from wounded vets, not a single such appeal had yet been heard. Again, the theme of betrayal and lack of respect and appreciation was striking, and again veterans' advocates protested that the disability ratings were manipulated to save money. Unheard appeals included such cases as that of Army Specialist Cristapher Zuetlau, whose military career ended when he wrenched his back so severely that he could barely walk. In a rather paradoxical ruling, the Army had decided he was no longer able to serve but also that his disability was too mild to qualify for long-term care by the military. As a result, his health care had been transferred to the VA, his family was cut off from government health care, and he had no retirement benefits.

As vets continued to struggle with the VA bureaucracy in an effort to obtain appropriate disability ratings and actual care, the VA itself began to acknowledge that it was having serious difficulties finding ways to provide *effective* ways to alleviate emotional pain.[31] According to top VA therapists like the wonderfully candid Dr. Patricia Resick, director of the Women's Health Sciences Division of the National Center for PTSD and the VA Boston Healthcare System, there were two major, unmet needs: (1) for developing and testing new treatments for substance abuse and other emotional or behavioral problems and (2) for finding ways to put treatments into practice in ways that actually helped servicemembers and veterans. Despite the impressive-sounding claims of some therapists that they do evidence-based practice, as described in chapter 3 there are major impediments to putting the outcomes of research into practice. The candor of some VA officials with regard to these failings was an important step forward. Ultimately, if we do not acknowledge what is not working and what we do not know, we cannot expect to begin to make progress.

Dr. Bruce Rounsaville, a Yale University professor of psychiatry and director of the VA Connecticut-Massachusetts Mental Illness Research Education and Clinical Center, has described a host of problems with putting research into practice. To begin with, he says, "Even the best ideas need to be tested in real-world settings . . . [and] evidence-based treatments are developed in narrow patient populations and require a large number of specific skills and techniques for one disorder. It's daunting to learn." He also described the trial-and-error basis of much treatment, pointing out that a treatment package for any one veteran could include "four or five general strategies, and it is hard to know whether all of them are needed for efficacy. . . . That takes added time and resources." He also noted that there are unknowns about what kinds of treatment work best with which therapists. Finding trainers and supervisors presents yet another challenge, because clinicians "have their biases" and it is hard to get them to switch away from practices they have followed for years.[32]

With the VA sorely needing some encouraging news, in a February 2009 article one of their spokespersons stated that its suicide prevention hotline had taken calls from nearly 100,000 vets or their family members and friends since its 2007 inception.[33] Most striking was the claim that "more than 2,600 veterans have been 'rescued' through the hotline." The press release did not include mention of what criteria were used to set apart the

2,600 from the 100,000 calls, and nothing was said about how they defined those rescues. Even if the number was accurate, however, statistics at the time were indeed showing vets from current wars to be significantly more likely than people in the general population to kill themselves. Furthermore, Chairman of the Joint Chiefs of Staff, Navy Admiral Mike Mullen, said in a public lecture that, despite wanting to support vets who are suicidal, in some cases they hadn't "quite figured out yet" how to do that. Interestingly, Mullen advocated increasing the amount of rest and time at home that troops have in between deployments, because "officials recognize the high tempo of deployment rotations as being a likely factor for the increased suicide rates," but there was no indication at that time that those increases were being implemented. With longer times at home off the table, it was perhaps unsurprising that figuring out how to prevent suicides continued to seem difficult.

In April 2009, President Barack Obama said that the incidence of suicide among active duty service members and veterans was growing. He proposed a major increase in funding for the VA—$25 billion over five years—in order to provide more services for those diagnosed with PTSD and TBI, as well as other mental health services.[34] He noted that "sometimes the deadliest wounds are the ones you cannot see, and we cannot afford to let the unseen wounds go untreated." The funding was to be used to increase the number of Vet Centers and mobile health clinics and for initiatives to educate vets and their families about their options for care.

Apparently seeking innovative ways to help, Dr. David Kearney at a VA hospital in Seattle began teaching "mindfulness-based stress reduction" techniques to vets in attempting to help them deal with anxiety and other problems through meditation, yoga and deep-breathing exercises."[35] The VA's Dr. Harold Kudler believes that the mindfulness approach, which involves focusing on the present moment, is helpful, because, as one soldier said, it reminds veterans that their combat memories are not the totality of who they are.[36] The data from Dr. Kearney's careful study suggest that this approach helped somewhat to reduce negative moods and to increase active behavior.[37] In a telephone interview on May 12, 2010, Dr. Kearney said that he felt that the approach had been helpful because, among other things, it involved teaching "lovingkindness meditation, compassion for self and others."[38] These techniques, he reported, helped vets deal with the intense anger and hypervigilance they felt as a result of combat experiences and involved rigorous training to counteract the military training to be constantly on alert and prepared to defend or kill. This is apparently an unusual program within the VA system, although I have some reason to wonder whether nontraditional approaches might be more common than the VA's public announcements would suggest: At a social gathering, I met a bright, caring psychologist who works at a VA facility and who told me about his approach, which was not the traditional one of labeling vets mentally ill and prescribing talk therapy and drugs. Instead, he described encouraging the vets to identify the problems with which they wanted help and then working with them to find solutions that fit their needs. During that discussion, he agreed that I could interview him later for this book, as long as I did not mention his name or the facility where he works. However, he did not respond to the phone and email messages I sent him to request an interview.

In August 2009, an article in the *Seattle Times* underscored "an unsettling new reality" for VA service providers: Owing to the frequency of repeated deployments, in contrast to previous wars, they were now often treating vets who were headed back to war.[39] This was confronting them with an ethical dilemma: What to do if they thought that emotional problems or "other unhealed wounds" could put their patient or others at risk on the front line, especially if the military was pressuring them to send as many soldiers as possible back to service? And what to do if a vet wanted to go back to war but the provider thought it was contraindicated? (These dilemmas are portrayed in poignant and vivid detail in Pat Barker's novel, *Regeneration*, about the dynamics between psychiatrist W. H. Rivers and the antiwar poet and soldier Siegfried Sassoon.)[40] One of the many complicating factors was that the VA's privacy policy only allows the disclosure of VA records to the military in limited circumstances. So soldiers' medical care could be fragmented, with VA doctors treating them while they are in civilian life but Army or other service doctors treating them if they are called up subsequently. Unsurprisingly, crucial information often gets lost. Thus, "Army doctors and commanders generally do not have access to VA medical records that might help them assess whether a veteran should return to front-line duty."[41]

August 2009 brought a *New York Times* article with even more alarming news about suicides: The toll had continued to rise, despite the VA's hiring of hundreds of additional therapists, and multiple deployments were again named as a major causal factor.[42] The report was all the more worrying, because there were no reliable figures for suicides by veterans who had left military service, since the VA could only systematically track suicides among its hospitalized patients and "does not issue regular suicide reports." Thus, even the already distressing numbers seemed to be underestimates. Those individuals attempting to examine academically the plight of war veterans would encounter additional hurdles in that same month. Researchers studying how to treat "the psychological wounds of war" among vets of current wars were having tremendous difficulty persuading vets to participate in their research.[43] They attributed this shortage to the stigma of seeking help for emotional troubles. In one study, researchers needed 440 couples for intensive couples counseling but had recruited only ten since the beginning of the year, and in another study calling for 135 male veterans, only thirteen had been attracted so far.

Then came still more information that cast the VA in a bad light: In April 2010, Adam Liptak reported in the *New York Times* a U.S. Supreme Court decision that deadlines for filing certain documents in court cases should be rigidly adhered to and showed that this rigidity was unfairly penalizing thousands of war veterans who were appealing the VA's rejections of their claims. Veterans often have difficulty meeting those court deadlines precisely because of psychological problems and cognitive impairment from their war trauma. Furthermore, Liptak noted, many veterans file appeals themselves, without help from lawyers, and the fact that they win 80 percent of the time reflects that their cases are usually meritorious. He quoted a judge who called "ironic and inhumane" the decision to be inflexible about these deadlines for veterans who have served their country, when courts have the leeway to be flexible.

On April 24, 2010, in a Department of Defense press release,[44] there came the announcement that, because more than 6,000 veterans were committing suicide every year, the VA was "redoubling its outreach to veterans and promoting its toll-free suicide-prevention hotline." The hotline was established in 2007, and Dr. Janet Kemp, the VA's National Suicide Prevention Coordinator, was quoted in the 2010 press release as saying that another 10,665 had made unsuccessful suicide attempts in 2009 but that the numbers had come down. She said the hotline had stopped 7,000 suicides in progress, but she gave only "anecdotal evidence" (describing a single case) that the VA's campaign to reduce suicides had had an impact.

In his 2009 book, *The War Comes Home*, journalist Aaron Glantz opined that "nearly everyone in the military system has an incentive to short-change the soldier."[45] He noted that military psychologists were overworked because of understaffing and "an ever-increasing torrent" of soldiers suffering the emotional consequences of war trauma, who were receiving only one hour of individual therapy a month and often seeing a different therapist each time. Between January 2000 and September 2004 the VA's patient-to-doctor ratio had grown from 335:1 to 531:1. To try to compensate for these shortages, Glantz wrote, therapists were freely prescribing psychiatric drugs, and he quoted Jason Forrester from the advocacy group Veterans for America as saying that it was "not uncommon for us to meet soldiers on over fifteen to twenty different medications at once." (Laypeople often understandably ask whether that kind of heavy prescribing of drugs is not a form of malpractice, but though it usually ought to be, rarely is any doctor charged for that reason.) One mother bemoaned that she had watched her daughter go to Iraq "to make things better" and then watched her come home to be "left behind by the VA system." "They're drugging them and not fixing them," she said.[46]

Despite the myriad problems plaguing the VA, in August 2009, VA secretary Eric K. Shinseki proclaimed that "[t]he hidden wounds of war are being addressed vigorously and comprehensively by this administration as we move VA forward in its transformation to the 21st century."[47] He announced that the VA was then publishing a proposed regulation in the *Federal Register* to make it easier for a veteran to claim service connection for PTSD by reducing the evidence needed about whether the stressor claimed was related to fear of hostile military or terrorist activity (for instance, instead of having to prove they were wounded in combat, they might be able to prove that they continue to suffer terribly because of having spent a long time in a zone where anyone could have been an enemy). But despite this upbeat claim about still more VA efforts to help vets, their press releases did not include concrete evidence of increasing benefits to those they aimed to serve. In fact, in contrast to Shinseki's assertion, on April 5, 2010, Michelle Dillow, one of the vets described earlier in this chapter who had not in previous years found VA staff to be helpful, described her more recent, negative experience in a VA facility. She had begun a new job that she found boring and was in a relationship with someone who verbally abused her. She hit a low point and felt no motivation to do anything. When she went to the VA and told a provider, "This isn't me," he simply put her on antidepressants for the first time in her life. She stopped taking them after three weeks because "they turned me into a zombie, made me numb." She flushed the pills down the toilet and "figured if this job and guy are making me that depressed, I'm going to get rid of both. It worked. I learned I could find solutions to my problems." She is in a new job that she loves and got out of the hurtful relationship, but none of that was with help from anyone at the VA.

In June 2010 the military and the VA were said in a DoD press release to be increasingly using digital technology to treat PTSD, with the VA creating an Internet-based chat line for people to discuss emotional upset. It is cause for concern that an official quoted in the release said that "Stress is a fact of life, and we want to reframe the issue to one of stress control," given the presentation of war trauma as resulting in the mild-sounding "stress" and given the implication that war, the cause of the upset, is simply a fact of life that has consequences that one must "control" rather than attempt to prevent.[48]

Some much more encouraging news appeared in July 2010, when journalist James Dao wrote in the *Seattle Times* that the VA was preparing to make it easier for vets who were diagnosed with PTSD to receive disability benefits.[49] The aim was to reduce vets' burden of proof that their emotional upset had been caused by specific traumatic events and that those events had been part of regular combat. This was tremendously important, because "the current rules discriminate against tens of thousands of service members—many of them women—who did not serve in combat roles but nevertheless suffered traumatic experiences." If the new rule went into effect, it would require vets only to prove that they had "served in a war zone and in a job consistent with the events that they say caused their conditions." As this book was in production, many were hoping that the new rule would be followed right away.

On August 30, 2010, an Associated Press article brought the news that Seroquel, "a potent antipsychotic drug" that the VA has given to thousands of soldiers diagnosed with PTSD since the current wars began, can cause sudden heart failure leading to death.[50] Purchases of the drug place it in the list of the VA's top drug expenditures, and the military's spending for it has increased more than sevenfold since 2001, when the war in Afghanistan began. Since several soldiers had died while on the medication, some military families were asking Congress to investigate. In the article, we read about Andrew White, who returned from nine months in Iraq beset with insomnia, nightmares, and constant restlessness. He took Seroquel and two other psychiatric drugs, but the nightmares persisted. This should not be surprising, given that the likely causes of his anguish may not have been addressed, that he was most likely solely put on drugs. What did the doctors do? They increased his Seroquel dose repeatedly, until finally this 23-year-old was taking more than 1,600 milligrams per day, "more than double the maximum dose recommended for schizophrenia patients." White died in his sleep, and VA officials concluded that he had died from "a rare drug interaction," but the combination of drugs he was taking—Seroquel, an antidepressant, an anti-anxiety pill, and a painkiller for which he did not have a prescription—is known to be common for vets.

We can hope that the military and the VA will look at the real causes of suffering that veterans experience and find ways to help alleviate or even prevent some of it. Fortunately, we need not wait for them to come through, because there is much that every citizen can do, and that is the subject of the next chapter.

6 What Every Citizen Can Do to Help

I thought the point was we were all in this together.
—Wendy Wasserstein, *The Heidi Chronicles*[1]

Only connect.
—E. M. Forster, *Howards End*[2]

You'd think for me my War has passed
  Pay attention! It has not.
  What troubles me now is a blood soaked dream,
  Can't stop the flow at will.
  As thousands of Vets, we fear the worst.
  Mirrored in The Wall for us still.

—David E. Jones, "War Drums"[3]

Every citizen can help our returning soldiers. Every vet deserves help in grappling with the shock of the loss of innocence that comes with the recognition of evil, as well as with the grief; guilt and shame; sense of betrayal and mistrust; rage; isolation, alienation, and numbing; and moral, spiritual, and existential crises that are often parts of the trauma of war. This is about love of humankind, of those who suffer because we as a nation looked the other way as they were sent to risk their lives and forfeit peace of mind, or because we have not truly known them when they returned. It is about the human need to be seen not (or not only) by a professional but by someone with no theory, no framework, no agenda but to see them and bear witness to what they, the vets, have been through. Gary Jacobson, a Vietnam veteran with a Web site about Vietnam (http://pzzzz.tripod.com/namtour.html), says that until he began to talk about his war trauma, thinking about the memories on his own "didn't work well . . . was too painful . . . too confusing. I didn't understand it, and could not get a handle on it."[4] But he found that "It is healing to talk about the traumas of war, and to get the demons of combat that we warriors who have stood in battle have buried so deep, out in front of us, out on our terms where we can easier deal with them."

What Jacobson wrote illustrates the general principle, borne out by high-quality research, that social connection and social support ease people's pain.[5] One's social environment matters greatly for one's identity, status, role, well-being, thinking, and emotional functioning. Thus, this chapter is about transforming the social context for veterans, and so it is about community, about the importance of talking and listening to a vet as a step toward helping that person come back into connection with an earlier community or a new one.[6]

Although in this chapter and this book I have wanted to speak primarily to the many laypeople who would like to be supportive, everything in this chapter could also be implemented by the military, the VA, and therapists outside the military system. Most of it is about citizens asking veterans if they would like to tell their stories: how to locate a vet, how to ask the initial questions, how to listen and respond, and how to deal with some of the common kinds of problems that can come up as veterans speak. The chapter ends with a sampling of resources that might be helpful as we hear from the vets' stories what kinds of needs they have other than to be heard. But in considering what interested individuals, groups, and organizations throughout the United States can do to help, the fundamental issues to keep in mind are (1) we should do all we can to keep from labeling vets mentally ill and treating them as though they were, and (2) the most important first step is to ask them to tell us their stories.

Before proceeding with the main part of this chapter, I'd like to explain something about its context. Since I began writing books and articles for the general public, some of my professional colleagues have made to me what they intend to be the demeaning statement, "You do pop psychology." It's fine with me if they want to call it that, as long as it is clear that I detest jargon and cant, and I detest the presentation as "science" that which most definitely is not. In my decades as a psychologist and professor, I have never encountered a concept in my field that cannot be fairly easily and accurately explained to a sixth-grader. There is no need or justification for mystification about psychology and psychiatry. Nevertheless, I have seen enormous harm done because people— patients, their families, even other therapists—have fallen for that mystification and believed they should not question what the authorities asserted. In tandem with this observation, since I graduated from my Ph.D. program in 1973, I have watched society become increasingly shaped by psychiatry, from the ways people raise their children to the ways they interpret their own feelings to the nature of friendship and the very limited uses to which friendship is put (such as friends assuming they cannot help each other because they are not therapists). I have seen a society filled with people who have increasingly come to pathologize everything—themselves, their parents, their children, the problems of their friends, characters in books and movies. And I have seen that same society turn increasingly to labels and solutions that sound scientific, that have fancy or obscuring terms. But as Robert Whitaker documents in exquisite and painful detail in his book, *Anatomy of an Epidemic*,[7] these recent decades of "new and better treatment," especially through chemistry, not only have not helped reduce the amount of suffering and mental illness (however one defines it) for most people but have increased it geometrically. The numbers of cases in which the former has actually been helpful are disturbingly small.

There is nothing wrong with applying sound science where it is relevant and helpful. The problem lies with much of what is currently passed off as science and scientifically based practice in the traditional mental health world. Furthermore, the overemphasis on science has made many tried-and-true methods for reducing people's suffering sound downright silly. What professional therapist wants to be heard saying that what vets need is not to be psychiatrically labeled, treated by a therapist, and put on medication but rather to be listened to with respect, care, patience, and support? That vets need to be told that the listener could very well have felt the same as the vet if they had been through what the vet went through?

So fasten your seatbelts, because in this chapter you will not find anything more than your grandmother or your best friend could have told you. I hope that the dissonance of knowing that I am a psychologist, then reading in ordinary words my statements about what I (and of course not only I!) have learned matters most in life—connection, respect, support, and understanding, will not be too unsettling. At three different times in my life I have gone to therapists with problems I was having, and although all three therapists were kind and intelligent, the best, most useful advice I received came from my parents, several key friends, and my now grown children. In my four years of graduate school, after being indoctrinated into all kinds of theories, techniques, and approaches that my trainers said were the best, most professional ones for helping people who were suffering, I have consistently been surprised by the way the simplest, most strength- and health-oriented kinds of action are what end up helping most. That is not to say they always help everybody but that they should be the first approaches tried. Even the helpful things that the three therapists said to me were all things that any layperson could have said, such as "I can see that you're upset, but it's not crazy to be upset, given what just happened to you."

When I used to have therapy patients myself, it was clear to me that nothing they found helpful was anything I had learned in my training; some was what I had always known, and some I had learned from living my own life, listening to other people, and reading. My mother was a stay-at-home mother while raising my brother and me, and not only was she good for me to talk with when I had problems, but she was also the person to whom other people's children would come when they were upset and needed help. After I left home, she began and completed a master's degree in guidance and counseling and began to counsel people in an office. Recently, as I watched her listen to a vet who was feeling terribly sad and anguished, I saw both that she was more helpful than any other therapist I had ever seen and that nothing she did that helped him was anything she had learned in her training.

Increasingly over the years, I have been alarmed to hear—even overhear in restaurants—people describe the way they flee from talking with friends about personal problems: "She was upset when her boyfriend dumped her, but I told her to go see a therapist, because I haven't been trained to help," or "I was so sad when my father died, but I didn't think I should impose on my friends like that. I mean, how often can you expect your friends to listen to you say that now, six months after your father died, you *still* feel overcome by grief?" What does the professionalizing of the handling of all human problems do to the nature of friendship in our society? This is not to say that there are never reasons to talk with someone other than a friend about one's troubles. For instance, if you are in a new place and have no close friends yet, or if you are being abused by a family member and don't feel ready yet to cope with the way that relatives and friends may react when you tell them, you might want to talk with a therapist or a spiritual adviser. I know that some people will say, "And surely if you are hallucinating or feeling paranoid, you should go see a psychiatrist!," but if you read Whitaker's book, you will see that the risks of being dealt with in ways that will make you worse far outweigh the chances they will make you better. Of course, friends and relatives also vary greatly in their abilities to help, and they too can do harm. The point is simply that wherever one turns for help, it is just not the case that a professional is more likely to help than a layperson, and professionals are as varied in their ability to help as any other group.

As you read this chapter, I hope you will put out of your mind the self-doubts that, because you are not a trained therapist, there is nothing you can do by listening to vets. Listening does not mean you will make no mistakes. We all make mistakes; they are part of life. Later in the chapter, however, I describe some of the common pitfalls and bumps in the road and make some suggestions about what to do about them.

How Listening Can Help

When you want to talk and release the load
  When you need someone to "hear"
  Not only the hill that shadows the Soldier
  But I as well . . . am near.
—David E. Jones, "A Fight Within"[8]

It might seem obvious that relationships with others are helpful to people who are suffering, but it is important to know that both solid research and numerous experiences bear this out. For instance, in a recent *British Medical Journal* article, the authors reported that a review of a large number of studies showed that social connectedness and social support lead to happiness.[9] Indeed, there is a huge research literature about this subject, including, for instance, work by Edward Diener[10] and J. Coyne and G. Downey.[11] Every time a person asks a vet to tell their story, that is an important form of reaching out, connecting, expressing interest and support, showing respect for the vet's experiences. There is healing power in not only listening but also remembering what the speaker says.

In a *New York Times Magazine* article, Ethan Watters described the ways that people in different cultures help each other cope with trauma differently.[12] More communally oriented cultures regard it as the community's role to help the traumatized person heal and reintegrate. Considering what Watters wrote makes it clear not just how wrong but how very simplistic—and thus disrespectful to the vets—it is for us to decide that what they are experiencing is unequivocally Posttraumatic Stress Disorder (PTSD) or other mental illness and that therefore we know what they need. Watters notes the dangers of imposing assumptions about trauma and healing on others, and he reports that the World Health Organization has begun recommending "psychosocial support" for disaster areas. There used to be something in the United States called friendship, before therapy took over every situation other than those that inspire only happiness. And in many cultures around the world, and even in subcultures within the United States, friends help each other through terrible times. These are things we ought to do for each other, to help each other through this life.

Many years ago I learned something about the power of respectful listening after a woman, without provocation, physically attacked me. I had never been physically attacked, and the episode was not only violent but also bizarre. Never until then had I had flashbacks, and that was when I learned that flashbacks feel so different from memories, because during a flashback one has no sense that the events are not happening *now*; one is completely immersed in the horror of the original trauma. When I told Rabbi Debra Brin that I could not seem to break free of the upset and that some of those closest to me expressed skepticism about how the attack had come about and whether I was describing it accurately, she asked me to invite three very close friends to my house. The first thing she did was have them sit around me and listen, just listen, as I described every detail of the attack. Suddenly I was going through the trauma not alone but with people who cared, and suddenly I was speaking to people who respected me and believed what I said. I felt the healing start, and I never had another flashback to the attack.

This story also illustrates that no one is an island. Each of us is embedded in a social context, and each of us is in contact with others who may or may not help us feel good about our identity, our feelings and interpretations of what happens in our lives, our status, our roles, and our functioning. What Rabbi Brin achieved was to change my social context at a crucial time by bringing very close to me the people who would provide respect and support.

David Oaks, head of MindFreedom International, has worked for decades with people who have been harmed in the mental health system. In a recent article about military veterans, pointing out that when there are problems or scandals in the mental health system, for 200 years "the usual position of caring people" has been "The system needs more money," Oaks urges readers to "go deeper" than that and understand that

real alternatives that work often go very deep indeed. For instance, consider "peer support." We all intuitively know that good peer support can help. "It takes a village to heal a mind," doesn't it? But WHY? Well, one reason is that we are forming really deep and complex mutual connections between one another, and that can help with recovery and healing.

It's really difficult for the current market system to supply that. You can't "buy a village" off the shelf. Real healing may take really deep connections between people, real COMMUNITY CHANGE.[13]

Why Storytelling Matters

To learn these [veterans'] stories is both civilian duty and commemoration.
—Caroline Alexander, journalist[14]

It is healing to talk about the traumas of war, and to get the demons of combat that we warriors who have stood in battle have buried so deep, out in front of us, on our terms where we can easier deal with them.
—Vietnam veteran Gary Jacobson[15]

Everyone has the story of their life, as William Randall writes eloquently in *The Stories We Are: An Essay on Self-Creation*.[16] This is not a story *from* one's life but rather the story we tell ourselves about who we are and how our life has been. Whether we are conscious or unconscious of our story, it helps determine the things we remember and the things we try to forget, as well as how we interpret them. For instance, do we selectively remember the aspects of our childhood that were happy or difficult? Which aspects do we consider part of our main story and which tangential? If we think of our childhood as having pretty much been happy, then the painful or embarrassing times that we recall we regard as exceptions, and vice versa. However we choose or otherwise end up with a particular story, that story is a major part of who we feel we are. If we feel that we are not seen and respected for who we are, in some way we feel we don't exist. Since so much of life is about connection, about how we relate to other people, if no one sees who we are or understands our story fully, or if others want to know only a bit of it, then in some important ways we disappear.

The use of psychiatric diagnoses for vets distances the person assigning the diagnosis from the vet and tends to limit what the diagnostician learns to how well the vet fits the various lists of symptoms in the psychiatric categories. David Jacobs and David Cohen object to this practice, pointing out how important it is to capture information beyond what is in the diagnosis: "[A] personal problem involves someone's story, a first-person drama-like narrative in which the narrator is the protagonist."[17] In other words, listening to life stories helps far more than assigning diagnoses when we want to understand the sources and nature of a person's distress. As Athar Yawar wrote in a 2009 article in the British medical journal *Lancet*,

We would, as a society, achieve a great deal by listening to patients' demands for good food, companionship, respect, practical support, and gainful activity. As doctors, being with the patient is one of the most powerful healing tools we have. It can sound trite; but the phrase describes receiving the patient's humanity, and allowing it to come through crisis intact and enriched, without the loss of dignity and self almost inherent in labeling.[18]

The combination of most Americans' aversion to facing the realities of war and the reluctance of many vets to bring up their stories has led to the veiling of so much about war. In turn, the hidden nature of many Americans' war experiences has constrained the stories war veterans can construct about their lives. Secrecy, in and of itself, can intensify upsetting experiences, making them seem as though they *ought* to be concealed, as though they are too shameful or otherwise horrific to be mentioned. Opening secrets up to daylight in cases like those often takes away at least some of the shame and tends to decrease the isolation of individuals who have kept their stories under wraps. The fact that secrecy itself can exacerbate problems was brought home to me when I worked in a clinic for children with learning disabilities. We would begin each assessment by calling the parents and child into the room and asking, "What brings you here today?" Often, at least one parent would look shocked and become agitated, casting their eyes in the direction of the child and looking at us as if to say, "Can't you see that the child is right here?! Surely you don't want to talk about the problem with the child in the room!" By the time most children have been identified as having learning problems, they are old enough to realize that they are struggling more than the other children in their class. For the parents not to speak of that struggle in front of the child implies that it is profoundly shameful. In our clinic, then, when parents responded that way, we wanted to remove some of that shame and fear right away, so we immediately turned to the child and said, "Reading is hard for you, right?" In this way, we conveyed the message, "No matter how anyone else acts about your problem, we do not think it is so terrible that we have to shroud it in secrecy."

Simply asking someone—virtually anyone—to tell their story can convey another powerful message: "Your story matters. You are important. I *want* to spend some time listening to you." My colleague, Karen Glasser Howe, has for decades included as a requirement in one of her courses that her students interview their mothers about their life stories.[19] Often the mother's immediate response is, "Oh, well, there's not much to tell." But once the interview gets under way, the stories and the emotions that go with them come pouring out. When students in my courses do these kinds of interviews, they often tell me that a major turning point in their relationships with their mother was the moment they asked to hear her life story. This is especially the case for mothers with histories of having lived through terrible times. Veterans tend to have many intensely disturbing feelings and experiences, but this constellation is too often ignored. As one vet after another has told me, "The only question people ask when they hear you've been to war is, 'Did you kill anybody?,' and people do not want to hear more once they know the answer to that question." To have someone ask to hear their story *as they wish to tell it* is a unique experience for many vets.

Sadly common in vets' experiences are atrocities they saw or even committed themselves, sometimes unknowingly, such as killing an innocent civilian after being misinformed that the person was an insurgent. A different kind of atrocity haunted the vet who told me that as he ended a mission that was legitimate within the parameters defined by his war and involved an attack on people who were clearly about to attack his men, he noticed that a child had been watching the slaughter. The look in her eyes has never left him. Trauma expert Judith Herman has written, "The ordinary response to atrocities is to banish them from consciousness. Certain violations of the social compact are too terrible to utter aloud: this is the meaning of the word unspeakable."[20] But the fact that something is considered too terrible to divulge tends to compound the shame, guilt, and fear. The act of telling a person who will listen and not judge but try to understand what it was like for the vet is a way to begin to reduce the load of what one Vietnam veteran described to me as the heavy rucksack filled with the jagged rocks of unvoiced memories. Burdens shared are often burdens lightened.

Beyond a certain point, isolation can be dangerous for almost anyone, depriving people of chances to connect, give and receive support, and check out whether their perceptions, interpretations of events, and feelings match those of anyone else. For veterans to be locked in alone with nightmare memories is all the more difficult. It leads some to question whether their memories are even accurate and many to believe they are crazy. The wholesale pathologizing of war trauma by assigning its sufferers one or more psychiatric labels, along with the fact that so many vets know this happens, may even hear it from family and friends, makes it even worse. Telling their stories often helps vets feel more assured that what they remember is real, not imagined, and the reactions (even respectful silence and a slight nod) of a caring listener can make them feel less crazy. The power of storytelling became clear to a top military psychiatrist, who reported that in the twelve hours after some actors gave a dramatic reading about war experiences, two soldiers and three Marines asked if they could tell their own stories.[21]

Transmitting one's story to someone else means that person, too, can tell it, and someone who hears it from that teller can tell it forward. Telling stories, if done enough, can change the culture in ways favorable to helping vets by creating a more receptive context, a sense of shared responsibility, a heightened awareness of the horrors or war and their impact. We can hope that this social transmission might even change public perceptions and attitudes toward vets and wars. In these ways and in the same way as any creation, storytelling thus carries whispers of immortality.

Can Nontherapists Really Help?

At the level of our daily lives, one man or woman meeting with another man or woman is finally the central arena of history.
—Athol Fugard, Georgetown University commencement address[22]

In our Scripture, it is written that when you do not have hope, you look for it in the face of your friend.
—James Gordon, Gaza psychologist[23]

In considering the suggestion for nontherapists to help veterans who are suffering emotionally, it is important to look at the practicalities. As reported in chapter 4, the Army acknowledges being "overwhelmed" by the problems of soldiers returning from war, despite its continual announcements that it is trying to hire still more military therapists.[24] In chapter 5 we saw a similar pattern for the VA. Furthermore, a 2008 RAND study showed that about half the veterans of current wars who were suffering from emotional trauma had not even sought treatment.[25] We have already discussed some of the reasons for their reluctance to seek treatment, including fear of breach of confidentiality, fear that seeking treatment will make them appear weak or cowardly or will interfere with their military careers, and fear that they will be considered mentally ill. Some of these concerns also apply to seeing a therapist outside the military or the VA. Furthermore, with the heavy use in the current wars of National Guard and Reserve troops,[26] many of today's vets originally came from small towns, where they are far from therapists if they return. At a purely practical level, then, even if there were plenty of military or VA therapists available to see all of the suffering vets who seek help, and even if every one of those therapists were 100 percent effective in providing help, many vets simply will not see a professional. This fact alone should make it clear that, as a nation, we need to draw on the resources of nontherapists and certainly of people outside the military.

In chapter 5 we heard about Michelle Dillow, who, after her return from active duty in Iraq, was so haunted by the constant danger in which she had lived and the losses of people she cared about there that she could not sleep. She had felt so anguished and enraged that, for fear of lashing out at or burdening her loved ones, she did not speak to them of her troubles, just held everything in. This made her feel increasingly isolated and increasingly ashamed of herself for what she saw as her failure to adjust and stop "being crazy." Visits with a therapist whom she described as very nice but not helpful got her nowhere. Dillow was asked to give a lecture in a college class about war, and during her talk, a student she had never met made a comment about the soldier seeming to be too hard on herself. Taken totally by surprise by this outreach, which came not from a therapist who spoke in jargon or was paid to talk to her, Dillow slept peacefully that night for the first time in the months since she returned from Iraq. I tell this story about Michelle because it is the kind of story I so often hear from veterans who have spoken to sympathetic listeners from the community. When I speak with vets as "just a person," not in my role as a psychologist, and certainly not doing anything I was trained to do, not doing anything beyond listening and making a very occasional comment or asking a very occasional question such as anyone might, it is not uncommon that I hear from them later that the night of our first meeting, they begin to be able to sleep. I have also heard a great many such comments from vets who spoke with people who have had no training as therapists.

In his classic book, *Man's Search for Meaning*, concentration camp survivor Viktor Frankl[27] describes how inmates of the camp often stopped believing that liberation would come, so that when it did come, they could hardly register its reality. What helped these victims of extreme torture?

[W]hen one of the prisoners was invited out by a friendly farmer in the neighborhood, he ate and ate and then drank coffee, which loosened his tongue, and he then began to talk, often for hours. The pressure which had been on his mind for years was released at last. Hearing him talk, one got the impression that he *had* to talk, that his desire to speak was irresistible. I have known people who have been under heavy pressure only for a short time . . . to have similar reactions.[28]

Related to this, psychiatrist Sally Satel describes her discovery that the treatment of vets at a VA Medical Center was misguided because it took them too much out of their communities.[29] Speaking of his own life, Marine Nathaniel Fick has written, "The main lesson of my experience is that the recovery process takes time, and *healing only happens in community"* (my italics).[30] Numerous experts stress the paramount importance of help from nonprofessionals. In an article in the journal *Clinical Psychology*, the authors first point out that there is no evidence that any particular traditional approach to dealing with trauma is actually helpful (and that there is evidence it may even be harmful), then say,

> There is consensus . . . that providing comfort, information, support, and meeting people's immediate practical and emotional needs play useful roles in one's immediate coping. . . . [T]he most appropriate early intervention . . . should be . . . supportive and non-interventionist but definitely not as therapy or treatment.[31]

Some of the authors of the *Iraq War Clinician Guide* say simply that "the most important initial needs of returning veterans are to be heard, understood, validated, and comforted in a way that matches their personal style. . . . There is much to be learned by listening carefully and intently."[32] Veteran and psychologist David Collier believes that nonmilitary people who are not therapists can "absolutely" be helpful to vets by listening without judging. World War II war correspondent Ernie Pyle understood this, believing that "the experience of the combat soldier is so terrible that you, the civilian, can never redeem it, but you must at least try to see it and know it."[33]

It is not surprising that the psychiatrized nature of our culture makes so many nontherapists feel they are out of their league when trying to help people who have been through as much horror as war veterans have. It is true that not every nontherapist, like not every therapist, can help every vet, and some nontherapists, like some therapists, will make mistakes. No approach is free from risk, because all involve interactions between two flawed (because human) beings. But if we consider the pros and cons of outreach from the community compared to those of psychotherapy with someone who is regarded as an expert and with psychotropic drug treatment, perhaps the risks of the first seem not quite so serious. And of course, any vet speaking to a layperson who does not feel better can always go to a therapist and give that a try as well. In principle, there is a huge array of things that might help a veteran, but a concern in this book is why the pool of potential helpers has been largely regarded as restricted to psychiatrists and psychologists. Everyone knows people whose conversations with friends or family members have been helpful, even transformative. The same can be true of vets. Even reading a book, article, or poem can have a major impact. Many adult women in the middle of the twentieth century who were unhappy staying home with their children had been isolated by their silence, each believing herself to be the only unhappy housewife, each considering herself inadequately feminine, insufficiently womanly. Often, those women who read Betty Friedan's 1963 book, *The Feminine Mystique*,[34] were transformed by learning thereby that huge numbers of women felt the same way. The reason Alcoholics Anonymous and similar twelve-step programs have more beneficial effects than virtually any other approach, whether delivered by mental health professionals or others, is that they rely on the combination of nontherapists helping each other and storytelling, empathic listening, and nonjudgmental support.[35]

There are several ways in which a nontherapist can convey messages that make a difference to vets in a way that therapists cannot. First, some therapists might try to erase the power differential that exists between themselves and their veteran patients because the former *are* therapists and thus assumed to know more about patients than they know about themselves, to have all the answers. But between a layperson and a vet, this particular power differential does not even rear its head. Laypeople are not being paid to listen to the vet, do not come from a training program in which they learned certain interpretations of people's experiences, and are not expected to have all the answers. This can create a more comfortable setting in which the listener and vet can interact. When a nontherapist listener clearly respects and tries to understand what a veteran says, the vet does not have to wonder what professional framework of interpretation might be getting in the way. (This is not to say that all therapists are dogmatic, of course.) Related to this, it is widely known that a major activity of therapists is to assign psychiatric labels to people and to treat as illness anything other than serenity and happiness. Although vets might be concerned that laypeople have absorbed these activities from the broader psychiatrized culture, they at least know that nontherapists do not have a professional stake in pathologizing them. Laypeople who listen and respond to vets outside a pathologizing framework reduce the isolation of vets that comes from their belief that they are crazy or at the very least have reacted weirdly to war. So many vets have told me that the best thing anyone has ever done for them is to say something along the lines of, "If I had been through what you just described that you went through, I would be feeling the same way you are. I don't think you're crazy. In fact, if you hadn't been this upset, I would have wondered why."[36]

Another function nontherapists can often serve better than therapists is to draw from their own life experiences in ways that promote connections between themselves and veterans. For a nontherapist to say, "I think I would have reacted just as you did to seeing someone close to me blown away," can reach the vet directly without the vet having to wonder, "Is the therapist saying this because that's what therapists are supposed to say?" Some therapists talk about their own lives, but many are trained to avoid this at all costs. A nontherapist is freer than many therapists to say, for instance, "I think I may be able to understand at least a little about your flashbacks or nightmares. Ever since eight years ago, when a car smashed into the front passenger side of my car where my daughter was sitting while I was driving, I panic and swerve to the left, even crossing the yellow line, every time a car comes toward me from that direction. It's just like the wreck is happening again."

Still another helpful function that nontherapists can serve is related to the phobia about death that pervades our culture. Most people believe there are things one talks about in a therapist's office that one would probably not discuss in the "real world." Thus, when a layperson is willing to listen to vets talk about their encounters with death, it helps break through a taboo that keeps vets terribly isolated. As Marcia Hill has written, some healing takes place when a person can speak what was not supposed to be spoken, because this helps make the previously unspoken memories real.[37] Possibly, it also makes them less frightening and less shameful. Further, Hill suggests, the powerlessness so many people feel when at war can be compounded if they feel powerless to speak up in order to help themselves or anyone else. Speaking of the forbidden, then, can be a way to regain some sense of one's power and effectiveness.

Nontherapist civilians can play another important role precisely because they are not veterans themselves. Although veterans, beginning most notably after the Vietnam War, have often found it helpful to talk with other vets, and such connections are in many ways extremely positive, there is a danger involved in limiting one's close relationships to other vets only. It is the same kind of danger that one sees in other groups, such as those composed of survivors of child sexual abuse: The identity of group members comes to be, or remains, wholly associated with the trauma.[38] Although sharing common or similar experiences and feelings about those experiences can help make vets feel understood and supported by other vets, if their identity does not eventually expand into other realms, serious problems can result. One problem is that associating only with other traumatized vets solidifies their sense of being nothing but a traumatized person, to the extent that they lose sight of their capacities for enjoyment, growth, change, developing connections with others and engaging with the rest of the world. Their feeling of being irretrievably different from those who did not go to war becomes entrenched. They find it harder to break out of the military's attack-defend mode and its strict hierarchies. Interacting with people who are neither therapists nor vets can help servicemembers experience other perspectives and bring out other parts of themselves, since we discover who we are partly by noticing what various people elicit from us.

Getting Started

Directions I do not provide with this, you only need a heart.
  And if you understand a Vet, you've made a small . . . small start.
—David E. Jones, "Needless to Say"[39]

It takes some time to heal the wounds
  but a good place here to start.
  Compassion in a trusting voice,
  that holds an open heart.
  No one can tell me what I must feel,
  or when to forget the past.
  No one can say it's over now,
  the memories will last.
—David E. Jones, "Endings"[40]

Anyone who has seen the worst of humankind's horrors needs and deserves tenderness and understanding. So many veterans have been trained to believe that they do not, should not, need either, that it is not soldierly, not masculine. Before we ask them if they want to tell us their stories, then, it is good to take some time to focus quietly on this: that listening means that you value their story, their feelings, and their struggles at least as much as you value your own time; that even if they do not feel they ought to need to speak, you believe it is legitimate and indeed important for them to have the opportunity to do this, should they choose to do so; and that you do not consider it weak or inappropriate for them to let you know what plagues them.

Be aware every moment of the potential that your listening has to matter to the vet. Even the VA's *Iraq War Clinician Guide* makes this clear: "At the end of the day, the most important initial needs of returning veterans are to be heard, understood, validated and comforted in a way that matches their personal style. . . . There is much to be learned by listening carefully and intently."[41]

Many servicemembers do not believe that someone who has not been through what they went through could possibly understand, and they may try to shut them out.[42] But Dr. David Collier, who has a long history of working with veterans, believes that veterans can often sense which civilians they can trust enough to open up to them in an interview: "You know when you meet somebody the first time and are evaluating 'What do I think about the person across from me? Do I think this person is respectful and has qualities of compassion where they can hear information and not be particularly shocked?'"[43] Graham Berman, a decades-long practitioner of healing through listening, notes the power of feeling understood: "When we are being understood, we know we are, and when we are being slightly misunderstood, we know that, too," and "We learn to trust our own feelings and what is real or not real by having an understanding person react in a way that confirms or disconfirms what we're feeling."[44] In corresponding with one vet who was telling me his stories partly in person and partly by email, the fact that I have never been at war and the question of whether I could fully understand what he told me came up. I responded,

When you tell me what war was like, I listen carefully and absolutely believe what you say, and when you are describing tragic or terrifying events, I do think I get that they are tragic or terrifying. Are there details and dimensions and certainly nuances I probably fail to understand? Undoubtedly so. But the same, I think, is true of any two people who have, for instance, each lost their father, because the fathers would not have been identical, nor would their children, nor would the father-offspring relationships. I know that the pain of not being fully understood can be great, but I think that being partly understood by someone who cares can be healing, at least partially so.

In this connection, it can be helpful to mention to vets the principle Gloria Steinem has elucidated, that people with different histories can trade abilities, and this "makes our differences into sources of learning from each other."[45]

Finding a Vet

Once you decide to make the commitment to listening to a veteran's story, how do you locate one? Veterans may be living in your neighborhood, you may see them in restaurants wearing hats or jackets that identify them as vets, or you may find them through community groups, religious organizations, or friends of friends. Some write letters to the editor of print or online media. Check out the VA's program of foster homes for veterans who do not want to live in institutions.[46] Consider contacting the groups or organizations for vets or their families that are listed at the end of this chapter.

Laying the Groundwork

1. You may want to begin by saying why you wanted to hear a vet's story, and of course you may have various reasons. You may have or have had a relative who is or was a vet, you may consider it important for Americans to hear stories about our wars, or you may be interested in people's stories in general.

2. Assure the vet that whatever they say will be kept confidential. Since nontherapists are not bound by rules of confidentiality, it will be up to the vet to decide whether to believe in this assurance from a layperson. Needless to say, it is essential to be able to make this promise in good faith. Since your purpose in meeting with the vet is not to get information to give to other people for any reason but solely to help this vet, there should be no reason to think of telling anyone else. The only exception to this could be if your interviewee tells you anything that is so horrific that you begin to have nightmares or to feel agitated, overcome by sorrow, or have other very difficult responses to deal with. This possibility is addressed in a later section of this chapter, "Common Problems and How to Handle Them."

3. You may want to say that you have not served in the military yourself but that you have no political agenda for doing this interview other than to listen to the vet's own story. Some vets will worry that you may judge them harshly because of their roles in the war, so it is important to convey that your wish is not to judge but rather to learn from them.

Beginning the Interview

Some vets will begin talking—and talking about the war—right away. If the vet you interview does not, it is good to have more than one option in mind, including saying, "Now I'd like to hear whatever you would like to tell me about your time at war." If the vet seems at all uncomfortable, you might ask, "If it is hard to talk about the war, do you want to tell me something about what makes it hard? What concerns you?" Of course, some of the reasons for difficulties in getting a conversation going may concern trust, so simply spending a fair amount of easy time together may be required at first, with more neutral topics of conversation. This would give both parties a chance to become more comfortable and more confident in each other. More difficult material may emerge only after such a preliminary stage is set.

If the vet is uncomfortable, then instead of asking what makes it hard to talk about the war, you could first ask, "Would you like to begin by telling me something about your life before you joined the military? Or about how your life has been since coming home? We don't have to start with the war itself." If the vet prefers to talk first about prewar times, you can just ask for their life story, beginning with where and when they were born and going right up to the point when they joined the military. Questions that can help to engage the person and may be relevant when you reach the war-related part of the story include: "What were your greatest strengths? What things made you the happiest? What were the most difficult problems you had to deal with before going into the service? What were the ways that you coped when you encountered problems? Who were the people you were closest to? Did you have people you could talk to about just about anything?"

If vets have worries about opening up about the war, it may be because they fear appearing too weak or having been too violent, because they have done things they consider shameful, because they have never been able to resolve moral conflicts or crises of meaning, because they believe that you will not understand or will not respect them, or because they are reluctant to burden or upset you. One way to begin to respond to many of these concerns is to say to the vet that you do not regard it as your job to judge them but primarily to listen and try to understand how it was for them and how it is now. You may want to say that after reading about some of the worst things servicemembers have gone through, you know that at least some of the most troubling ones will not come as a surprise to you, though the details of what this storyteller experienced may. And in response to their concern about burdening or upsetting you, you can say that life includes both the good and the disturbing and that so many members of the military have had to go through so much, that you consider it the least you can do to be open to hearing their story. You can say that as an adult, you regard it as your responsibility to figure out how to deal with your feelings of upset and that many vets have long had to struggle alone with what they actually experienced, not just what they were hearing secondhand, as you are. You can also consider saying, "I am an American, so I take some responsibility for what happened to you, and frankly, I will feel better if telling me what you went through is helpful to you." Just providing a chance for vets to speak their fears about opening up can help take away some of their force and sting. But it may take time for the vet to feel ready to talk very much. Be prepared to wait, and indicate your willingness to listen for a long time. Do not feel that you are failing to do the right thing if they do not open up immediately or even in the medium term.

General Guidelines

The best thing that you can do is to make it safe for the vet to talk and hear themselves talk. You do this by not saying much and by not saying things that are judgmental or pushy and by not giving advice. Giving advice, especially early on, can destroy the listener's sense of being understood.[47] Most vets will be quick to recognize a person who is respectful and focused on listening and understanding their story and their perspective. Remember that trust develops *gradually* as one feels understood.[48] And at some point, it may be all right to ask questions, but it is crucial first for the vet to feel listened to for a long time without feeling rushed, and what the vet needs to say first must be the priority. Feeling understood helps people strengthen their sense of who they are, so it is good to let who they are emerge in the way it tends to come from the speaker. Related to this, do not try to get the vet's whole story or even one of the stories all at once and in coherent form. To push for that can overwhelm the teller.

Dr. David Collier, a psychologist who has worked for decades with vets through the VA's Vet Centers, located in their communities rather than in medical centers,[49] suggests that vets make lists of topics they want to talk about as they come up, whether it is during the interview times or when they are at home. This keeps them from feeling pressured to remember everything on the spot and especially when the listener is someone they are just getting to know and especially if they have not previously told their stories. Furthermore, putting things in writing can make vets feel their experiences are more manageable. For one thing, once they have made notes in black and white, they do not have to worry about forgetting those things. For another, writing down a few notes about experiences or feelings reduces their nebulousness and can help bring some order to them that makes it easier to talk about them.

Dr. Collier also talks about the value of loving another person—in the sense of love for humanity—to help that person get through painful times and move toward healing. He believes it is essential to think in those terms and not to limit our thinking to concepts like "empathy," for it is the broader and deeper feeling for people that he believes leads to recovery. This means, he says, "I am not trying to get anything from you, just here to affirm that you have value because you are also a human being. It is done genuinely from the heart and makes the other person feel heard."[50]

Be aware of the value of your silence. Silence from a supportive listener can allow veterans to find out who they are now. Many have had to flee from or cut off feelings in order to get through the war trauma, and your silence now allows them the chance to get back in touch with those feelings without being pressed to do anything but speak, feel, and wait. Try to be comfortable with long silences, even very long ones, and fill them with respect for the veteran's need for them. If you become uneasy when the vet is silent, you might be tempted to jump in and speak just to break the silence and reduce your own anxiety, but to do so can break the vet's train of thought or feeling and limit the directions and depth of the conversation. It can make the interview go where you want it to go rather than where the vet needs it to go. It can convey the wrong messages about the importance of the vet's perspective and needs, and it can put distance between you and the vet. On the other hand, there may be times when the vet seems to feel pressured to keep talking or to stick with a very difficult topic or feeling, and at those times, you might want to speak in order to give the vet the option of moving to another subject or just waiting awhile before continuing the interview. If this sounds as though I am saying, "Stay silent always . . . except sometimes, and sometimes speaking can push vets in a direction other than where they need to go," I understand that it can be difficult to judge when to do each. Do not assume that it is always possible to know ahead of time the best thing to do. However, one way to take care is that instead of speaking about whether they would like to switch topics or wait awhile, you can sometimes find nonverbal ways to give them options. So, for instance, you could just nod supportively to try to indicate that whatever they choose to do is fine, or you could raise your eyebrows in a way that shows you wonder if they are all right.

Although military training and war experiences do not eliminate vets' capacities to feel love, compassion, fear, grief, or guilt, for many, they may dramatically reduce the capacity to *recognize* such feelings in themselves or to *allow others to see them*. For this reason, it is especially important, when a vet is having any of these feelings or seeming to struggle against having them, for the listener to wait patiently and calmly and to watch for chances to affirm their validity and importance.

Be careful not to tell the vet what to feel. In fact, don't even ask, "Are you or were you feeling X?" that can be answered yes or no. Instead, ask open-ended questions, such as, "What was that like for you? How did you feel then?" In other words, ask questions for *clarification*, but *make as few assumptions as possible* about their emotions. Playwright Joshua Casteel has said that vets have to

[find] words to explain [their] experiences...but [they] can't have those words imposed on [them]. They have to be self-generated, and I think that means more than anything a willingness to be quiet until they come and friends who are willing to stay with [them] but allow [them] to be quiet so they [the words] come on their own.[51]

One way you can help vets elucidate their experiences without your telling them what to feel is to ask, "What would you want to say to another vet who had been through exactly what you had?" Remember that the storyteller cannot possibly convey to you all of the relevant details and context, and it may take you a long time to understand how they have handled and labeled these feelings since their time at war; so if you guess about those feelings, you run a big risk of getting it wrong. It is not that it would always be disastrous to guess wrong but simply that the focus should be on listening and asking whenever possible, rather than jumping in to shape the way the interaction goes or trying to translate the vet's language or experience into your own. Best to leave that to the vet.

One topic about which I have found that even suggesting a different perspective can be utterly counterproductive is that of survivor guilt. Do not say to a vet, "You shouldn't feel guilty that they died, and you lived, because you didn't make that happen! And look at all you've got to live for!" If knowing it was not their fault has not taken away their guilt, your telling them that will not help and can make them feel you do not understand or care how devastated they feel. Also, sometimes expressing grief about the deaths of treasured friends in the form of guilt is a way of introducing some sense of control (even though the reality of how they died may not warrant it) over losses about which their powerlessness feels unbearable. And a vet who has not yet found reasons to go on living after loss will not find those reasons by hearing us say they have much to live for. For us to say that they have much to live for runs the risk again of making them feel we do not understand. For those still swamped by survivor guilt or a sense that life is meaningless, the best that we can do at this moment is to make it a bit easier for them to grieve and thereby have at least a chance to move through and beyond it over the longer term. Grief, after all, cannot be sidestepped but must be lived through and worked through. What helps people grieve is knowing that one of two things is true: (1) I have enough inner resources to go into the sorrow and come out at the other end, or (2) I have enough support from one or more other people that I feel I can go into the sorrow and come out at the other end. We can help provide that second condition, because the sharing of grief can lead toward healing.

What applies to grief applies in general to other strong feelings the vet has, in that fear, rage, alienation, and other emotions are normal responses to harsh realities of one sort or another, and, as with grief, it may take substantial time for a person to regain some footing by dealing with these feelings. The process varies among individuals but is likely to be helped along when we can reduce vets' isolation and avoid pathologizing labels and other vehicles of avoidance and distancing.

Watch for opportunities to let the speaker know that their feelings about past or current experiences make sense to you, seem human and healthy and understandable rather than bizarre or "crazy." This has to be sincere, so say it only if you mean it. Otherwise, keep listening, and assume that as you hear more about what happened and how the person felt, you will understand the vet's reaction more. When I advise, "Say it only if you mean it," that does not necessarily mean literally speaking such words as, "That makes perfect sense to me" or "I think I would have felt the same way," because often, your clear willingness to go on listening and the absence of expressions of disapproval or shock will be enough to convey the important messages. This approach is also helpful in counteracting the part of military training that can make servicemembers feel weak and overly dependent for needing to talk and for needing connection. In fact, it might even be counterproductive to express approval, because that can sometimes convey the message that you consider yourself in a position to judge the vet—and if you can judge something to be positive, you can raise the vet's concern that you might judge something else to be negative. The better course is probably to keep listening, pay respectful attention, and so on, so that vets can find their own way.

Be aware that it may not be solely the war trauma itself that causes the vet's current anguish but rather the interplay with other factors such as problems in primary relationships (such as a spouse's failure to listen in a caring way), financial strain, and physical health problems.[52] Each of these can block the speaker's progress in trying to recover from the trauma. With regard to problems with life partners, emotions underpinning many fights between returned veterans and their spouses are usually the needs for more love and reassurance of being loved, and that can be the case for both partners.[53] Many nonveteran spouses are unable to provide this, either because of their own personal limitations or because they are already having to bear extra burdens, including dealing with children who are thrown by the other parent's absence and return, caring for the physical injuries of the veteran, supporting the family financially while the vet struggles to find a job, and, for partners of male veterans, trying to figure out how to make the vet feel "like a man" even though he may be injured, deeply distressed, or unemployed. (Although this is not, strictly speaking, within the topic of this book, it could only be helpful to vets' loved ones—and thus probably to vets—for communities to focus on creating a supportive network on a massive scale for those who are vets' spouses, friends, and helpers, as is done for caregivers to the ill, the old, or partners of addicts.)

Make sure that your relationship with the vet does not consist only of the sharing of what haunts them. Both expression of unspoken or rarely-spoken horrors *and also* exploration of ways to move from the realm of death and destruction to the realm of life, growth, and creativity can be important elements of these interviews. Watch carefully for indications that the vet engages, or longs to engage, in life-affirming activities of any kind. These can range from saying a friendly "Hello" to the barista at Starbucks to volunteering to be a Big Brother or Big Sister to creating in the arts to political activism.[54] They are powerful opposites of the aspects of war that involve destruction, death, and powerlessness. Therefore, they carry the potential for healing, and the listener can comment on the way the vet has chosen to do things that bring connection and joy or poetry into the world. Dave Jones explained how he got through his pain about Vietnam without using drugs or alcohol to escape:

I wrote poetry instead of shooting fifty bucks up my arm or drinking to numbness. I posted it [on my Web site[55]] in December of 1997 not knowing there were so many others out there of every race, religion, thresholds of pain, guilt, loss and more. I found mothers and fathers, sisters, sons, children and just people of caring that responded to me. It had a profound effect on me as each e-mail made *me* feel better.[56]

Dave's use of his poetry to reach out to others in need is action, the opposite of the powerlessness he often felt in Vietnam. Sean Huze, a vet who wrote a play about Iraq,[57] says, "Writing a play and putting these feelings onto characters was a safe way for me to start the road home." Therefore, ask vets what matters to them, what helps them feel better when they are down, what makes them happy.

Related to being on the watch for life-affirming inclinations and activities, assume that everyone seeks emotional health. Many former soldiers I have met— including one who had recently gone AWOL—have discovered that they needed to avoid talking to people who did not care about them or who treated everything they said as signs that they were "sick." They found it more helpful to spend more time with people who cared and who, instead of looking for the most dismal interpretations of everything they did ("You are just planting the garden as a way to escape reality"), could both listen respectfully to their troubles and join with them in moments of creativity, connection, and joy.

Experts who study the body's response to threat say that after the body prepares to flee or fight, people need to act to discharge that energy. If they cannot take action, they are "not suffering from a disease" but are "stuck."[58] Vets' need to come unstuck, to stop feeling powerless and helpless, renders it especially important to allow them to choose what to speak to the listener about and when to say what. As Vet Center psychologist David Collier points out, time spent in the military is time spent following other people's orders and acting according to other people's priorities,[59] so providing vets opportunities to make their own choices is invaluable. These opportunities are also important because of the use of psychiatric labels and medications, which tend in many ways to make vets into passive objects. Related to this, referring to the sense of powerlessness engendered by trauma, Dr. Collier believes that victims have a "foreshortened sense of the future, a leaf-in-the-wind feeling."[60] He says that the way to health is to focus on how to *change* your future, another active approach. For this reason, vets who shows signs of interest in educating others about war or about political issues related to their experiences might be helpfully encouraged to consider becoming public speakers, politicians, or activists. Or they might consider taking as models Dave Jones and Gary Jacobson, who through their Web sites reach out to, support, and educate huge numbers of veterans and those who care about them.[61]

There is, then, a balance to seek between expressing/listening to narratives and reports about the past and engaging in talk and action focused on the present and future aimed at piecing together a life. The former is a necessary part of healing and of setting the stage for the latter; but the latter is also a way to place the past in a larger context and locate it in a way that makes sense. Both serve important functions, neither has priority over the other, the order in which they occur can vary, and there can be switching back and forth between them.

Rachel Yehuda, a professor of psychiatry at Mount Sinai School of Medicine in New York, has described the experience common to many vets of feeling they are both perpetrators and victims of violence in different ways.[62] Since most people before going to war are decent folk with no experience of killing, maiming, or being killed or maimed, not to mention with the kinds of confusions about who is right and who is wrong that characterize current wars in so many ways, it is not surprising that vets are reeling from both having killed other human beings and having been in danger of being killed. They may also be reeling from the strange combination of feelings of tremendous power, given that they had actual life-or-death power, and feelings of utter helplessness when they were the ones under attack. This is an arena in which expectations about masculinity can exacerbate the confusion. After all, if men are expected to relish their power, then what is a vet to do if he is shaken by some of the consequences of his power? The impossibility in war of avoiding situations in which one is powerless and helpless may be little comfort to those men who believed that a real man would have remained completely unafraid. Women vets, depending on the extent to which traditional expectations about femininity have shaped them, may have more complicated feelings about their power but have less trouble dealing with powerlessness and helplessness because these are consistent with traditional feminine roles. Naturally, however, the reactions of many men and many women are too complex and nuanced to be captured by the above description.

Another important guideline is to watch for opportunities to help vets consider what steps they took, in the midst of nightmarish conditions, to help or protect others. Too often, the memories that linger are only those of powerlessness, helplessness, or what the vets think of as their weaknesses. Captain William Nash, a Navy psychiatrist, tells soldiers, "Grief . . . can make us forget how random war is, how much we have done to protect those we are fighting with. . . . You have to help them reconstruct the things they used to believe in that don't make sense anymore, like the basic goodness of humanity."[63] Indeed, it is no wonder that vets who have forgotten their own goodness may lose sight of the goodness of humanity. It may help to keep in mind that not just vets but all human beings have biases in what we remember that may need correction and a rebalancing of themes and feelings.

Related to looking for strengths and creativity on which to comment, if the vet is like many in having trouble finding a job, keep in mind the way that work can meet many needs, including a sense of work identity, accomplishment and status (even if the latter is only in being employed rather than unemployed), and relationships with others. For unemployed vets it can be particularly important to spend some time focusing on what Helliker calls characteristics that cannot be stripped away, such as "virtue, integrity, honesty, generosity,"[64] and on their other strengths, including relationships with family, friends, and the wider community.

While keeping in mind the injunction against giving the vet advice, do be on the lookout for chances to *ask* if they are interested in finding out about various resources for help with practical problems. A list of some such resources appears at the end of this chapter. And you might even know someone, for instance, who would hire a vet if your interviewee is looking for work.

Be aware that more will be going through the veterans' minds than they can possibly convey to you. Imagine, for instance: A vet is trying to tell you about their vehicle hitting an IED. The vet cannot portray in words in as little time as it took to hit that IED the perceptions of all five senses and the emotions that went with them at that moment. Furthermore, because trauma is fragmenting, it can be hard for the teller to produce a story that feels coherent and that conveys the full horror of the experience. So be prepared to proceed slowly. Each time after the vet speaks, wait a long time, even a very long time. Sometimes it is in those silences that the most important material will come to the speaker's mind or that the speaker will gather strength to voice what has been unspoken. The importance of silence was referred to earlier, but it is worth stressing here: Do not worry about long silences being uncomfortable. This could not be more different from a cocktail party, since there is no need to keep up the pace and fill in gaps in conversation. Silences can be comfortable, indeed can be supportive and even healing, when they are filled with the listener's careful attention to what the vet needs to do at the time. Watch for a sign that the vet is ready to continue or wants a response from you. And then ask if it's OK for you to do whatever you want to do next, whether to ask for clarification or a definition or whatever—keeping in mind that what you want to do next should always be for the purpose of understanding as much as possible for the vet's sake and the sake of the connection between you.

Much of this relates to what Dr. Collier describes as the importance of the concept of pacing.[65] He says, "If people are going to talk about things that are difficult or traumatic, there is a tendency to think they will open up like you throw up," that everything will suddenly come pouring out. But, he says, even if that happens, it may not be a good thing. It may not change anything except that "you've gotten it out of your system at that moment." Thus, instead of doing anything to encourage the vet to produce an entire story about a terrible experience at once, allow the speaker to tell you bits at a time. Consider suggesting that the vet slow down and take some deep breaths when things get rough. Many veterans I have spoken with have described the importance of pacing in the way they tell their stories. Recall Michelle Dillow, whose story about her friend's death from an IED appeared in chapter 2. The first time we spoke, she had told me that no one in the Army with her in Iraq showed or spoke about their grief about the death from an IED of a soldier they called "the big guy," whom they all had loved. Not until our fourth conversation, two years after the first one, did she disclose that in all the times she had told anyone that story, she had never until very recently been able to tell the most nightmarish fact about his death: The IED had blown his body in half. She had never forgotten that fact but had not been able to report it until she felt generally stronger and more secure about the directions her life was going.

When the storyteller is clearly upset, it is a good idea for the listener to stick to simple responses. The vet's upset can be from various feelings the memories bring back, it can be from frustration about the fragmented nature of the memories or the difficulty the speaker has in conveying them to the listener, or it can be from being flooded and overwhelmed as trauma survivors often become when trying to focus on painful material. Some vets may become totally silent and go deeply into themselves, so that you may feel they have become unreachable. If just continuing to listen or wait in total silence does not feel adequate, consider asking, "What's happening now?" or "What can I do?" because that leaves the control in their hands. They are likely to respond that they just want you to keep listening or to give them time to struggle through. However, they may need to take a break and resume the interview in a few minutes or even some days later, so consider asking if they would like to do that, and let them know you will be available to them at future times, too. Do not feel that it is your failing or your fault that makes it impossible for them to tell their story straight through. Many people who have talked with vets have said that those times of total withdrawal are the times they (the interviewers) felt most powerfully what war does, the extent to which the feelings it creates can overcome the soldiers and to which they can become unsayable. If a vet becomes very withdrawn, however, do not remain silent indefinitely. Dr. Collier recommends voicing some observation of just what you see (without interpreting it in any way), such as "I notice you are preoccupied" or "You have a tear in your eye," and then asking what you can do: "Do you want to stop and take a breath? Want me just to sit here with you? What can I do?"[66] He suggests having at the ready the address of the nearest

Vet Center or other resources where people are used to working closely with vets in nonjudgmental ways and offering to accompany them to one of these places *if* the vet is interested in that (see the resources section at the end of this chapter).

When the vet's speech comes in fragments, be aware that the very consistency of you as a listener can help reduce the fragmenting; you become a person whose mind and heart contain the bits of the trauma, and you can provide some unity, some continuity related to the trauma, because you were not the one who was traumatized, even though some fragments will be hard for you to put together with others, hard even for you to register or imagine experiencing completely. As the vet begins to speak what has been unsayable, just listen, be with the person one moment at a time. That is the beginning. The sharing of the fragments breaks the horrible isolation that plagues so many vets, the sense of being locked in a room alone with what has till now been unspeakable. As Aaron Glantz writes, "Soldiers heal best when they can come up with a coherent narrative that puts their experiences in perspective."[67] Realize that it may take a long time for the vet to be able to speak about the fragments until they begin to form into such a narrative. And understand that to speak about trauma can be terrifying, because it makes it real, makes it harder to go back to suppressing or distancing oneself from one's feelings. As with going into feelings of grief, talking about trauma can mean needing to find the strength to face the reality. There is the fear of not being able to turn off intensely negative feelings once one starts to let them come out. That the listener does not fall apart will help, as writing can: Vets can experience in the continuity and wholeness of the listener something beyond the assault of their memories and the powerlessness they have often felt.

The combination of the vet speaking in fragments and using words and phrases whose meaning you do not know—military terms, special languages of particular wars—can make it impossible for you to grasp their stories fully at first. Do not worry about this, but let the veteran know that you are committed to listening as fully and coming to understand as fully as possible but that that may take some time. Expect to feel fragmentation within yourself as you register a fact here, an intense feeling there, the shock of the losses or moral crises the speaker is describing to you, as you try to keep hold of or pull together the various details the vet tells you. But understand that it will come together bit by bit as you are able cognitively and emotionally to integrate the facts and feelings. In fact, as you listen, chances are the vet will become gradually able to do some of this integration. In the words of Tony Stanton, "You just can't organize yourself without a connection to another human being."[68] Do not rush either the speaker or yourself to put the bits together; the human mind and heart were not made for this formlessness, this powerlessness, so it takes time for the trauma's shape and meaning to become clearer.

A word about physical contact is important. Because of the very personal nature of much of what the vets may tell you—including about losses, the nature of injuries to their bodies, feelings that overwhelm them—and the degree of their suffering, you may feel inclined to take their hand, hug them, or make some other physical contact in an attempt to comfort or reassure them. But when people are suffering, it is a good idea to take your cue from them, letting them indicate whether even a caring hand on a shoulder or forearm will be helpful or whether it might take them out of their story, be misinterpreted in its intention, or be in a sense "too much kindness" so that more emotion comes pouring out than they are ready for. If you can think in terms of not making physical contact or at least deferring it for a long time, you will probably discover how powerful and comforting are simple, attentive silence and waiting. Usually, listening with all your heart and focusing completely on the vet's story, giving silent respect, is the best thing you can offer. Pat Barker describes a vet who is ambivalent about telling his story and the beneficial effect of his listener's respectful attention:

And so he swayed to and fro: sometimes guarding his knowledge jealously, sometimes sharing it freely, sometimes spitting it out with a bitter, angry pride, sometimes almost with gratitude to Rivers, *whose obvious interest in what he was being told seemed to confirm its value* [my italics].[69]

If vets ask you what you think about their stories, keep in mind that what may seem minimal to you may trigger a flood of wrenching images and emotions in them. So if you say that what they are telling you is devastating, they may feel horrible for having "burdened" you, assuming that it is harder for you to deal with than it really is or that it is more than you can manage. A helpful response can be to focus on what you are learning rather than on overwhelming feelings you might be having. One might say, then, "I had no idea. It is a completely different world. It is remarkable how few people are aware of what goes on. I so appreciate your telling me."

Guilt is a subject veterans often raise, and when they do, it can be helpful to consider that, in the words of psychologist Dr. Nikki Gerrard, "Guilt is a terminal word."[70] What she means by that is that when people say they feel guilty, that often leaves them with no way to move on. Guilt

Table 6.1
Summary of general guidelines

Mostly, just listen, respect, and bring love of humanity to the interview

• Do not give advice.

• Do not judge (even positively, except very rarely) or challenge.

• Trust the power of pacing: Do not rush the vet.

• Suggest that the vet take deep breaths when things get rough.

• Allow them to come to trust you gradually.

• Trust the power of silence.

• Trust the power of your genuine respect and compassion to come through.

• Stick to simple responses to what the vet says.

• Suggest that before or between interviews, they jot down notes of what they want to tell you.

• Assume that in everyone there is some drive toward emotional health.

• Find an opportunity or two to let them know you do not think they are crazy or their feelings are bizarre.

• Find ways to say that you notice what they do that is resourceful, life-affirming, or future-oriented.

• Be open to hearing about factors other than the war that upset the vet.

• Listen for signs that the vet feels like both victim and perpetrator of violence.

• Listen for signs of positive, helpful steps the vet took toward others during the war.

• Listen for indications the vet could use help with practical matters.

• When they are upset, ask, "How can I help?" or "What can I do?"

• Be prepared to take breaks of a few minutes or even days or weeks.

• Be patient with yourself if you have trouble grasping information or dealing with emotions.

• Use physical contact very sparingly.

• Raise the possibility that they feel something other than or in addition to guilt, such as shame or fear.

---

is often considered to be impossible to overcome. However, Gerrard notes, what people call guilt is often—wholly or partly—something else. As noted in chapter 2, this is often shame, and it is sometimes fear. It can be helpful to ask the vet something like, "If instead of 'guilty,' you were going to choose a different word for what you felt, what would that be?" If the answer is "shame," the listener can ask two questions: (1) What is the standard that you feel ashamed for having failed to meet? and (2) In front of whom do you feel ashamed about this? Often, in considering how to answer these questions, vets realize that the standard may be one that no human being could ever meet, such as being completely physically and emotionally invulnerable, and that they actually may not care all that much about the person they believe would shame them. If vets say they feel fear rather than or instead of guilt, the act of saying that often helps them recognize that their fears were understandable, human ones.

Topics to Watch For and to Consider Raising

Some themes and issues come up often in listening to vets. If they do not raise them on their own, you may want to consider bringing up any or all of the following, many of which can put them in the role of potential teachers and holders of wisdom who can help educate others about war and coming home:

• You may want to talk about the combat and other directly war-related experiences, but do you want to describe first some of the other factors, like the weather, the geography, the living conditions, animals and insects, other things that were hard to deal with, such as hazing or harassment?

• Did anything prepare you in any way for the emotional and moral aspects of what you experienced at war? Do you have suggestions about what could be done to prepare others?

• Are there things you feel you have learned from your experiences either in the military or because of returning home after your time at war?[71]

• What have you found helpful in coping with the memories of war?[72] With problems you have encountered in coming home? What has been hurtful?

• What would you like other people to know about war? About returning home?

• Did any of your views about life change because of your time in the service? (This could include any of the following: loss of innocence, confusion about what is morally right and wrong, greater clarity about right and wrong.)

• Did being in the military—or coming home—change your views about the meaning of life,[73] about what matters, your values and priorities? How would you describe your current spiritual life? Where do you find meaning?[74]

• Were you ever in a situation in which you felt powerless or helpless? How did you deal with that?

• What were the best things about your time in the military? Those who are lucky become tempered by the grief and terror through which they have lived. What were the worst things about your time in the military?

• What are the best things about your life now that you are back home? What are the most difficult?

• How do your family and friends deal with your reactions to your war experiences?[75] Who has and has not been supportive since you came home?

• What is your current work situation?[76]

• Are there ways that you currently do things with or for other people, either formally through an organization or informally?[77]

Common Problems and How to Handle Them

• Vets sometimes say, "I don't want to tell you the worst things that happened to me, because I don't want to hurt you." Let them know that in telling you what happened to them that was devastating, they will not damage you. Say that hearing about it may make you feel sad and pained for them and that you share their horror and grief and their sense of the impossible positions they were in, but that is different from *being* a vet, because you did not have the experiences directly. This can be a good time to let them know that to hear another person's story can, instead of breaking us, make us stronger because of the connection we form with them and the greater understanding of a part of life we have not known about before.

• A vet stops speaking in the middle of telling a story, looks away from you, and is silent for a long, long time. Vets who were traumatized may sometimes variously pull away from connection with you, shut down emotionally, go numb, show grief or rage. Do not be afraid of any of this unless it appears that the vet is in danger of becoming violent, in which case of course it is important to try to keep some physical distance from the vet while speaking gently to ask, "Where are you?" and to remind, if it seems appropriate, "You are not back in combat." Of course, if you feel you are in real danger because of a vet's rage, your safety has to take precedence over everything else, and you should get away or get help. Understand that these states are ways that people cope with what they feel they cannot bear, and remember that you are there in part to bear witness and to make sure that they know they are not alone. As noted earlier, a long silence is a time to wait patiently, but after awhile, say briefly that you are concerned, that they have just changed, that you wonder what they would like you to do to help.

• In the middle of a story, a vet's voice suddenly becomes almost unrecognizably rough, the eyes taking on what is sometimes called the thousand-yard stare. Vets who were traumatized may have flashbacks, when they feel that the awful events are actually happening at the moment, and such sudden changes of voice, facial expression, or posture can signal that they have gone into one of these experiences. Often traumatized vets try to keep troublesome feelings from becoming overwhelming by going emotionally numb, detaching feelings from their memories, or otherwise managing to block out the trauma. Sometimes, their blocking out goes on for decades, only to be "triggered" at some point, at which time they go into a flashback. Vets themselves often cannot predict what will trigger a breakthrough of the shut-out memories and feelings. Interviewers need to be aware that these breakthroughs can occur and that those are times when vets will especially need patience, respect, empathy, and support. Over time, part of the healing process involves vets coming to recognize some of their common triggers. Dr. Collier described the way people can help vets achieve this kind of understanding. For instance, like Merrill, who was described in chapter 5, a vet Dr. Collier knew would start to panic when his car was in traffic. With help in focusing on what in that environment caused the triggering reaction, the vet realized that it was the smell of diesel coming from other vehicles that reminded him of that smell from his combat zone. Just being aware of such triggers can help vets find ways at least to reduce their effects. One vet told me that children spraying each other with water from a hose triggered his traumatic memory of the spray of tracer rounds from machine guns. When he sees children at play with a hose, he says, "I don't participate. I don't squirt them with the hose, and it is time then to go inside or find something or somewhere to go." Psychiatrist Graham Berman observes that people who are suffering, given adequate support and compassion, are more likely to come up with these sorts of solutions than are other people to do it effectively for them.[78]

• A vet tells you that she unknowingly and under orders shot a civilian. Immediately, she accuses you of thinking she did so intentionally and relished the experience. You genuinely do not feel this way. Vets who felt betrayed by their government or the military during their service or by loved ones since coming home may expect you to betray them by failing to understand what they are saying, by failing to care, by thinking ill of them, by mocking or judging or doubting them, by being fed up with listening to them. You may certainly say to the vet that you do not believe she willingly killed the person, but your continued, calm, caring presence will help as much as anything to give her the chance to learn that you are not betraying them in any of these ways. Keep in mind Dr. Collier's confident statement about the importance to vets of "anybody who has a sincere heart and wants to be helpful to someone."[79]

• You will probably glimpse a terrifying world that you have never imagined. You will likely learn that in ways that never entered your mind, the world is not safe; you will wonder why you didn't know, and you will find it painful now to know. You may wish you had gone on not knowing. Knowing that what the vet who sits before you is telling you is what actually happened to them will almost certainly shake you more than learning about that world in any other way, such as by watching a film. What can help is first, finding someone you can trust, someone you can expect to be supportive, and telling them what is happening to you. In order to protect the confidentiality you promised the vet, do not disclose the vet's name or where the vet served or any specifics that are not necessary to convey what you are finding hard to deal with (and it is hard to think of an instance when such specifics would be necessary). Also, remind yourself of why you are doing this work with vets and why it matters to you and to the wider world (maybe review chapters 1, 2, and 7, as well as this one). Work with only one vet at a time, then take a break of weeks or months before contacting the next one if you plan to work with a second. And make sure that you have sources of enjoyment and strength in your own life. You might consider telling the vet that you have just gone through, to some lesser degree, no doubt, some of the same loss of innocence that so jolted them. Just as their telling you of their stories can help lift some of the heaviness their burdens put on them, so your telling them of your new understanding can be helpful to you. I do not advise telling the vet this, however, until you have spent time on your own or talking with others about how you feel, so that any initial shock and rawness have begun to dissipate. Otherwise, you risk increasing their concerns about having hurt you by telling their stories. What you and they stand to gain once you can tell them calmly what you have learned is the increased connection of two people who see the world in something of the same way, and you can let the vet know you appreciate the role they have taken in teaching you important truths.

• Related to the previous point, some of what a vet tells or shows you may move you to shed tears or to cry out in horror. Do not assume that this will harm the vet. Extreme conditions cause intense feelings, and that should be cause for neither surprise nor shame. It is crucial not to expect the vet to take care of you at those times, but if your attitude is that it can be important to the vet to see how their words affect you and that you do not expect them to take care of you, these heartfelt expressions of feeling can increase your connection with them and be helpful to them in other ways. It is a way to validate their feelings, as long as this happens only occasionally and thus does not turn the focus of your conversations too often to your feelings and needs.

Opening Hearts

Know that once someone who has been at war describes to you having seen someone's head blown off or having watched a friend's body catch fire, these images will never leave you. Before you contact a vet and ask to hear their story, take many deep breaths, and realize that once you start to listen, you will lose whatever innocence you may have, and your life will never be the same. I remember driving down a desert road in the sun one day and driving down the same road the next day—the difference being that on the first, I did not know how innocent I was, and by the second I did. The difference has brought a sadness that sometimes seems unbearable, and I have asked myself hundreds of times how I could have known in some general way about war for sixty-two years but never come close to what those who have been through it have gone through. Yet I know how blessed I am not to know with the immediacy with which they know. The change in what the listener knows does matter. It reminded me that the poet Susan Griffin wrote that when she gave birth to a daughter, "my heart opened to myself and all the suffering of women seemed unreasonable to me."[80] In a somewhat similar way, the vets who opened their lives and hearts to me have given me the gift of knowing how much more suffering the world holds than I had ever imagined and how important it is to try to make the suffering stop.

The word that has repeatedly come to my mind when listening to vets' stories is *sacred*. Definitions of *sacred* include words and phrases such as "regarded with great respect," "reverently dedicated to some person [or] purpose," "secured against violation," and "properly immune from violence, interference, etc."[81] The intensity of the original experience the storyteller is recounting and of the pain that inhabits the vet while remembering and describing that experience are part of what make the telling and listening sacred. So, too, does the frequent combination of the tenderness, vulnerability, and humanity that underlies the pain and the strengths that have enabled the sufferer to come this far. And the privacy of many vets' experiences, their reluctance to tell them for fear of being thought weak, cruel, or crazy or for fear of burdening others, makes their telling all the more sacred when they do begin to speak. Their stories can also be private in the sense that the traumatic memories can feel impossible to describe fully, in part because most of their listeners will not have been there and do not know how it looked, sounded, smelled, felt, and tasted. This makes the relating of one's story risky, because there is no way to know how much the listener will be able to grasp and appreciate. I often feel awe as vets talk, and I want the time of the telling to be protected from interference, the slightest suggestion of disrespect or distraction, and certainly the infliction of further pain.

A Note about the Military and the VA

For the military and the VA, implementing the kinds of suggestions in this chapter would require changing their own cultures (a tough job, admittedly) to incorporate a more honest acknowledgment of the emotional effects of war and a wider repertoire of responses—beyond drugs, pathologizing, and shaming—to those who are suffering.

The military and the VA stand to gain much from such an approach. They would, for instance, avoid the rage directed against them for failing to listen, failing to understand the impossible positions in which they put soldiers and vets by setting superhuman standards and ignoring soldiers' and vets' needs. In addition to asking to hear soldiers' and veterans' stories, the recommendations for therapists both in and out of the military would include depathologizing, at least a more judicious use of psychotropic drugs, individual therapists' recognition of the limits of what they can do, and encouragement of therapists to incorporate a more community-based approach to helping vets.

Additional Resources: A Partial and Idiosyncratic List

In the course of interviewing a veteran, you may want to turn to further resources, either to help the vet or because of your own interest. This book's chapters have extensive endnotes, so it's a good bet you will find readings, Web sites, or films cited in the notes that correspond to a topic of interest. In addition to those, you may wish to inspect the subsequent, nonexhaustive list of materials—books, films, and organizations—I have come across in the course of my work on this book.

Applying Critical Thinking
Some of the resources listed at the end of this section include materials I would not myself want to use but that are helpful in other ways. As with

everything, users of these materials should consider their contents from a critical thinking approach, keeping in mind the inordinate influence that the mental health establishment and the drug companies tend to have on even people who have the best of intentions. For instance, you may find that a particular organization makes heavy use of psychiatric labels or says that everyone with war trauma has PTSD but also does great work in finding places for homeless vets to live.

In addition to availing yourself of some of these resources, you might want to take action yourself. For instance, you might want to find a number of people willing to come together to urge other civilians to interview vets and in other ways to find out what their needs might be and help ensure that these needs are met. Forming such groups, writing letters to editors of print and online publications, working through elected representatives at all levels of government, religious groups, social clubs, or citizens' organizations such as Chambers of Commerce are ways to refashion communities so that they make a more public commitment to helping vets. The aims of helping could include anything mentioned in this chapter (see especially the General Guidelines in table 6.1 and the sections on common themes and common problems that come up in interviews), as well as, for instance, helping veterans form self-help groups; encouraging high school administrators and existing community and religious groups to invite vets to speak about their war experiences; exploring possibilities for education or political action groups composed of vets and civilians together; helping vets find jobs and homes; and urging vets to volunteer for Big Brother/Big Sister or similar organizations as one of many possible ways to resume exercising their powers to nurture and create rather than to destroy.

Organizations and Services

Acupuncturists Without Borders

www.acuwithoutborders.org

Offers more than twenty-five free clinics for veterans nationwide to help with the effects of emotional trauma.

Black Veterans for Social Justice

www.bvsj.org

Assists those making transition from active duty military to civilian life.

Coming Home Project

www.cominghomeproject.net

Provides compassionate care for current wars' vets and families. The staff consists of veterans, therapists, and interfaith leaders.

Department of Health and Human Services Suicide Prevention Hotline

www.suicidepreventionlifeline.org
1–800–273-TALK, with a special feature for veterans (veterans press 1).

Fisher House Foundation

www.fisherhouse.org
888–294–8560

Donates homes that enable family members to be close to a loved one during hospitalization for an unexpected illness, disease, or injury.

GI Rights Hotline (Run by the American Friends Service)

www.girightshotline.org
girights@girightshotline.org
877–447–4487

Assists with GIs' rights, military discharges and military counseling, filing of complaints and grievances, and matters related to going AWOL or UA.

Give an Hour

www.giveanhour.org

A network of mental health professionals reaching out to troops and their families.

Homes for Our Troops

www.homesforourtroops.org
866–7-TROOPS

Raises donations of money, building materials, and professional labor and coordinates building homes for severely injured service members to provide maximum freedom of movement and the ability to live more independently.

The Icarus Project

www.theicarusproject.net

Helps people who have been given psychiatric diagnoses find alternative ways to overcome alienation and suffering.

Intrepid Fallen Heroes Fund

www.fallenheroesfund.org
800–340-HERO

Provides financial support for dependents of US military personnel lost in the performance of duty.

Iraq Veterans Against the War

www.ivaw.org
215–241–7123

Among other things, offers writing workshops, with the results compiled as publications, performances, and exhibits.

Medical Foster Homes ("Adopt a Vet")

www1.va.gov/GERIATRICS/Medical_Foster_Home.asp

A caregiver in the community takes a veteran into their home and provides twenty-four-hour supervision as well as needed personal assistance. The VA provides comprehensive primary care through the interdisciplinary home care team, and the veteran pays the caregiver.

Miles Foundation

www.hometown.aol.com/milesfdn
877–570–0688

Toll-free helpline staffed by people who advocate for victims of military sexual assault and domestic violence.

Military Families Speak Out

www.mfso.org
mfso@mfso.org

Organization of people opposed to the wars in Iraq and Afghanistan who have relatives or loved ones who are currently in the military or who have served in the military.

MindFreedom International

www.mindfreedom.org

Organization of psychiatric survivors.

The National Center for Posttraumatic Stress Disorder

www.ncptsd.va.gov/ncmain/index.jsp

National Coalition for Homeless Veterans

www.nchv.org
800-VET-HELP

National Lawyers Guild Military Task Force

www.nlgmltf.org
415–566–3732

Assists with military law issues.

National Military Family Association

www.nmfa.org
800–260–0218

Supports spouses and children of service members.

National Veterans Foundation

888–777–4443

Toll-free hotline for veterans having trouble adjusting to civilian life.

Real Warriors campaign by the Defense Department

Service members interested in telling their stories as part of the campaign may send an e-mail to DCoE.Realwarriors@tma.osd.mil.

Salute, Inc.

www.saluteinc.org
847–749–2768

Provides financial support and assistance to service members and veterans.

Service Women's Action Network

www.servicewomen.org

Helps women veterans, including with healing after service.

SOFAR: Strategic Outreach to Families of All Reservists

www.sofarusa.org
help@sofarusa.org, jldarwin@aol.com

A pro bono project to provide support and services to the extended families of Reserve and National Guard members deployed in Afghanistan, Iraq, and Kuwait.

Soldiers Project

www.thesoldiersproject.org
818–761–7438

Therapists who volunteer to help.

U.S. Vets Inc.

www.usvetsinc.org

For homeless vets.

Vet Centers

www.vetcenter.va.gov
800–905–4675, 866–496–8838

Small storefront centers operated by the VA but that are accessible, less dogmatic, and less bound by the mental health system's traditional practices.

Veterans across America

www.veteransacrossamerica.org
212-684-1122

Works with veterans and their families to provide access to business and employment opportunities they do not have.

Veterans for Common Sense

www.veteransforcommonsense.org
201-558-4553

An advocacy organization.

Veterans for Peace

www.veteransforpeace.org
314-725-6005

Includes men and women veterans from past and current wars.

Veterans for Social Justice

http://www.veteransforjustice.com/phpBB3/index.php

Gordon Sturrock has helped create a Web forum for military vets who support peace and social justice.

Vets4Vets

www.vets4vets.us
520–319–5500

Nonpartisan project to create support groups of vets.

VetStage

www.vetstage.org
818–308–6296

Arts troupe that helps veterans express themselves.

Veterans Upward Bound

www.veteransupwardbound.org

Offers college preparation programs.

Wounded Warrior Project

www.woundedwarriorproject.org
877-TEAM-WWP

Publications

Coleman, P. *Flashback: Posttraumatic Stress Disorder, Suicide, and the Lessons of War.* Boston: Beacon Press, 2006.

Crawford, J. *The Last True Story I'll Ever Tell: An Accidental Soldier's Account of the War in Iraq.* New York: Riverhead Books, 2005.

Engel, R. *War Journal: My Five Years in Iraq.* New York: Simon & Schuster, 2008.

Fassihi, F. *Waiting for an Ordinary Day: The Unraveling of Life in Iraq.* New York: PublicAffairs, 2008.

Fitzgerald, F. *Fire in the Lake.* Boston: Little, Brown, 1972.

Grossman, D. *On Killing: The Psychological Cost of Learning to Kill in War and Society.* New York: Back Bay Books, 1996.

Junger, S. *War.* New York: Twelve, 2010.

Kovic, R. *Born on the Fourth of July.* New York: McGraw-Hill, 1976.

Kraft, H. S. *Rule Number Two: Lessons I Learned in a Combat Hospital.* New York: Little, Brown, 2007.

Marlantes, K. *Matterhorn: A Novel of the Vietnam War.* New York: El Leon Literary Arts/Atlantic Monthly Press, 2010.

Massey, J. *Kill! kill! kill!.* Paris, France: Editions du Panama. 2005.

Rieckhoff, P. *Chasing ghosts: Failures and Facades in Iraq: A Soldier's Perspective.* New York: NAL Trade, 2007.

Shay, J. *Odysseus in America: Combat Trauma and the Trials of Homecoming.* New York: Scribner, 2003.

Sherman, N. *The Untold War.* New York: W. W. Norton, 2010.

Tolstoy, L. *War and Peace.* New York: Random House, 2007.

Trumbo, D. *Johnny Got His Gun.* New York: Citadel, 1939.

Veterans for America. *The American Veterans' and Servicemembers Survival Guide.* http://www.veteranstoday.com/2008/12/22/the-american-veterans-and-service-members-survival-guide.

Veterans for America, 2010. Veterans for America, a nonprofit group, has produced a 599-page guide for veterans about practical issues, including housing, education, vocational rehabilitation, and citizenship. http://www.picosearch.com/cgi-bin/ts.pl?index=411973&calln=2&doc0=0&query=survival+guide&search.x=0&search.y=0&opt=ANY.

Workman, J., and J. Bruning, J. *Shadow of the Sword: A Marine's Journey of War, Heroism, and Redemption.* New York: Presidio Press, 2009.

Web Sites

Ken S. Pope's Web site, Resources for Troops and Veterans, Their Families, and Those Who Provide Services to Them:
http://kspope.com/torvic/war.php

Dr. Pope is an award-winning psychologist who has written extensively about ethical issues in psychology, as well as about a vast array of political issues as they intersect with psychology. This Web site is listed first here because of his vast array of relevant articles and listings of both nonmilitary and military organizations that might be helpful to vets.

David E. Jones's Web site of poetry about war, love, and family:
http://webspace.webring.com/people/l1/11bravovet

Gary Jacobson's Web site about the Vietnam War:
http://pzzzz.tripod.com/namtour.html

Films

All Quiet on the Western Front (feature)
Battle of San Pietro (documentary)
Blackhawk Down (feature)
Brothers (feature)
Coming Home (feature)
Flags of Our Fathers (feature)
Ground Truth, The (documentary)
Hidden Wounds (documentary about Iraq veterans; info@fanlight.com)
Hurt Locker, The (feature)
J'accuse (silent feature)
Letters from Iwo Jima (feature)
Platoon (feature)
Saving Private Ryan (feature)
Soldier's Story, A (feature)
Stop Loss (feature)

7 This Matters Desperately

No man is an Island, entire of itself; every man is a piece of the Continent, a part of the main . . .

—John Donne, *Devotions*[1]

We are all in the same boat, in a stormy sea, and we owe each other a terrible loyalty.

—G. K. Chesterton[2]

Thou shalt not stand idly by.

—Elie Wiesel, "Against Indifference"[3]

Can you begin to see now what this Soldier sees.
  Can you feel what he feels here?
  Do you understand the cries he hears
  of Friends that were so dear?
  For if not, go back and read again,
  read deep into the lines.
  And you may touch this Soldier's heart,
  Leave an imprint on his mind.
  For I am on your table now,
  your knife cuts quick and deep.
  I've laid my soul in front of you,
  No secrets here I keep.
—David E. Jones, "Perspectives"[4]

Share a Soldier's life today
  And talk with him awhile . . .
  And here the task begins anew
  To touch another's soul
  To listen to their memories
  Two lives today are whole.
—David E. Jones, "Scorners"[5]

I can remember thinking that war was so horrible that, at last, thank goodness, nobody could ever be fooled by romantic pictures and fiction and history into marching to war again.

—Kurt Vonnegut, *Bluebeard*[6]

The stories of veterans matter because of the massive, human, emotional carnage that is fast building in the United States and elsewhere as Johnny and Jane come marching home from our current wars and as the suffering of veterans from earlier wars goes on. We cannot rely on even the best of therapists to make it all better, because that simply will not happen, any more than it happened after the Vietnam War or the Gulf War or even after earlier ones. We do not need untold numbers of veterans from Iraq and Afghanistan—and, heaven forbid, future wars—swelling the ranks of the homeless, the suicidal and homicidal, the drug- and alcohol-addicted, the tormented. We do not want our world laced with former soldiers who endure lives of isolation, shame, guilt, panic, and despair. It doesn't have to happen, and we do not have to stand idly by and watch it happen.

One soldier, who has a gorgeously life-affirming spirit but who recently went through another time of intensified anguish, tells me that he now lies in his bed all day, heavily medicated with dangerous drugs that have not helped him for months. This is the vet who sent me months ago the message quoted earlier in the book about what an extremely large number of psychiatric medications had and had not done for him over the years: They had never helped him at all but had repeatedly precipitated or helped precipitate his serious and terrifying attempts to kill himself. That this news of him arrives at the same time as more reports of the often life-threatening dangers of these drugs and the overprescribing of them for veterans is devastating. I wrote just above that we must not stand idly by, but in the face of the power of the mental health, pharmaceutical, and military establishments, there are times when our hands are tied, when we ′t know how to help people break out of the fortress of fear that to try ing besides drugs or therapy is risky or simply naive. When we or when we try to act but to no beneficial effect, we must at ′o talk, to educate ourselves and as many others as will listen. ly touched by Michelle Dillow's story of how haunted ′ce and loss of innocence she experienced while at tion after returning home, and her struggles with had been struck by the many similarities so many other vets. With Michelle's kind ′ript about it. The play, called *War&Therapy*,

was first performed at the Capital Fringe (Washington, D.C.) Festival in July 2010 and at the Edmonton International Fringe Festival the following month. A discussion with the audience followed each of the twelve performances, and three themes that emerged are worth mentioning here. One was the almost universal extent to which people responded in the same ways, whether they were veterans, veterans' loved ones, or people who had never served in the military and regardless of their political views about current wars or any wars. I believe that this near universality was because the climax of the story is the vet's simple, honest telling of what happened to her at war and after coming home. The humanity and pain in that story spoke to me as I learned of them, and they were what impelled me to write both that play and this book. A second theme applies to those audience members who had not served in the military. They were stunned by exposure to the details of war experiences and disturbed by watching the vet's anguished struggles. One woman said she felt the silence had been broken. A member of a Canadian audience wrote afterward: "I saw the harsh reality of a soldier's life: at war and post-war. I realized that during war a soldier is required to FIGHT a very real enemy. Afterwards, they are forced to shift to yet another war. An internal one."

The third theme that appeared was the depth of the pain that most veterans continue to endure in silence. Every veteran who spoke in the post-performance discussions spoke through tears and with quivering chin, and that certainly included the men, even the one who came wearing a crisp uniform decorated with at least a dozen medals. One man who was probably in his eighties and had served in the American military during World War II said that war is not in human nature, because no matter what you feel about the enemy, once you know you have killed another human being, it haunts you. Then, although not a word of criticism had been spoken about veterans or about the politics or morality of any war, another man, who was undoubtedly a vet himself and probably in his sixties, rose from his seat and announced that he was leaving. The reason, he said, was that the previous speaker's words had desecrated the memories of those who had fought for liberty, as in World War II. Every word of the play and every word of the discussion had been spoken out of concern and respect for veterans' suffering, but it seems likely that this man feared that to speak the truth about anything bad that happens during wartime is to challenge the integrity and motives of anyone who has been in a war. I found it tragic that this man could not hear what was actually said, for such global, impermeable pictures of war as all-good do not correspond to the truth, and for vets and civilians to speak freely about the realities in all their starkness and complexity is to move us as individuals and as a society toward health and strength.

Closeting vets behind therapists' doors and silencing them with drugs makes all of us morally sick, because it keeps private and hidden the consequences of war. For those of us lucky enough not to have been in combat or had a loved one in combat, it insulates us from the hardest facts about how war destroys human hearts and souls. If we keep ourselves innocent of what has happened to veterans and what they live with back at home, we cut ourselves off from profoundly important parts of the human condition. This insulation is part of what Judith Shklar[7] has described as the notion that humankind marches inexorably toward perfection, which encourages us to focus attention away from "the darker recesses of the human condition" and to regard those recesses as anomalies. A graphic example of the turning away from the dark side has been the suppression during most of the wars in Afghanistan and Iraq of photographs of the bodies of American soldiers from these wars. The suppression has been so great that that this kind of current photographic record is more sparse than that of the Civil War.[8] But as two professionals working with a woman veteran who served at war as a nurse have observed, the woman has stories she finds hard to tell, but such stories are exactly what need to be heard for future generations to avoid repeating this kind of distress.[9]

How far from the realities of that dark side are even people who are supposedly aware of important political and social issues was brought home to me by a throwaway comment I heard on National Public Radio on March 20, 2010. On my local NPR station during a fundraising drive offering gifts to people who donate funds, someone mentioned that it was the anniversary of the start of the war in Iraq. One of the announcers emitted a little laugh and said, "Gee, I wonder what kind of gift is appropriate for that." He meant it as a joke. The very fact that he could even utter that as a joke reflects how far we are from understanding what war is doing. And in August 2010, I had another experience that stunned me by the lack of awareness of the very existence of many veterans: As I drove up to a Starbucks, a man who was probably in his late thirties burst out of the door, wild with rage and furiously talking to himself. Once I was inside the coffee shop, I heard two men who were also probably in their thirties talking angrily about the man who had just raced out. After saying to them I understood that the incident had been terribly upsetting, I couldn't help but wonder aloud, "Maybe he's a veteran." Both men replied immediately, "Oh, no. He's too young." They could only have thought that if they had blocked out of consciousness all of the Americans who have been sent to fight wars since the days of Vietnam.

To hear veterans' stories can help individual vets, to be sure. That in itself would be sufficient reason to do this work. And as seen in chapters 4 and 5, and given a strong perception that, in the words of Iraq veteran and activist Paul Rieckhoff, "Very few people on [Capitol Hill] want to spend money on veterans' issues,"[10] it is all the more important that, in addition to advocating for much better funding for job training, education, housing, and other services that provide real help, we engage in the project of listening.

Beyond the help for individual vets, listening is important for the rest of us as individuals and collectively. As more civilians hear more stories, we can start a national dialogue that begins with getting the veterans' war stories more generally known, with making them frequent topics of conversation at informal gatherings, at meetings and conferences, as subjects in the arts. This will create a widely known body of information, an archive, about the emotional consequences of war. It can serve as a basis for other useful work, including open analysis of the effects on soldiers and vets at times when truth-telling gets short shrift. The range of issues that can be analyzed and questions asked is nearly infinite. As one example, we would benefit from a hard look at the contrast between military language and expectations and servicemembers' experiences. Many soldiers and vets have noted how stunned and troubled they were when, during basic training, they were given rifles with bayonets and told to run around a field jabbing their bayonets and yelling, "Kill! Kill! Kill!" These vets have also said that there is no room in the military for them to express, never mind grapple with, those feelings. What are they supposed to do with the incongruity between how they are expected to feel and how they really feel? One veteran told me he dealt with the expectations by "becoming a machine." But when he came home from war, what was this gentle soul to do with his machinelike past? When soldiers and veterans who have reservations about "Kill! Kill! Kill!" pick up the newspaper published for the Fort Benning, Georgia, community and see its title, *The Bayonet*, how do they feel? On a different level, how does the use of the word *troops* help to cover up the effects of war? It takes us a significant step away from war's realities, because the announcement that "six troops were killed in Kandahar" does not call to mind the same images as if the announcement were that "six human beings were killed in Kandahar" and certainly not as if it were that "six people who had barely begun to live have died, and their deaths leave enormous, unfillable voids in the lives of their loved ones."

It is not only the cover-ups, problematic images, and incongruous messages about killing that warrant concern. We cannot keep sending people to war, where they are trained to be violent, and have them come home, where they too often grapple alone with what to do with their violent feelings and all that training to produce hair-trigger, precise responses that damage or destroy. And we wonder why we have a violent society, and we fail to consider that this explains a part of it.

Let us consider another example of the kinds of questions that creating a larger database of veterans' stories can usefully raise. What is the cost to the children whose parents are sent to war, especially in light of the expectation that not just the soldiers but entire families will be upbeat and optimistic about the soldiers' service? The media rarely carry reports of servicemembers themselves (especially high-ranking ones) expressing concern about the children. One exception is Major Kevin Becar, who "began choking up" while telling a journalist about his anguish on a brief visit home from Iraq, when he spent time with his eleven-year-old son and was about to go back: "The last couple of days as he looks at me, I know he's thinking about me leaving. He's starting to act differently. . . . It just kills me to think how tough this is for him."[11] Yet Major Becar is supposed to feel like a good American, perhaps even a hero, for leaving his son and putting himself at great risk for being maimed or killed. These are major moral dilemmas. Who helps Major Becar grapple with his? Who assists and supports him in going beyond the knee-jerk choices he is pressured to make that are based on, "If my country fights a war, then it's good for me to go, and that must come before everything"? We often hear the results of attempts to reconcile the two with statements such as, "You go to Iraq or Afghanistan and risk your life and try to kill other people *in order to make the world safer for your children.*" Whether or not one believes that for the United States to prosecute wars in these countries makes the world safer for the American children of those who fight the wars, it does not require rocket science to realize that (1) at least some wars are wrong or misguidedly fought; (2) there are other ways to make the world safe for one's children besides fighting wars in distant countries, and these other ways do not involve risk to life and limb or the leaving of one's children for long periods of time; (3) for young children, the abstraction of "Daddy or Mommy fights in Kabul to keep me safe in Cincinnati" is heavily overshadowed by the parent's absence, not to mention the troubling ways a parent who does survive and come back may be changed; and (4) children old enough to understand the abstraction of "fighting over there to keep children safe back home" or "fighting evil over there to make the world a better place" can feel disloyal to the parent if they do *not* accept that these statements are true and important, and this sense of disloyalty can prematurely make them retreat into rigid ways of deciding what matters.

A different kind of question that can arise from hearing vets' stories is how we as a society determine priorities or allow considerations of war to determine them. Television, YouTube, and other Web sites sometimes show heart-wrenching scenes of parents who have been deployed to war returning home to surprise their children for brief periods of time. Some such surprises are heavily publicized and take place, for instance, at major sports events or in school classrooms in front of all children in a class.[12] The pressure is on the children to be simply elated. But how is it for the deployed parents to be on display and put their children on display like that, knowing that the children may be angry that the parents have been away? Then, too, these dramatic, public homecoming surprises help fuel unrealistic expectations, so that when the returned warrior and the child go home, if the soldier simply wants to sleep or is on edge or, often, distant or angry, the contrast with the initial encounter can be painful. It is worth listening to vets talk about the whole range of ways their being at war, or even in the military, quite apart from being deployed, has affected their families and put pressure on them. One telling example of problematic priorities is that in at least some of these surprise scenarios, the deployed parent returned home but did not immediately go to spend time with the child, because it was considered desirable to conceal their presence in order to spring the reunion on the child in some very public way some days later. It is also worth exploring whether this and other kinds of public displays involving members of the military help gloss over the disturbing realities of war, contributing to the belief that these stories have happy endings, since rarely are they accompanied by much footage about how the children have suffered the extended separations and their fears of never again seeing their parents alive.

Gary Lord, a second-grade teacher at Whispering Pines Elementary School in Boca Raton, Florida, understood the importance of teaching his young students to begin to listen to vets—in ways appropriate to their ages, of course.[13] He told each of his seven- and eight-year-old students to interview a vet, asking when and where they served in the military, why they wanted to join, what were their responsibilities, what was their most exciting moment, and whether they participate in current Veterans' Day activities. Depending on our own attitudes about war in general or about the wars in which these veterans fought, some of these questions could be replaced with others, or more questions could be added, but this assignment served at least five important purposes: to make it clear that soldiers are real people, listen to some of what they have felt, collect some factual information about them, pave the way for hearing more from vets, and show civilians that their interest is helpful to veterans. Mr. Lord's exercise is in keeping with the recent upsurge nationally in encouraging people to ask their parents and grandparents to tell their stories, with the sense that we lose much that is precious if we do not ask and do not listen.

We now teach schoolchildren about slavery and HIV/AIDS. We need to teach them, as befits their ages as they grow, the truth about war. "I am a soldier defending my country" calls up images that are morally pure, ethically unquestionable, emotionally unconflicted, even aesthetically appealing. "My windshield shattered at the same time that the blood and brains of my driver filled the vehicle" destroys some of those images. This includes the hell of what in chapter 2 I called Daniel's Choice, when as an infantry sergeant, Daniel had to choose exactly where to tell his artillery to fire when the enemy was approaching his platoon and thus how many and which of his men to risk killing, since some would surely die. Still more of the falsely simplistic and easy, clean images of soldiers are destroyed when we hear the "Please stop" story, the one after which a soldier's VA psychologist begged him, with tears in his eyes, "Please stop." Here is part of that story: After some of the most horrific scenes from a battle fought by "25 men who had breathed together for months on a truck," some of the men burning from white phosphorus dropped on them, some terrified of dying and screaming for their mothers, seeing some of their "brothers" killed in action, seeing some wounded in action, one private jumped on a truck and yelled to others to leap on as he rammed other vehicles—some carrying wounded friends—over the cliff into oblivion in order to save at least some. The soldier telling me the story said that after all that, a few feet down the road they saw small children and bicycles, and "I still see their faces at night and I still see every dark-eyed, dark-haired child with those same eyes." He said that when he had gotten that far in telling his therapist the story and had begun to tell a bit more, the doctor was asking him to stop, so he ceased speaking: "I stopped living the story for him, but I live with it and more every night."

When the therapist, whose job was to help bear such burdens, said, "Please stop," the soldier left, so shaken by the lack of support, by the intimation that no one could go on in the face of such memories, that he wandered the parking lot for six hours, unable to find his car. No one should ask a veteran to stop. It is too cruel to them, and it keeps us too unjustifiably innocent. I had seen *Saving Private Ryan* and *Blackhawk Down*. I had heard some pretty terrible war stories. But until I met Daniel and heard his Daniel's Choice story, and until I heard the "Please stop" story,

I knew much less than I assumed I did, and I am sure that that remains true even now.

Since beginning the work that led to this book, every time in the past seven years that I have heard another story which I am sure must be the last, terrible surprise about war, I hear a shattering story of a new kind. They are the kinds of stories from which we want to turn away, but what we need is to come as close to them as we can, step by step. We begin to know a small part of a reality we have tried not to see if we become completely quiet, alone, and call to mind someone we dearly love and want to keep safe, think of times of tenderness and times of laughter we have shared with them, then picture their arm blown away at the shoulder, imagine lifting them to us as they bleed, their weight against our body, imagine cradling that wounded place against our chest, knowing that at any moment they could die, and knowing that we must race against time to try to get them to lifesaving help . . . and seeing the light of life leave their eyes.

People hearing that I am writing this book have asked whether World War II vets suffered less than vets from Vietnam on, since most people have heard less about the emotional pain of the former. Some people have the impression that World War II veterans have suffered less because World War II was considered a "good war," in which it was clear who the enemy was and clear that the enemy was perpetrating genocide. It is true that World War II vets came home to a nation that celebrated them, and that has been much less the case for veterans of wars since then. After all, the Allies had won, American soldiers were heroes, America was seen as the shining promise, vets came home to all kinds of support from the GI Bill, and they were supposed to be happy and get on with their lives. Certainly, there has been more questioning of the Vietnam War and the current wars than of World War II, despite the attempts of some to suppress dissent as unpatriotic, and that may have made it easier for some recent vets to talk about the suffering their wars caused them than it was for World War II vets. Furthermore, soldiers who fight the enemy directly rather than, for instance, by bombing them from above seem to suffer more later on,[14] and in the wars in Iraq and Afghanistan, servicemembers are in almost constant actual or potential, direct contact with the enemy. In addition, since guilt about killing is a major contributor to veterans' anguish, it is important to note that, whereas in World War II only 15 to 20 percent of military personnel fired at the enemy, that figure increased to 55 percent during the Korean War and to 90 to 95 percent during the Vietnam War.[15] However, we cannot conclude that World War II vets suffered less. People of both sexes from the World War II generation were more likely than vets of later wars to have been raised to keep their emotions to themselves, and so responses may not have been very empathic for those who did open up more. Changes in what people, including men, are encouraged to say about their feelings, as well as changes in diagnostic and treatment practices, make it impossible to do the kind of study that could definitively answer the question about whether vets from different wars suffered differently. However, that World War II veterans probably bottled up a great deal seems clear from the reactions of veterans on encountering each other on the fiftieth anniversary of D-Day and at other reunions; some who may never have shed a tear since the war broke down simply at the sight of someone else who had been in the war at the same time and in the same place as they. Some did not even see each other but just had their anguish triggered by hearing about the celebrations of the anniversary.[16] We will never come close to knowing what vets from earlier wars actually suffered. Further-more, J. M. Whiteley has reported that after the end of World War II, there was an unprecedented demand for psychologists to respond to veterans' personal problems,[17] and Steven Spielberg has said that he made his recent television series about World War II's Pacific battles because his uncle and father were telling him "how hellacious [World War II] was, and it just wasn't jibing with what was coming out of Hollywood."[18] It is clear that at least some veterans of World War II were no less anguished than others have been. My friend Trina Mascott, whose husband was wounded during the Battle of the Bulge and spent a long time recovering in a military hos-pital, reports that she saw World War II vets' glazed stares and heard their screams in the night well after they left the war. And in fact, nearly every time I speak to a World War II vet or someone close to that vet, I hear another story of someone haunted by what they saw. As Battle of the Bulge veteran James E. Wibby recently wrote, "We don't talk too much about the battle, but it's one of those things that kind of sits in the background. Every now and then a story creeps out."[19]

A major difference between the current wars and World War II must be marked well: Far fewer Americans—less than half of 1 percent of the population—are taking part in the wars in Iraq and Afghanistan than did so in World War II, when 12 percent participated. This lower participation rate only increases the likelihood that the truths of vets from Iraq and Afghanistan will remain hidden.[20]

Terrible news from the military and the VA about the increasing rates of suffering among veterans continues to arrive nonstop. As I proofread the manuscript for this book just three months after it went into production, I am now worried that the problem is even greater and more widespread than I had feared three months ago. As I was going over this chapter, I had to go back to chapter 5 to report information I just received about yet another dangerous practice involving the VA and psychiatric drugs. And between now (August 2010) and the time the book is published (spring 2011), I shudder to think what more news will reach us.

The truth about war must become as much a fully seen and fully known part of our culture as any other truth. We have more to lose if we fail to achieve this change in culture, because we thereby cut ourselves off from the knowledge of the greatest physical, emotional, and moral dangers that lurk for humankind. And as a country, and as a world, we come to greater harm from dangers that catch us unnecessarily and unjustifiably unawares. By educating ourselves about war's truths, by telling the stories to others, by connecting with those who lived and live those truths, we connect with more of the full web of human experience. If we as citizens do not open our ears and our hearts, then as a nation we will not truly and fully face the realities, the consequences, of war, and as a nation we will go to war again as fast and as effortlessly as we have these recent times. As all of these veterans live every moment with the nightmares of their pasts, they also help to shape all our futures. We cannot turn our backs on them now. We ignore them at our peril. We engage with them in hope for us all.

Afterword

In October 2010, correcting page proofs for this book, I have my last chance to make additions. I had hoped that between August, when I corrected the copyedited manuscript and sent it off to the publisher, and the page proof stage, some good news would arrive. A couple of encouraging signs appeared, combined with more that were alarming.

September 10, 2010, brought a *Los Angeles Times* report by Tony Perry that the 2009 Marine suicide toll was the highest since record-keeping began and gave the Marines the highest suicide rate of any of the U.S. armed services.[1] Encouraging was that the article included citation of back-to-back deployments as a crucial factor in the rise in suicides and that the "dwell time" ratio, or number of months at home between deployments to number of months deployed, was being increased from 1:1 (e.g., seven months at home, seven months deployed) to 2:1 (14 months at home for seven deployed). In the same article, other factors cited included relationship, family, and money problems and a sense of isolation, each of which is often related directly to war, but that relationship is not noted by the authorities who mention them.

Another *Los Angeles Times* article, this one by Alexandra Zavis, appeared on September 20 with the story about how hard many veterans are finding it to get jobs and keep them. Some prospective employers fear hiring vets who are suffering emotionally, because they fear they will commit acts of violence, or they do not want to give the vets time off to obtain care that they need.[2]

Two days later, an encouraging sign of increased willingness to acknowledge the effects of war appeared in a DoD press release, when the Navy Surgeon General, Vice Admiral Adam M. Robinson, Jr., voiced the view that no one comes back from being in or near to combat without some emotional trauma. It was also helpful that he does not use the word *disorder* to refer to upset that results from trauma.[3] And the following week, in a

CNN story about suicides, an Army official was quoted as acknowledging that the simultaneous fighting of two wars, the pace of Army operations, was the primary factor leading to military suicides.[4]

On October 11, James McKinley wrote in the *New York Times* about the role of overworked Army therapists' overreliance on psychiatric drugs and these drugs leading some servicemembers to become listless and deeply withdrawn, while the suicide numbers only increase.[5] One possibility that warrants a good, hard look is that the increase in suicides *results* at least partly from the effects of some of these drugs, a possibility Martha Rosenberg explored the same week as McKinley's article appeared. In "Are We Giving Soldiers Drugs That May Make Them Kill Themselves?"[6] Rosenberg reported that, according to the Army itself, more servicemembers were killing themselves than were dying in combat, that "The unprecedented suicide rates are accompanied by an unprecedented rise in psychoactive drug rate among active duty-aged troops." Noting that the use of such drugs had increased by 85 percent since 2003 and that many servicemembers take multiple drugs, Rosenberg cites an internal review showing that "the biggest risk factor may be putting a soldier on numerous drugs simultaneously, a practice known as polypharmacy." She points out that the psychiatric drugs most commonly used in the Army are known to cause not only suicide attempts (as she reports, they carry FDA-mandated suicide warning labels) but also other problematic behavior, such as domestic violence.

On October 26 there appeared on the defensetech Web site[7] the announcement that the DoD had developed a new "app" or system for using smartphones to take notes about their emotions so that they could later give accurate reports to therapists. The principle of making it easier for servicemembers to record emotions sounds good and might indeed help some people, as can any attempt either to record or to put in artistic form emotions that feel overwhelming and fragmenting. As the unnamed writer of the announcement on defensetech's site suggested, the news was about the Pentagon going high-tech in this new direction, but use of technology is not the same as effective use of technology, and it appears far too early to know whether this application will be helpful, harmful, or some of each, depending on the person and the situation. It is simply not known to what extent the psychological survival of any particular individual during a traumatic time is helped or hindered by their focusing on, rather than dissociating from, the intense sources of trauma. It is known, however, that many trauma victims describe dissociating rather than focusing more intensely on the terrifying experiences as an important way they survived emotionally and even helped resist the negative effects of the trauma. Furthermore, someone whose convoy has just been blown up by an IED might feel that to relax their vigilance about danger or their efforts to help wounded comrades in order to spend time jotting down their own feelings would be out of the question.

On October 28, the DoD released the transcript of a panel discussion after a screening of the documentary film, *WARTORN 1861–2010*, which deals with war-caused emotional trauma.[8] Describing the film as presenting the reality of such trauma, military specialists made announcements during the panel—such as that of General Pete Chiarelli, Vice Chief of Staff of the Army, that "we had over 900,000 folks take the global assessment tool, which measures resiliency. And we know we can teach people to be more resilient"—that would have seemed impressive and encouraging, had one not known about the long, largely unproductive history of a wide variety of efforts to use new tools and techniques (as described in chapters 4 and 5 and in this Afterword). The same is true for General Chiarelli's statement that

We're proud of the research that's being done at MRMC, the Medical Research Materiel Command, that is looking at things like biomarkers, which will be able to help us work our way through this horrible problem we have with the comorbidity, or sharing of symptoms, between post-traumatic stress and PTS [TBI, traumatic brain injury] with a simple test that would allow us to know whether an individual was suffering from a concussion or mild TBI [traumatic brain injury].[9]

And here is what Buddy Bucha, Army captain of 101st Airborne and recipient of the Medal of Honor for service in Vietnam, told the panel about how agonizing the problems continue to be for so many, indeed saying that no one escapes unscathed:

It doesn't matter if you have four stars or no stripes. Man or woman, you have this problem. You don't know when it's going to manifest itself, but it will. If you see behavior that you can't explain, a four-star general or private, old man, young man, you say, what were they thinking? That's bizarre. They committed murder. They weren't murderers before we got to them, but they committed murders on our watch. How can they explain?[10]

Similarly poignant, in light of what is known, is the series of claims and implications about success of treatment made by Dr. Kate Chard, director of the PTSD and Anxiety Disorders division at the Cincinnati VA medical center, that

We know that there are gold-standard therapies that work for our veterans and active-duty service members. I personally have been part of a rollout that's trained almost 3,000 therapists in the VA alone, but also now we've trained almost 500 therapists in the Department of Defense to do these therapies so that we can have a seamless transition, so that every single service member that is suffering can start these therapies while still in active-duty service. And then if they choose to, they can come back to the VA hospitals, to the vet centers, to all the facilities. We have over 150 separate hospitals that have clinicians actively trained. And we're prepared to help individuals regain their life and reduce the stigma and create hope that they can get better.[11]

How wonderful it would be if all those good intentions had borne better fruit.

An October 29 article on The World Can't Wait site[12] brought a powerful reminder of the rigidity in at least some realms of the military about what it means to be a man. The headline captures the kernel of the story: "Traumatized troop seeks help: NCO tells him, 'Get the sand out of your vagina!'"

Finally, on November 11—Veteran's Day—investigative journalist Aaron Glantz reported a stunningly high rate of suicide in World War II veterans.[13] In California, he writes, WWII-era vets are killing themselves at nearly four times the rate of people of the same age who did not do military service, and it is about double the rate of veterans returning from the U.S.'s current wars.

Glantz quoted Ken Norwood, an 86-year-old retired architect and WWII vet who fought in Europe and spent a year as a Nazi prisoner of war, as saying that even after all these years, "Some little incident will trigger a recollection about some event in combat," he said, "like a DVD playing back in my head. I just let it play until it's over. I've gotten used to it." In fact, his flashbacks have worsened over the years. And addressing the common belief that WWII vets were not emotionally scarred by war as vets of more recent wars have been, Patrick Arbore, the founding director of the Center for Elderly Suicide Prevention and Grief Counseling, says in the article that instead of showing their emotional devastation, most World War II veterans self-medicated with alcohol:

"This was the only way they could contain the trauma," Arbore said. "They never, never, never talked about it, but they would go to the American Legion religiously and get drunk."

At Legion halls, "one would hope that they'd be sharing stories and communicating," Arbore said, "but if you go there you see these older veterans sitting several seats away from each other, just sitting there drinking." . . .

And when old age begins to lead to physical maladies and diminished mental capacity, "that defense that they have held on to for so many years begins to slip away."[14]

The vets of current wars and others since WWII must not be sent into a future in which, like the WWII vets, they will still suffer so intensely more than six decades after they served their time.

Even in the face of the torment suffered by veterans and those who care about them, it is clear that it will require clarion calls from enormous numbers of us to focus those with the power to make changes at the top on what veterans really need, what really helps, and what unforgivably does them further harm.

Notes

Prologue

1. M. Atwood, *The Blind Assassin* (New York: Anchor, 2000).

2. P. J. Caplan, "For Anguished Vets, the Listening Cure," *Washington Post* (Outlook section), September 5, 2004, B02.

3. Published in Toronto in 200x by Thomson Gale.

4. P. J. Caplan, "Vets Aren't Crazy; War Is," *Tikkun*, September–October 2007, 44–48, http://www.tikkun.org/magazine/tik0709/frontpage/vets.

5. P. J. Caplan and J. B. Caplan, *Thinking Critically about Research on Sex and Gender*, 3rd ed. (Boston: Allyn and Bacon, 2009).

6. M. Twain, letter to President Timothy Dwight, Yale University, June 26, 1888, reprinted in *Hartford Daily Courant*, June 29, 1888, 5.

7. P. J. Caplan, "Defying Authority: The Liberation and Poignancy of Questioning the Status Quo," Distinguished Career Achievement lecture, Association for Women in Psychology conference, San Diego, March 14, 2008.

Chapter 1

1. V. Frankl, *Man's Search for Meaning: An Introduction to Logotherapy* (New York: Washington Square Press, 1959) (lines 256–258 on Kindle).

2. H. S. Sullivan, *The Psychiatric Interview* (New York: W. W. Norton, 1970).

3. American Psychiatric Association, *Diagnostic and Statistical Manual of Mental Disorders–IV* (Washington, DC: American Psychiatric Association, 1994).

4. D. Kersten, "Invisible Wounds," *Govexec.com*, July 1, 2005, http://www.govexec.com/features/0705-01/0705-01s3.htm.

5. Associated Press, "More Troops Developing Latent Mental Disorders," July 28, 2005, http://www.google.com/search?ie=UTF-8&oe=UTF-8&sourceid=navclient&gf ns=1&q=More+Troops+Developing+Latent+Mental+Disorders.

6. "Cory," posting in response to "PTSD: A Marine's Story," NPR, November 17, 2010, http://onpointradio.org/2009/11/ptsd-a-marines-story.

7. E. Showalter, *The Female Malady: Women, Madness, and English Culture, 1830–1980* (New York: Penguin, 1985).

8. Barry Romo, telephone conversation, May 12, 2010.

9. P. Carter, "A Veteran," *New York Times*, May 9, 2010, 8. Marine Nathaniel Fick describes this "war whose burden is borne almost exclusively by the tiny minority in uniform and their families." N. Fick, "Coming Home—to What?" *Boston Globe,* August 28, 2005.

10. S. Shane, "A Flood of Troubled Soldiers Is in the Offing, Experts Predict," *New York Times*, December 16, 2004, A1.

11. M. Winerip, "Vietnam's Damage, Four Decades Later," *New York Times* (Styles section), September 6, 2009, 1, 2.

12. J. E. Stiglitz and L. J. Bilmes, *The Three Trillion Dollar War: The True Cost of the Iraq Conflict* (New York: W. W. Norton, 2008).

13. As just one example, B. Bender, "Veterans Forsake Studies of Stress" (*Boston Globe*, August 24, 2009, http://bit.ly/vE2uy), reported that soldiers at Fort Carson were also found to be involved in a rash of crimes, including murders, beatings, rapes, DUIs, drug abuse, domestic violence, shootings, stabbings, kidnappings, and suicides.

14. P. J. Caplan, "Ambiguity, Powerlessness, and the Psychologizing of Trauma: How Backlash Affects Work with Trauma Survivors," *Journal of Trauma Practice* 5 (2006): 5–24.

15. Frankl, *Man's Search for Meaning* (lines 256–258 on Kindle).

16. A. Kleinman, *What Really Matters: Living a Moral Life amid Uncertainty and Danger* (Oxford: Oxford University Press, 2006).

17. C. W. Hoge, J. L. Auchterlonie, and C. S. Milliken, "Mental Health Problems, Use of Mental Health Services, and Attrition from Military Service after Returning from Deployment to Iraq or Afghanistan," *Journal of the American Medical Association* 295, no. 9 (2006): 1023–1032.

18. Suicide Risk Management and Surveillance Office, Army Behavioral Health Technology Office, *Army Suicide Event Report (ASER): Calendar Year 2006* (Tacoma, WA: U.S. Department of Defense, 2007).

19. Associated Press, "22,000 Vets Call Suicide Hotline in Its Opening Year," *USA Today*, July 28, 2008, http://www.usatoday.com/news/washington/2008 -07-28-Vets-suicide_N.htm.

20. U.S. Department of Defense, "U.S. Army Releases 2008 Suicide Data, Highlights Efforts to Prevent Suicide," press release, January 29, 2009; idem, "Army Creates Suicide Prevention Task Force during 'Stand Down,'" press release, March 6, 2009; and idem, "'Super Coaches' to Assist Servicemembers with Psychological Problems," press release, March 24, 2009.

21. U.S. Department of Defense press releases, January 29, 2009, March 6, 2009, and March 24, 2009. The quotation is from the March 24, 2009, press release, "'Super Coaches' to Assist Servicemembers with Psychological Problems."

22. U.S. Department of Defense, "'Super Coaches' to Assist Servicemembers with Psychological Problems."

23. A. Glantz, *The War Comes Home: Washington's Battle against America's Veterans* (Berkeley and Los Angeles: University of California Press, 2009); and M. S. Kaplan, N. Huguet, B. McFarland, and J. Newsom, "Suicide among Male Veterans: A Prospective Population-Based Study," *Journal of Epidemiology and Community Health* 61 (June 2007): 619–624, http://jech.bmj.com/cgi/content/full/61/7/619.

24. National Coalition for Homeless Veterans, "Facts & Media: Background & Statistics," National Coalition for Homeless Veterans, 2010, http://www.nchv.org/ background.cfm.

25. Ibid.

26. According to the VA (http://www1.va.gov/homeless/page.cfm?pg=1), homeless veterans tend to be older and better educated than other homeless people, and about 56 percent of homeless veterans are African-American or Hispanic.

27. National Coalition for Homeless Veterans, "Facts & Media: Background & Statistics."

28. National Coalition for Homeless Veterans, "Facts & Media: FY 2010 VA Budget Includes $3.2 Billion for Homeless Vets," January 4, 2010, http://www.nchv.org/ news_article.cfm?id=650; Glantz, *The War Comes Home*, and Kaplan et al., "Suicide among Male Veterans," 619–624.

29. A. J. Mansfield, J. S. Kaufman, S. W., Marshall, B. N. Gaynes, J. P. Morrissey, and C. C. Engel, "Deployment and the Use of Mental Health Services among U.S. Army Wives," *New England Journal of Medicine* 362, no. 2 (2010): 101–109.

30. See also S. J. Danish and B. Antonides, "What Counseling Psychologists Can Do to Help Returning Veterans," *Counseling Psychologist* 37 (2009): 1076–1089. The authors note, citing the APA Presidential Task Force on Military Deployment Services for Youth, Family, and Service Members (2007), that the divorce rate for Army

families nearly doubled for enlisted personnel and nearly tripled for officers between 2001 and 2004; that more than 40 percent of those deployed at that time had children; and that 72 percent of the children were under twelve years of age. Regarding unemployment, see T. Baldas, "DOJ Cracks Down on Discrimination against Returning Injured Soldiers" (*National Law Journal*, May 6, 2009, http://www.law.com/jsp/nlj/PubArticleNLJ.jsp?id=1202430498762&hbxlogin=1), who reports that the Department of Justice has had to ride herd on employers who discriminate against returning, injured soldiers, making it hard for them to get their old jobs back, demoting them, or denying them work altogether.

31. "Stopping 'Stop-Loss,'" editorial, *New York Times*, May 22, 2009, 7.

32. Mansfield et al., "Deployment and the Use of Mental Health Services among U.S. Army Wives," 101–109.

33. G. Zoroya, "Troops' Kids Feel War Toll," *USA Today*, June 26, 2009.

34. P. Lester, K. Peterson, J. Reeves, L. Knauss, D. Glover, C. Mogil, N. Duan, et al., "The Long War and Parental Combat Deployment: Effects on Military Children and At-Home Spouses," *Journal of the American Academy of Child and Adolescent Psychiatry* 49, no. 4 (2010): 310–320, quoted in Zaroyo, "Troops' Kids Feel War Toll.".

35. Zoroya, "Troops' Kids Feel War Toll."

36. Ray Parrish, telephone conversation, September 10, 2008.

37. Ray Parrish, telephone conversation, May 13, 2010.

38. VA Watchdog.org, VA's Deadly PTSD "Drug Cocktail" Is Back in the News," 2010, http://www.vawatchdog.org/10/nf10/nfmar10/nf030910-5.htm.

39. R. Rosenheck, L. Frisman, and A. M. Chung, "The Proportion of Veterans among Homeless Men," *American Journal of Public Health* 84, no. 3 (1994): 466–469. See also G. Gamache, R. Rosenheck, and R. Tessler, "Overrepresentation of Women Veterans among Homeless Women," *American Journal of Public Health* 93, no. 7 (2003): 1132–1136.

40. B. Bender, "More Female Veterans Are Winding up Homeless; VA Resources Strained; Many Are Single Parents," *Boston Globe*, July 6, 2009.

41. National Coalition for Homeless Veterans, "Facts & Media: Background & Statistics."

42. L. Alvarez, "Newest Veterans Are Hit Hard by Economic Crisis," *New York Times*, June 26, 2009, http://www.nytimes.com/2008/11/18/us/18vets.html?pagewanted=1&_r=1&partner=rss&emc=rss.

43. J. Shapiro, "The Span of War: PTSD among Poor Soldiers: Herold's Story," *Morning Edition*, NPR, July 7, 2005, www.npr.org/templates/story/story.php?storyId=4732666.

44. E. Goode, "When Minds Snap," *New York Times*, November 8, 2009, 1, 4.

45. B. L. Litz and S. M. Orsillo, "The Returning Veteran of the Iraq War," in *The Iraq War Clinician Guide*, 2nd ed., ed. R. G. Lande et al. (Washington, DC: National Center for PTSD and the Department of Veterans Affairs, 2004), 21, http://www.ptsd.va .gov/professional/manuals/iraq-war-clinician-guide.asp.

46. As someone with the user name "William" wrote, "It is stunning that almost a century after the book *All Quiet on the Western Front* . . . we seem to be oblivious to the true nature and cost of war," "PTSD: A Marine's Story," NPR, November 17, 2010, http://onpointradio.org/2009/11/ptsd-a-marines-story.

47. Glantz, *The War Comes Home*, 223.

48. American Psychological Association, "Materials Released to Help Build Resilience in Wartime," *Monitor on Psychology* 34, no. 5 (May 2003): 14.

49. P. Barker, *Regeneration* (London: Penguin, 2008), 211.

50. I do not refer to those who believe with reason that we must seek ways to protect ourselves from terrorist attacks, which differs in important ways from believing that anyone very different from Americans is dangerous to us.

51. K. Vonnegut, *Bluebeard* (New York: Dell, 1987), 171.

52. Cable News Network, "'Nightline' Airs War Dead amid Controversy: Owner Ordered Affiliates Not to Broadcast Program," *CNN.com*, May 1, 2004, http:// www.cnn.com/2004/SHOWBIZ/TV/05/01/abc.nightline.

53. Ibid.

54. UNESCO, "The Seville Statement on Violence," 1991 (with commentary by David Adams), http://www.culture-of-peace.info/brochure/titlepage.html.

55. Ibid., 6.

56. Barry Romo, telephone conversation. May 12, 2010.

57. P. J. Caplan, *The New Don't Blame Mother: Mending the Mother-Daughter Relationship* (New York: Routledge, 2000).

58. P. J. Caplan, *They Say You're Crazy: How the World's Most Powerful Psychiatrists Decide Who's Normal* (Reading, MA: Addison-Wesley, 1995).

59. J. Hogan, "Culture-Shock and Reverse Culture Shock: Implications for Juniors Abroad," ERIC doc. ED233268, 1983, http://www.eric.ed.gov:80/ERICWebPortal/ custom/portlets/recordDetails/detailmini.jsp?_nfpb=true&_&ERICExtSearch_Search Value_0=ED233268&ERICExtSearch_SearchType_0=no&accno=ED233268.

60. Caplan, *They Say You're Crazy*; and idem, "What the Supreme Court Doesn't Know," *CounterPunch*, October 2, 2006, *www.counterpunch.org*. See also my letter to

the editor, http://psychdiagnosis.net/notScientology.html, and my "Questionable Grounds for Exclusion," *Monitor on Psychology* 38, no. 1 (January 2007): 4.

61. Caplan, *They Say You're Crazy.*

Chapter 2

1. G. Orwell, *In Front of Your Nose, 1945–1950 (Collected Essays, Journalism, and Letters of George Orwell)*, ed. I. Angus and S. Orwell (Boston: Godine, 2000).

2. M. Gellhorn, interview by P. Williams, reporter and producer, in *War Reporters* (Hamilton, NJ: Films Media Group—Films for the Humanities, 1991).

3. P. J. Caplan, "Ambiguity, Powerlessness, and the Psychologizing of Trauma: How Backlash Affects Work with Trauma Survivors," *Journal of Trauma Practice* 5 (2006): 5–24.

4. www.barrypopik.com/.../never_doubt_that_a_small_group_of_thoughtful _committed_citizens_can_change.

5. J. Tobin, *Ernie Pyle's War* (Lawrence: University Press of Kansas, 1997), 4.

6. Ibid., 90.

7. P. W. Tuerk, A. L. Grubaugh, M. B. Hamner, and E. B. Foa, "Diagnosis and Treatment of PTSD-Related Compulsive Checking Behaviors in Veterans of the Iraq War: The Influence of Military Context on the Expression of PTSD Symptoms," *American Journal of Psychiatry* 166, no. 7 (2009): 762–768.

8. N. Fick, *One Bullet Away* (Boston: Houghton Mifflin, 2005), 18.

9. Ibid., 22.

10. Ibid., 51.

11. Tobin, *Ernie Pyle's War*, 88–89.

12. Quoted in S. Anderson, "Bringing It All Back Home," *New York Times Magazine*, May 28, 2006, 36–56, 63, quotation at 42.

13. K. Holmstedt, *The Girls Come Marching Home: Stories of Women Warriors Returning from the War in Iraq* (Mechanicsburg, PA: Stackpole Books, 2009), 53. See also L. Kaufman, "After War, Love Can Be a Battlefield," *New York Times* (Sunday Styles section), April 6, 2008, 1.

14. S. Corbett, "The Permanent Scars of Iraq," *New York Times Magazine*, February 15, 2004, 56.

15. B. Bender, "Veterans Forsake Studies of Stress," *Boston Globe*, August 24, 2009, http://bit.ly/vE2uy.

16. J. Gettleman, "Soldier Accused as Coward Says He Is Guilty Only of Panic Attack," *New York Times*, November 6, 2003, http://www.nytimes.com/2003/11/06/us/soldier-accused-as-coward-says-he-is-guilty-only-of-panic-attack.html?pagewanted=1.

17. Quoted in A. Carroll, *War Letters: Extraordinary Correspondence from American Wars* (New York: Scribner, 2001).

18. A. Glantz, *The War Comes Home: Washington's Battle against America's Veterans* (Berkeley and Los Angeles: University of California Press, 2009).

19. S. Shane, "A Flood of Troubled Soldiers Is in the Offing, Experts Predict," *New York Times*, December 16, 2004.

20. Quoted in D. Filkins, "His Long War," *New York Times Magazine*, October 18, 2009, 36–47, 54–55, 57, quotation at 43.

21. J. Dao, "Gone for a Soldier," *New York Times*, June 27, 2010, A1, A20–21.

22. Glantz, *The War Comes Home.*

23. J. Hammer, "Death Squad," review of *Black Hearts: One Platoon's Descent into Madness in Iraq's Triangle of Death*, by J. Frederick, *New York Times Book Review*, March 14, 201, 1, 10. .

24. Hammer, "Death Squad."

25. J. Straziuso, "Soldiers in Afghanistan Also Battle Extreme Elements," *News-Leader* (Springfield, MO), June 23, 2006, 7A.

26. K. Vonnegut, *Bluebeard* (New York: Dell, 1987). And war correspondent Dexter Filkins in "The Shrine down the Hall" (*New York Times Magazine*, March 21, 2010, 34–47) writes, "You step inside the barracks thinking big, burly and deep-voiced. And what you get are chubby faces and halfhearted mustaches and voices still cracking. . . . No one mentions the possibility of death" (34).

27. T. McNally, interviews of S. Huze, P. Rieckhoff, and J. Massey, *Battlefield Iraq* (interview transcript), January 20, 2006, http://www.uruknet.info/?p=19785.

28. Anderson, "Bringing It All Back Home," 36–56, 63, quotations at 63, 41.

29. Glantz, *The War Comes Home*, 34.

30. Associated Press, "Marine Unit Finds Scars of War Run Deep," *USA Today*, October 9, 2006, 11A.

31. D. Filkins, *The Forever War* (New York: Knopf, 2008).

32. B. Carey and D. Cave, "Who'll Counsel the Counselors? Military Faces Therapy Overload," *New York Times*, November 8, 2009, 1, 27.

33. Daily Press, "Invisible Casualties," July 18, 2004, http://www .informationclearinghouse.info/article6514.htm.

34. Y.-C. Shen, J. Arkes, and J. Pilgrim, "The Effects of Deployment Intensity on Posttraumatic Stress Disorder: 2002–2006," *Military Medicine* 174, no. 3 (March 2009): 217–223. http://findarticles.com/p/articles/mi_qa3912/is_200903/ ai_n31513622/?tag=content;col1.

35. J. Brothers, "When Our Troops Come Home," *Parade Magazine*, April 16, 2006, 4–5, quotation at 5.

36. A. Rogers, *The Unsayable: The Hidden Language of Trauma* (New York: Random House, 2006), 262–263.

37. Ibid., 262.

38. D. Filkins, "The Army You Have," *New York Times Book Review*, October 25, 2009, http://test.pathologyportal.org/site~/NYTReviewFourthStar.pdf. Foreign correspondent Dexter Filkins has described how otherwise talented generals made disastrous decisions in Iraq "that brought America to the brink of defeat," including "pulling American troops from the streets and replacing them with Iraqi soldiers who were unwilling or incapable of fighting for their government," the results being "anarchy and civil war." See also K. Johnson and R. Hampson, "Combat Stress Takes Toll" (*USA Today*, June 15, 2006, 1A, 7A), who report that as early as 2006, Army officials were saying that when a war's goal seems unclear or unreachable, the negative emotional effects on service members increase.

39. Filkins, "The Army You Have," believes that the magnitude of the disaster in Iraq has been underreported, with the generals responsible for it continuing in the face of "catastrophe" to assure the public "that their strategy was working. Even a glance into the Iraqi streets proved otherwise" (16). In "Collateral Damage" (*Nation*, November 3, 2008, 25–30), Chris Toensing, editor of *Middle East Report*, writes about American soldiers' discoveries that conditions in Iraq were not as clear-cut as they had been led to believe, and in many ways were alarmingly bad. See also F. Kaplan, "Challenging the Generals," *New York Times Magazine*, August 26, 2007, 34–39. America's junior officers are fighting the war on the ground in Iraq and losing faith in their superior officers. The former have more combat experience than the latter and do not trust the superiors' orders, partly because of the increases in length and number of deployments. And J. S. Gordon, in "Cases without Borders: For Gaza Psychologist, Hope amid Despair," *New York Times* (January 13, 2009), reports that the occupation plan for Iraq was seriously faulty from the beginning, something the soldiers there soon learned.

40. See, for example, M. Benjamin, "Friendly Fire in Iraq—and a Coverup," *Salon.com*, October 14, 2008, http://www.salon.com/news/feature/2008/10/14/ friendly_fire/index.html. Holmstedt in *The Girls Come Marching Home* relates the

story of a woman soldier who was shot at four times in the Army, three times by Americans and once by Iraqi celebratory fire.

41. Examples include the Bush administration's failure to provide adequate armor for vehicles in Iraq and what Eisenhower called the "calculated risk" he took with the lives of soldiers in what became the Battle of the Bulge, the latter described by C. H. Philips in "Battle of the Bulge: Fortunes of War: How the 101st Airborne's Good Luck Helped Win the Battle of the Bastogne," Military History Online, June 23, 2003, http://www.militaryhistoryonline.com/wwii/articles/bastogne.aspx.

42. D. E. Jones, *A Soldier's Story: The Power of Words* (Bloomington, IN: AuthorHouse, 2006), viii.

43. Ibid., 88.

44. From Bob Lange's poem "When Were You There?," in Jones, *A Soldier's Story*, 137.

45. C Hedges, "What War Looks Like," *New York Times Book Review*, May 24, 2009, 5.

46. J. Gettleman, "Soldier Accused as Coward Says He Is Guilty Only of Panic Attack."

47. P. Barker, *The Ghost Road* (New York: Plume, 1995), 172.

48. U.S. Department of Defense, "Defense Department Kicks Off Sexual Assault Awareness Month with Campaign, Web Site," press release, April 3, 2009.

49. M. Mitka, "Military Sexual Trauma, *Journal of the American Medical Association* 304, no. 2 (July 14, 2010).

50. S. Corbett, "The Women's War," *New York Times Magazine*, March 18, 2007, 40–55, 71–72.

51. K. Williams, "A Soldier's Story," *New York Times Magazine*, August 21, 2005, http://www.nytimes.com/2005/08/21/magazine/21QUESTIONS.html.

52. J. Sullivan and C. Pope, "Oregon Veteran among Troops Suffering Sexual Trauma," *Oregonian*, October 12, 2008. See also M. Elias, "15% of Female Veterans Tell of Sexual Trauma," *USA Today*, October 28, 2008.

53. Elias, "15% of Female Veterans Tell of Sexual Trauma."

54. Sullivan and Pope, "Oregon Veteran among Troops Suffering Sexual Trauma."

55. Ibid.

56. U.S. Department of Defense, "Defense Department Kicks Off Sexual Assault Awareness Month."

57. Holmstedt in *The Girls Come Marching Home* recounts the story of a woman who told her platoon sergeant that another soldier had sexually assaulted her, and the sergeant said they needed to keep the perpetrator in the service because they needed him to work.

58. Sullivan and Pope, "Oregon Veteran among Troops Suffering Sexual Trauma." .

59. Ibid.

60. Williams, "A Soldier's Story."

61. See, for example, J. Larkin, *Sexual Harassment: High School Girls Speak Out* (Toronto: Second Story Press, 1994); L. E. Walker, *The Battered Woman* (New York: Harper & Row, 1979); and D. E. H. Russell and R. M. Bolen, *The Epidemic of Rape and Child Sexual Abuse in the United States* (Thousand Oaks, CA: Sage, 2000).

62. S. J. Cozza, D. M. Benedek, J. C. Bradley, T. A. Grieger, T. S. Nam, and D. A. Waldrep, "Topics Specific to the Psychiatric Treatment of Military Personnel," in *The Iraq War Clinician Guide,* 2nd ed., ed. R. G. Lande, B. A. Marin, J. I. Ruzek, et al. (Washington, DC: National Center for PTSD and the Department of Veterans Affairs, 2004), 4–20, http://www.ptsd.va.gov/professional/manuals/iraq-war-clinician -guide.asp.

63. Ibid.

64. I. Pivar, "Traumatic Grief: Symptomatology and Treatment in the Iraq War Veteran," in *The Iraq War Clinician Guide,* 2nd ed., ed. R. G. Lande, B. A. Marin, J. I. Ruzek, et al. (Washington, DC: National Center for PTSD and the Department of Veterans Affairs, 2004), 75–78, http://www.ptsd.va.gov/professional/manuals/ iraq-war-clinician-guide.asp.

65. N. Banerjee, "Few But Organized, Iraq Veterans Turn War Critics," *New York Times*, January 23, 2005, 14.

66. Jones, "Scars of War," in *A Soldier's Story*, 23.

67. D. Cave, "A Combat Role, and Anguish, Too," *New York Times*, November 1, 2009, 1, 32.

68. Ibid.

69. Shane, "A Flood of Troubled Soldiers Is in the Offing": Paul Rieckhoff, who served as a platoon leader in Iraq, going on hundreds of combat patrols, tried to warn about this as early as 2004: "In the urban terrain, the enemy is everywhere, across the street, in that window, up that alley. . . . It's a fishbowl. You never feel safe. You never relax." C. S. Smith, "Big Guns for Iraq? Not So Fast" (*New York Times*, August 28, 2005, section 4, 1), reported that the United States was holding off on giving the Iraqi military heavy weapons and vehicles for fear they would be used against Americans. See also Banerjee, "Few But Organized, Iraq Veterans Turn War

Critics," about the difficulty of distinguishing friend from foe. See also D. Filkins, "Where the Shadows Have Shadows," *New York Times*. February 5, 2006, section 4, 1, 3. Corbett, "The Permanent Scars of Iraq," says there are estimates that 25 percent of soldiers on a war's front lines will experience combat stress, but in Iraq there are no front lines. Alfonso Batres, who was the psychologist in charge of readjustment counseling services for the VA's Vet Centers, said, "It's just like Vietnam. They have to be on guard with everyone; they're always facing an unknown" (41).

70. Corbett, "The Permanent Scars of Iraq," 39.

71. Tobin, *Ernie Pyle's War*, 135.

72. Anderson, "Bringing It All Back Home," 36–56, 63, quotation at 43.

73. Corbett, "The Permanent Scars of Iraq."

74. A character in the film *Flags of Our Fathers* says, "They may have fought for their country, but they died for their friends." The "father" of the Navy SEALs, Roy Boehm, wrote to his mother from Vietnam, "Please don't fear for me as my frogmen are devoted to me as I to them and protect me as if I were something sacred" (Carroll, "War Letters," 61). And see Barker, *The Ghost Road*: "[The group of soldiers constituted] a fragile civilization, a fellowship on the brink of disaster" (140).

75. See Glantz, *The War Comes Home*.

76. Tobin, *Ernie Pyle's War*, 148.

77. J. Key, "Our Heroes, This Day and the Year-Round," *USA Today*, November 6, 2009, 13A.

78. Jones, "The Wall, " in *A Soldier's Story*, 1.

79. Jones, "Brothers," in *A Soldier's Story*, 54.

80. For an excellent book about dealing with many kinds of guilt, see S. Carrell, *Escaping Toxic Guilt: Five Proven Steps to Free Yourself from Guilt for Good!* (New York: McGraw-Hill, 2007).

81. P. J. Caplan, *The New Don't Blame Mother: Mending the Mother-Daughter Relationship* (New York: Routledge, 2000).

82. N. Gerrard, "Guilt Is a Terminal Word: A Critical Analysis of Guilt in Relation to Women with a Focus on Mothers and Daughters," unpublished manuscript, Ontario Institute for Studies in Education, 1987 (available from author: 1904 Pembina Ave., Saskatoon, Saskatchewan, Canada S7K 1C3).

83. Jones, "58," in *A Soldier's Story*, 92.

84. Jones, *A Soldier's Story*, xii.

85. Glantz in *The War Comes Home* reports that more than five years after the war in Iraq began, most American soldiers knew that the invasion of Iraq had been based

on the false claims that there was a link between Saddam Hussein and the 9/11 attacks and that Iraq had weapons of mass destruction. Glantz also reports soldiers who were angry because in the military they had not learned skills that would transfer to work back home, as their military recruiters had promised they would. And veteran Jimmy Massey says, "My questions to my command became, how do you tell a 25-year-old Iraqi male who just witnessed his brother being killed at a checkpoint, how do you tell this young man not to become an insurgent? So I was very critical of our mission and what we were performing and the lack of humanitarian support to the Iraqi people" (interview by McNally, *Battlefield Iraq*). Holmstedt in *The Girls Come Marching Home* (149) writes that

Contractors like KBR provided . . . shower water that was not disinfected with chlorine or properly filtered; it was concentrated waste stream. . . . She wonders what exactly the contractors spent the money on. . . . [T]he contractors carelessly exposed troops . . .to E. coli, typhoid fever, and hepatitis. . . . McNeill and those she served with had grown used to an upset stomach and the smell of sulfur in the showers. . . . She carried a new M16 that was missing a part, so it wasn't a reliable weapon. She carried a gas mask with a "training" canister rather than the type that would actually work in an attack.

86. See the films *The Hurt Locker* and *Brothers* for vivid depictions, as well as K. Goetz, "Troubled Veteran's Call Leads to Firing; VA Patients Lament Loss of Psychologist," *Commercial Appeal* (Memphis, TN), 2009, http://tinyurl.com/awavgy.

87. R. Rogers, "Raising an Army of Counselors; Returning Combat Troops, New Vets, Families Targeted," *San Diego Union-Tribune*, January 3, 2009, http://tinyurl.com/9u7cvn.

88. Associated Press, "Domestic Abuse on Rise as Economy Sinks; Hotline Calls Up from Last Year as Are Cases of Shaken Baby Syndrome," April 11, 2009, http://www.wiminswatch.org/domestic-abuse-on-rise-as-economy-sinks.

89. K. Helliker, "You Might as Well Face It: You're Addicted to Success," *Wall Street Journal*, February 11, 2009. http://online.wsj.com/article/SB123423234983566171.html.

90. Caplan, *The New Don't Blame Mother*.

91. Ibid.

92. B. Carey, "The Struggle to Gauge a War's Psychological Cost," *New York Times*, November 26, 2005.

93. M. Murdoch and K. L. Nichol, "Women Veterans' Experiences with Domestic Violence and with Sexual Harassment while in the Military," *Archives of Family Medicine* 4, no. 5 (1995): 411–418.

94. A. G. Sadler, B. M. Booth, D. Nielson, and B. N. Doebbeling, "Health-related Consequences of Physical and Sexual Violence: Women in the Military," *Obstetrics and Gynecology* 96, no. 3 (2000): 473–480.

95. David Collier, telephone conversation, April 13, 2010.

96. S. Erlanger, "A Tank's-Eye View of an Unpopular War," *New York Times* (August 1, 2010), 5, 8.

97. Canadian Broadcasting Corporation, "Military Launches Mental Health Awareness Campaign," June 27, 2009, http://www.cbc.ca/health/story/2009/06/25/military-campaign025.html?ref=rss.

98. D. G. Faust, *This Republic of Suffering: Death and the American Civil War* (New York: Knopf, 2008).

99. Shane, "A Flood of Troubled Soldiers Is in the Offing."

100. Glantz, *The War Comes Home*, 12.

101. T. Perry, "Marine Denies a Role in 12 Haditha Killings," *Los Angeles Times*, September 7, 2007, A9.

102. Anderson, "Bringing It All Back Home," 36–56, 63.

103. McNally, interviews of Huze, Rieckhoff, and Massey, *Battlefield Iraq*.

104. Ray Parrish, personal communication, September 10, 2008.

105. M. Mazzetti, "War's Risks Include Toll on Training Values," *New York Times*, June 4, 2006, A10.

106. Ibid.

107. P. Coleman, "Pentagon, Big Pharma: Drug Troops to Numb Them to Horrors of War," *Alternet.org*, January 10, 2008, http://www.democracymatters.org/site/apps/nlnet/content3.aspx?c=lgLUIXOwGnF&b=3793717&ct=4915929&notoc=1.

108. P. J. Riga, letter to the editor, *New York Times*, August 9, 2009, 7.

109. M. Twain, "The Private History of a Campaign That Failed," *Century Magazine*, December 1885.

110. J. Shay, *Odysseus in America: Combat Trauma and the Trials of Homecoming* (New York: Scribner, 2003).

111. V. Frankl, *Man's Search for Meaning: An Introduction to Logotherapy* (New York: Washington Square Press, 1959).

112. B. Jayamaha, W. D. Smith, J. Roebuck, O. Mora, E. Sandmeier, Y. Gray, and J. A. Murphy, "The War as We Saw It," *New York Times*, August 19, 2007, 11. The authors of the piece are all soldiers who were concerned about what they described as lies coming from Washington, which were making it seem that the successes were greater and the failures much lesser than they actually were. Some vets I interviewed told me they were expected to say they had brought democracy to Iraq, but they were almost powerless to provide the subsistence resources— food, electricity, water,

jobs, safety—that provide the chance to think about and *choose* democracy rather than just to cope and survive.

113. For instance, consider the cover-up of the killing of Pat Tillman by friendly fire and distortion of the story so that he appeared to have died heroically in fighting the enemy, as well as the distorted story that made Private Jessica Lynch look like a hero.

114. A. Madhani, "Court-Martial Weighed in Discipline Cases," *USA Today*, October 12, 2009, 9A.Ten soldiers testified that two sergeants regularly punished them with verbal abuse and grueling exercise and that a private who killed himself had been hazed and treated roughly by them. The U.S. Army was weighing whether to prosecute the sergeants for maltreatment and cruelty to their troops.

115. Glantz in *The War Comes Home* reports other reasons for feeling betrayed, including the false promises made to "weekend warriors" who had signed up for the National Guard and Reserves before these wars began, never expecting to go into combat and then being sent on long deployments in war zones; the Pentagon's broken promises to recruits of tens of thousands of dollars for a college education and that they would be able to attend college anywhere they were based; and the Bush administration's active scaling back of veterans' benefits, including the health insurance lost by many veterans, bringing to a total of six million the number of uninsured veterans or their families. R. A. Oppel, Jr., "Courting Sunnis, G.I.s Hope for Relative Safety" (*New York Times*, July 17, 2005, 1, 4), pointed out that the Bush administration early in the occupation of Iraq marginalized Sunni leaders suspected of having ties to insurgents but quickly switched to courting those same Sunnis, and some American soldiers took note of that switch as well as of the discovery that working with Sunnis with checkered histories could involve "trade-offs that would be unacceptable in a Western country," going against values that many soldiers felt they were in Iraq to protect and defend. And A. Huffington, "We Have a Winner: Big Business with Cozy Federal Deals Will Rebuild Iraq as Needs at Home Go Begging" (*Los Angeles Times*, March 19, 2003), noted that the Bush administration was handing out more than $1.5 billion in government contracts to U.S. companies that stood to make huge profits from the rebuilding of postwar Iraq. Several veterans I interviewed felt betrayed to be risking their lives while knowing of the obvious profit motive behind numerous war-related enterprises in their wars. These included a Vietnam vet who expressed the bitterness many soldiers in Vietnam felt when they learned that the enormous numbers of sandbags they were ordered to use had little or no purpose but that General William Westmoreland was a major stockholder in the company from which the government purchased them.

116. B. Lange, "The Train," in Jones, *A Soldier's Story*, 124.

117. Jones, "Reasons," in *A Soldier's Story*, 56.

118. B. Lange, "I Don't Fit In Here Anymore," in Jones, *A Soldier's Story*, 128.

119. See Glantz, *The War Comes Home.*

120. Ibid., 163.

121. J. Crawford, *The Last True Story I'll Ever Tell: An Accidental Soldier's Account of the War in Iraq* (New York: Riverhead Books, 2005).

122. S. Shem and J. Surrey, *We Have to Talk: Healing Dialogs between Men and Women* (New York: Basic Books, 1998).

123. President's Commission on Care for America's Returning Wounded Warriors, *Serve, Support, Simplify: Report of the President's Commission on Care for America's Returning Wounded Warriors* (Washington, DC: President's Commission, 2007), http://www.veteransforamerica.org/wp-content/uploads/2008/12/presidents-commission -on-care-for-americas-returning-wounded-warriors-report-july-2007.pdf.

124. Caplan, *THE NEW Don't Blame Mother.*

125. Glantz, *The War Comes Home.*

126. D. Filkins, "My Long War," *New York Times Magazine*, August 24, 2008, 37–43, quotation at 43.

127. Caplan, *THE NEW Don't Blame Mother.*

128. M. J. Friedman, P. P. Schnurr, and A. McDonagh-Coyle, "Posttraumatic Stress Disorder in the Military Veteran," *Psychiatric Clinics of North America* 17, no. 2 (1994): 265–277, quotation at 274.

129. Holmstedt, *The Girls Come Marching Home.*

130. See http://www.womensmemorial.org/PDFs/StatsonWIM.pdf.

131. Holmstedt in *The Girls Come Marching Home* describes women feeling the need to pull themselves together and not show fear or upset.

132. P. J. Caplan and J. B. Caplan, *Thinking Critically about Research on Sex and Gender*, 3rd. ed. (Boston: Allyn and Bacon, 2009). See especially Preface to Third Edition.

133. Carey, "The Struggle to Gauge a War's Psychological Cost."

134. Ibid.

135. Holmstedt, *The Girls Come Marching Home*, 186.

136. Ibid., 233:

she was wearing her neck brace and that made it difficult for him to hold her. She couldn't even lean back against her husband's chest. So the speed at which they usually reconnected after a deployment was slowed. Having a wounded spouse was hard on Jason. He was feeling somewhat helpless because there wasn't much he could do to make his wife feel better. . . . Snavely started feeling overwhelmed. . . . when it was quiet and the only sounds were the two dogs snoring, her emotions would get the best of her. . . . There's no doubt that Jason's experience as a Navy corpsman who had served in Iraq was helpful. Snavely didn't have to spend a lot of time explaining what was going on with her physically and emotionally. . . . When she had a nightmare, he didn't drill her about it. He'd just hug her, wipe her tears, and tell her that it was okay for her to cry, that it wasn't a sign of weakness.

137. Corbett, "The Women's War," 49.

138. L. Alvarez, "Wartime Soldier, Conflicted Mom," *New York Times*, September 26, 2009, http://www.nytimes.com/2009/09/27/us/27mothers.html.

139. Ibid.

140. D. St. George, "Limbs Lost to Enemy Fire, Women Forge a New Reality," *Washington Post*, April 18, 2006, http://www.washingtonpost.com/wp-dyn/content/article/2006/04/17/AR2006041701618_pf.html.

141. Associated Press, "Discharge from Army Relieves Mother," *New York Times*, March 8, 2009, 20.

142. Ibid.

143. Holmstedt, *The Girls Come Marching Home*, 79.

144. Alvarez, "Wartime Soldier, Conflicted Mom," 1, 22.

145. Ibid., 22.

146. Holmstedt, *The Girls Come Marching Home*.

147. S. Danish and B. Antonides, "What Counseling Psychologists Can Do to Help Returning Veterans," *Counseling Psychologist* 37, no. 8 (2009): 1076–1089.

148. Cozza et al., "Topics Specific to the Psychiatric Treatment of Military Personnel."

149. See, for example, T. Reid and M. Evans, "Officer Accuses US of Racism," *Times Online*, January 12, 2006, http://www.timesonline.co.uk/tol/news/world/iraq/article787622.ece; and M. Prysner, "Racism and U. S. War," Mike & Friends Blog, December 26, 2009, http://www.michaelmoore.com/words/mike-friends-blog/racism-and-us-war.

150. D. Holthouse, "A Few Bad Men," *Intelligence Report*, Summer 2006, 122, http://www.splcenter.org/get-informed/intelligence-report/browse-all-issues/2006/summer/a-few-bad-men; and idem, "'Killing a Brown': New Evidence of Extremists in the Military," *Intelligence Report*, Winter 2008, 132, http://www.splcenter.org/get-informed/intelligence-report/browse-all-issues/2008/winter/killing-a-brown.

151. Associated Press, "Army General Apologizes for Tattoo Strip Search: National Guard Soldiers Ordered to Remove Clothes while on Duty in Kuwait," June 27, 2007, http://www.msnbc.msn.com/id/19196511.

152. J. A. Ruhman, H. Boxeth, and C. R. Shagin, Banished Veterans Web site, http://www.banishedveterans.info.

153. Holmstedt, *The Girls Come Marching Home*.

154. W. Curtis, "A Military Strategy for Combating Institutional Racism," *Black Issues in Higher Education*, January 23, 1997, http://findarticles.com/p/articles/mi_m0DXK/is_n24_v13/ai_20055254.

155. Unpublished reports of this research are available from the author. We are currently preparing reports for publication.

156. Glantz, *The War Comes Home*.

157. T. Lewin, "Drafted at 19, Opposing Military Recruiters at 61," *New York Times*, May 10, 2009, 19.

158. Lucerito Ortiz, personal communication, April 4, 2010.

159. B. MacQuarrie, "The Weekend Warriors' War," *New York Times Magazine*, April 23, 2006, 54–70.

160. A. Kleinman, *What Really Matters: Living a Moral Life amid Uncertainty and Danger* (Oxford: Oxford University Press, 2006).

161. S. Burnett, "Vets Visit Carson, Say Army Failing Traumatized Troops," *Rocky Mountain News*, May 17, 2007.

162. Jones, "Sorry . . .?," in *A Soldier's Story*, 29.

Chapter 3

1. See, for example, David E. Jones's exquisite Web site, http://webspace.webring .com/people/l1/11bravovet/, with its poetry, music, and graphics that move the heart and enrich the soul. For prose examples, see P. Barker, *Regeneration* (London: Penguin, 2008).

2. N. Bunnin and J. Yu, eds., *The Blackwell Dictionary of Western Philosophy*. Hoboken, NJ: Wiley-Blackwell, 2004).

3. P. J. Caplan, *They Say You're Crazy: How the World's Most Powerful Psychiatrists Decide Who's Normal* (Reading, MA: Addison-Wesley, 1995). See also J. C. Norcross and M. R. Goldried, *Handbook of Psychotherapy Integration* (New York: Oxford University Press, 2003), 94–129.

4. *Science Daily*, "Is Technology Producing a Decline in Critical Thinking and Analysis?" January 29, 2009, http://www.sciencedaily.com/releases/2009/01/090128092341.htm.

5. L. Hudson, *The Cult of the Fact: A Psychologist's Autobiographical Critique of His Discipline* (New York: Harper & Row, 1972); and P. J. Caplan and J. B. Caplan, *Thinking Critically about Research on Sex and Gender*, 3rd ed. (Boston: Allyn and Bacon, 2009).

6. C. A. LeardMann, T. C. Smith, B. Smith, T. S. Wells, and M. A. K. Ryan, "Baseline Self-Reported Functional Health and Vulnerability to Post-traumatic Stress Disorder after Combat Deployment: Prospective US Military Cohort Study," *British Medical Journal* 338 (April 16, 2009), http://www.ncbi.nlm.nih.gov/pmc/articles/PMC2671472.

7. There are some wonderful exceptions to this, including even within the military and VA systems. These are discussed in chapter 6.

8. K. S. Pope and M. Vasquez, *Ethics in Psychotherapy and Counseling: A Practical Guide*, 3rd ed. (Hoboken, NJ: Jossey-Bass/John Wiley & Sons, 2007). The excerpt referred to here is available at http://kspope.com/apologies.php.

9. National Institute of Mental Health, 2010, http://www.nimh.nih.gov/health/publications/post-traumatic-stress-disorder-easy-to-read/index.shtml.

10. S. Keitt, "Post-traumatic Stress Disorder and the Female Soldier," press release, Society for Women's Health Research, February 19, 2009, http://www.womenshealthresearch.org/site/News2?page=NewsArticle&id=8153.

11. Dear Abby, "Vet Needs Help with Post-traumatic Stress," *News-Leader* (Springfield, MO), November 22, 2006, 4C.

12. S. J. Landers, "Suicide Hotline Lets Veterans—and Families—Dial for Help," *American Medical News*, August 25, 2008, http://www.ama-assn.org/amednews/2008/08/25/hlsc0825.htm.

13. M. Elias, "Post-traumatic Stress Is a War within the Body, for the Military and for Civilians," *USA Today*, October 27, 2008, http://www.usatoday.com/news/health/2008-10-26-PTSD-main_N.htm.

14. For instance, see Z. Imel, M. Malterer, K. McKay, and B. Wampold, "A Meta-analysis of Psychotherapy and Medication in Unipolar Depression and Dysthymia," *Journal of Affective Disorders* 110, no. 3 (2008): 197–206.

15. R. Rogers, "Raising an Army of Counselors; Returning Combat Troops, New Vets, Families Targeted," *San Diego Union-Tribune*, January 3, 2009, http://tinyurl.com/9u7cvn.

16. It is hard not to wonder what might be the effect if those three thousand therapists also mounted a visible protest against the wars that are propelling people to their offices.

17. Caplan, *They Say You're Crazy*.

18. M. Hogan, "Speaking out for Her Family: Molly Hogan Interview," *MindFreedom Journal*, Winter 2009–2010, 9.

19. A. Glantz, *The War Comes Home: Washington's Battle against America's Veterans* (Berkeley and Los Angeles: University of California Press, 2009).

20. Caplan, *They Say You're Crazy.*

21. R. Verdon, ed., "Unraveling Illness Is First Step to Recovery," *Menninger Perspective*, no. 2 (2007): 7–9, quotation at 8.

22. Ibid., 9.

23. Caplan, *They Say You're Crazy*; S. A. Kirk and H. Kutchins, *The Selling of DSM: The Rhetoric of Science in Psychiatry* (Piscataway, NJ: Aldine Transaction, 1992).

24. S. Satel, "To Fight Stigmas, Start with Treatment," *New York Times*, April 20, 2009, http://tinyurl.com/dmmha9.

25. A. Yawar, "The Fool on the Hill," *Lancet* 373 (2009): 621–622.

26. S. J. Cozza, D. M. Benedek, J. C. Bradley, T. A. Grieger, T. S. Nam, and D. A. Waldrep, "Topics Specific to the Psychiatric Treatment of Military Personnel," in *The Iraq War Clinician Guide*, 2nd ed., ed. R. G. Lande, B. A. Martin, J. I. Ruzek, et al. (Washington, DC: National Center for PTSD and the Department of Veterans Affairs, 2004), 4–20, quotation at 22, http://www.ptsd.va.gov/professional/manuals/iraq-war-clinician-guide.asp.

27. Ibid., 8.

28. Ibid., 8.

29. Ibid., 11.

30. B. L. Litz and S. M. Orsillo, "The Returning Veteran of the Iraq War," in *The Iraq War Clinician Guide*, 2nd ed., ed. R. G. Lande, B. A. Martin, J. I. Ruzek, et al. (Washington, DC: National Center for PTSD and the Department of Veterans Affairs, 2004), 21–32, quotations at 23, 34.

31. J. I. Ruzek, E. Curran, M. J. Friedman, et al., "Treatment of the Returning Iraq War Veteran," in *Iraq War Clinician Guide*, 2nd ed., ed. R. G. Lande, B. A. Martin, J. I. Ruzek, et al. (Washington, DC: National Center for PTSD and the Department of Veterans Affairs, 2004), http://ncptsd.va.gov/ncmain/ncdocs/fact_shts/treatment_ret_iraq.html?opm=1&rr=rr124&srt=d&echorr=true.

32. "Executive Summary," in *The Iraq War Clinician Guide*, 2nd ed., ed. R. G. Lande, B. A. Martin, J. I. Ruzek, et al. (Washington, DC: National Center for PTSD and the Department of Veterans Affairs), http://www.ptsd.va.gov/professional/manuals/iraq-war-clinician-guide.asp.

33. See discussion in Caplan, *They Say You're Crazy.*

34. E. Watters, "The Americanization of Mental Illness," *New York Times Magazine*, January 8, 2010, http://www.nytimes.com/2010/01/10/magazine/10psyche-t.html?pagewanted=all.

35. Caplan, *They Say You're Crazy.*

36. Rogers, "Raising an Army of Counselors."

37. Elias, "Post-traumatic Stress Is a War within the Body."

38. D. Miles, "Officials Report Progress, Challenges in Treating Combat Stress," Armed Forces Information Service, Washington, DC, July 28, 2005.

39. E. Goode, "When Minds Snap," *New York Times*, November 8, 2009, 1, 4, quotation at 4.

40. M. J. Friedman, P. P. Schnurr, and A. McDonagh-Coyle, "Post-traumatic Stress Disorder in the Military Veteran," *Psychiatric Clinics of North America* 17, no. 22 (1994): 265–277, quotation at 271.

41. M. Linder, "Constructing Post-traumatic Stress Disorder: A Case Study of the History, Sociology, and Politics of Psychiatric Classification," in *Bias in Psychiatric Diagnosis*, ed. P. J. Caplan and L. Cosgrove (Lanham, MD: Rowman and Littlefield, 2004), 25–40.

42. American Psychiatric Association, *Diagnostic and Statistical Manual of Mental Disorders–III* (Washington, DC: APA, 1980).

43. Caplan, *They Say You're Crazy*, and Caplan and Cosgrove, *Bias in Psychiatric Diagnosis*.

44. American Psychiatric Association, *Diagnostic and Statistical Manual of Mental Disorders–IV* (Washington, DC: APA, 1994).

45. Glantz, *The War Comes Home*.

46. Litz and Orsillo, "The Returning Veteran of the Iraq War," 21–32.

47. M. deYoanna, and M. Benjamin, "'I Am under a Lot of Pressure to Not Diagnose PTSD': A Secret Recording Reveals the Army May Be Pushing Its Medical Staff Not to Diagnose Post-traumatic Stress Disorder. The Army and Senate Have Ignored the Implications," April 8, 2009, http://www.salon.com/news/special/coming _home/2009/04/08/tape/print.html.

48. J. Schogol, "Pentagon: No Purple Heart for PTSD," *Stars and Stripes* (European edition), January 6, 2009, http://www.stripes.com/article.asp?section=104&arti cle=59810.

49. American Psychiatric Association, *Diagnostic and Statistical Manual of Mental Disorders–IV*.

50. Caplan, *They Say You're Crazy*, and Linder, "Constructing Post-traumatic Stress Disorder," 25–40.

51. R. L. Spitzer, G. M. Rosen, and S. O. Lilienfeld, "Revisiting the Institute of Medicine Report on the Validity of Posttraumatic Stress Disorder," *Comprehensive Psychiatry* 49, no. 4 (2008): 319–320.

52. G. C. Lasiuk and K. M. Hegadoren, "Posttraumatic Stress Disorder: Part II. Development of the Construct within the North American Psychiatric Taxonomy," *Perspectives in Psychiatric Care*, May 2006, http://findarticles.com/p/articles/mi_qa3804/is_200605/ai_n17187842.

53. Caplan, *They Say You're Crazy*.

54. W. D. Spaulding, M. E. Sullivan, and J. S. Poland, *Treatment and Rehabilitation of Severe Mental Illness* (New York: Guilford, 2003).

55. E. Watters, "The Way We Live Now: Idea Lab: Suffering Differently," *New York Times Magazine*, August 12, 2007, http://query.nytimes.com/gst/fullpage.html?res=9A05EEDD113BF931A2575BC0A9619C8B63&sec=&spon=&pagewanted=1.

56. D. Summerfield, "A Critique of Seven Assumptions behind Psychological Trauma Programmes in War-Affected Areas," *Social Science & Medicine* 48 (1999): 1449–1462.

57. Ibid., 1455.

58. Linder, "Constructing Post-traumatic Stress Disorder," 25–40.

59. Caplan, *They Say You're Crazy*.

60. C. North et al., "Toward Validation of the Diagnosis of Posttraumatic Stress Disorder," *American Journal of Psychiatry* 166 (2009): 34–41.

61. Caplan, *They Say You're Crazy*.

62. D. Jacobs and D. Cohen, "Hidden in Plain Sight: *DSM–IV*'s Rejection of the Categorical Approach to Diagnosis," *Review of Existential Psychology and Psychiatry* 26 (2001): 81–96.

63. Ibid.

64. P. J. Caplan, "Call Me Crazy," theater script, 1996, available from author.

65. See http://www.google.com/search?client=safari&rls=en&q=permutation+formula+calculator&ie=UTF-8&oe=UTF-8.

66. Caplan, *They Say You're Crazy*.

67. Ibid.

68. Ibid., and M. Linder, "The Construction of Illness," in Caplan and Cosgrove, *Bias in Psychiatric Diagnosis*, 3–7. See also J. Poland and P. J. Caplan, "The Deep Structure of Bias in Psychiatric Diagnosis," in Caplan and Cosgrove, *Bias in Psychiatric Diagnosis*, 9–23.

69. Poland and Caplan, "The Deep Structure of Bias in Psychiatric Diagnosis."

70. Caplan and Caplan, *Thinking Critically about Research on Sex and Gender*, chap. 7.

71. Yawar, "The Fool on the Hill."

72. Caplan and Caplan, *Thinking Critically about Research on Sex and Gender*, 60.

73. United States Institute of Medicine, "Military Personnel with Traumatic Brain Injury at Risk for Serious Long-Term Health Problems," December 4, 2008, http://www.nap.edu.

74. Caplan and Caplan, *Thinking Critically about Research on Sex and Gender*, 58.

75. Ibid., 60.

76. Ibid., chap. 7.

77. W. Uttal, *The New Physiology: The Limits of Localizing Cognitive Processes in the Brain* (Cambridge, MA: MIT Press, 2001).

78. M. Hutson, "Neuro-realism," *New York Times*, December 9, 2007.

79. Caplan and Caplan, *Thinking Critically about Research on Sex and Gender*: in chapter 7 we describe in detail some of the major problems with knowing what we can learn from research about relationships between the brain and behavior or emotions.

80. E. A. Maguire, D. G. Gadian, I. S. Johnsrude, C. D. Good, J. Ashburner, R. S. Frackowiak, et al. "Navigation-Related Structural Change in the Hippocampi of Taxi Drivers," *Proceedings of the National Academy of Sciences of the United States of America* 97, no. 8 (2000): 4398–4403.

81. Elias, "Post-traumatic Stress Is a War within the Body."

82. P. J. Caplan, "Emotional Well-being," in *Our bodies, Ourselves* (New York: Simon & Schuster, 2005), 82–95.

83. Ibid.

84. A. Hochschild, *The Second Shift* (New York: Penguin, 1989).

85. P. Hanlon, "Prescription Drug Use for Mental Health Diagnoses on the Rise," *New England Psychologist*, August–September 2009, 8.

86. In *They Say You're Crazy* and elsewhere, I have written about the ways that the traditional therapy framework can make it hard for people to leave their therapist even if that therapy is failing to help them. This includes rigidly attributing the lack of progress to the patient's "resistance" or "trouble with authority figures." (It's not to say that these factors never operate but rather that it is too easy for therapists to blame their patients when therapy does not go well.).

87. J. D. Kraemer and L. O. Gostin, "Science, Politics, and Values: The Politicization of Professional Practice Guidelines," *Journal of the American Medical Association* 301, no. 6 (2009): 665–667.

88. M. Shuchman, "Spilling the Beans on the Pharmaceutical Industry," *Canadian Medical Association Journal* 179, no. 12 (2008), http://www.cmaj.ca/cgi/content/full/179/12/1309?etoc.

89. C. Goldberg, "Firms Tied to Some MDs Who Set Policy; Treatment Advice Focuses on Drugs, Researchers Find," *Boston Globe*, April 2, 2009, http://tinyurl.com/cysns5: "Virtually all the psychiatrists who wrote the latest clinical guidelines for how to treat depression, bipolar disorder, and schizophrenia had financial ties to drug companies."

90. American Psychiatric Association, *Diagnostic and Statistical Manual of Mental Disorders–IV*.

91. B. Carey and G. Harris, "Psychiatric Group Faces Scrutiny over Drug Ties," *New York Times*, July 12, 2008, http://www.nytimes.com/2008/07/12/washington/12psych.html?_r=1&pagewanted=print.

92. S. Rust and J. Fauber, "Are Doctors' Loyalties Divided? Drug Firms' Cash Skews Doctor Classes; Company-funded UW Courses Often Favor Medicine, Leave out Side Effects," *Milwaukee Journal Sentinel*, March 30, 2009, http://www.jsonline.com/news/42064977.html. See also E. Ramshaw, "University of Texas Officials Vow to Strengthen Ethics Rules for Researchers," *Dallas Morning News*, February 11, 2009, http://www.dallasnews.com/sharedcontent/dws/news/texassouthwest/stories/021209dntexresearchpolicy.77399bc.html.

93. D. Wilson, "Drug Maker Said to Pay Ghostwriters for Journal Articles," *New York Times*, December 13, 2008, http://www.nytimes.com/2008/12/12/business/13wyeth.html The article includes this: "The World Association of Medical Editors says ghost authorship—which it defines as a substantial contribution not mentioned in the manuscript—is 'dishonest and unacceptable.'"

94. *Medical News Today*, "Unfavorable Results of Clinical Trials Often Go Unpublished," January 21, 2009, http://www.medicalnewstoday.com/articles/136134.php.

95. *Medical News Today*, "New Study Finds Publication Bias among Trials Submitted to FDA," November 25, 2008, http://www.medicalnewstoday.com/articles/130606.php.

96. See Caplan, *They Say You're Crazy*, for a review. See also North et al., "Toward Validation of the Diagnosis of Posttraumatic Stress Disorder," who describe the vast majority of categories in the *DSM* as not having been scientifically validated.

97. *Medical News Today*, "Grassley, Dingell Call for Overhaul of FDA, Say Agency Should Be Able to Levy Fines, order Recalls, Limit Drug Industry Advertising," July 31, 2008, http://www.medicalnewstoday.com/articles/116749.php. See also J. A. Favole, "FDA Says It Erred on Doctor," *Wall Street Journal*, February 24, 2009, http://online.wsj.com/article/SB123544421394356087.html. This is an account of the FDA

barring from a drug-approval meeting a doctor known to be critical of the drug, which has been linked to "dangerous internal bleeding."

98. For instance, see a recent report that as the economy worsens, and people lose jobs while prices rise, they flock to see psychotherapists: A. Weston, "More People Seek Therapy as Economy Falters," *St. Joseph* (MO) *News-Press*, December 31, 2008, http://findarticles.com/p/news-articles/st-joseph-news-press/mi_8070/is_20081231/seek-therapy-economy-falters/ai_n47905622. Although one would not want to deny emotional support to people who are frightened about their economic situation, this article illustrates the tendency in the United States to consider everything except happiness a mental illness and therapists the answer to all troubles. In this case it is hard not to wonder what might happen to the economy if those who have lost their jobs or fear that they will would, instead of spending time and money on therapists, organize some political action aimed at providing more jobs, for instance, or even helped each other find jobs or started small businesses together.

99. Summerfield, "A Critique of Seven Assumptions behind Psychological Trauma Programmes," 1461.

100. U.S. Department of Defense, "Army Creates Suicide Prevention Task Force During "Stand Down,'" press release, March 6, 2009, http://www.defense.gov/news/newsarticle.aspx?id=53378

101. K. Goetz, "Troubled Veteran's Call Leads to Firing; VA Patients Lament Loss of Psychologist," *Commercial Appeal* (Memphis,TN), 2009, http://tinyurl.com/awavgy.

102. B. T. Litz, M. J. Gray, R. A. Bryant, and A. B. Adler, "Early Intervention for Trauma: Current Status and Future Directions," *Clinical Psychology: Science and Practice* 9 (Summer 2002): 112–130: "Many empirical questions pertaining to PD [psychological debriefing, the most common early intervention used for traumatized people] have not been subjected to scrutiny" (130).

103. Yawar, "The Fool on the Hill."

104. C. Courtois and J. Ford, eds., *Treating Complex Traumatic Stress Disorders: An Evidence-based Guide* (New York: Guilford Press, 2009).

105. David Collier, personal communication, April 13, 2010.

106. Caplan, *They Say You're Crazy.*

107. For instance, see G. Waller, "Evidence-Based Treatment and Therapist Drift," *Behavior Research and Therapy* 47, no. 2 (April 5, 2009). He describes the way that therapists trying to implement cognitive-behavioral therapy, one kind of approach often described as helpful to veterans, often fail to "implement the full range of tasks that are necessary for CBT to be effective." This kind of difference between what is seen in research and what happens in clinical practice is common, because clinicians, being human, are fallible.

108. A. E. Kazdin, "Evidence-Based Treatment and Practice: New Opportunities to Bridge Clinical Research and Practice, Enhance the Knowledge Base, and Improve Patient Care," *American Psychologist* 63, no. 3 (2008): 146–159.

109. Ibid., 149.

110. Litz et al., "Early Intervention for Trauma," write, "Many empirical questions pertaining to PD [psychological debriefing, the most common early intervention used for traumatized people] have not been subjected to scrutiny" (130).

111. Kazdin, "Evidence-Based Treatment and Practice," 149.

112. Ibid.

113. Ibid., 153.

114. Ibid., 150.

115. A. Kazdin, "Competence in Clinical Practice, Quality of Care, and the Burden of Mental Illness," *The Specialist (American Board of Professional Psychology)*, 2010: 13–16, quotation at 14.

116. J. Kreisman, "The Mythology of Evidence-Based Medicine," *Psychiatric Times*, February 4, 2010, http://www.psychiatrictimes.com/blog/couchincrisis/content/article/10168/1518990?verify=0.

117. N. S. Reiss, "Today's Psychiatrists Less Likely to Provide Psychotherapy Than Ever Before," *MentalHelp.net*, August 5, 2008, http://www.mentalhelp.net/poc/view_doc.php?type=doc&id=28897&cn=91. See also M. Moran, "Psychiatrists Lament Decline of Key Treatment Modality," *Psychiatric News* 44, no. 13 (2009): 8, http://pn.psychiatryonline.org/content/44/13/8.1.full; and N. Shnitzler, "Survey Shows Talk Therapy on the Decline," *New England Psychologist*, November 2008, 1.

118. G. Miller, "Is Pharma Running Out of Brainy Ideas?," *Science* 329, no. 5991 (July 30, 2010): 502–504.

119. G. Miller, "This Is Your Brain Off Drugs: Why Pharma May Be Cooling on Psychiatry Drugs," American Association for the Advancement of Science's *Science Insider* (July 28, 2010), http://news.sciencemag.org/scienceinsider/2010/07/this-is-your-brain-off-drugs-why.html.

120. S. Corbett, "The Women's War," *New York Times Magazine*, March 18, 2007, 40–55, 71–72, quotation at 72.

121. Ibid.

122. S. Corbett, "The Permanent Scars of Iraq," *New York Times Magazine*, February 15, 2004, 34–41, 56, 60, 66.

123. Glantz, *The War Comes Home*, 157.

124. S. Anderson, "Bringing It All Back Home," *New York Times Magazine*, May 28, 2006, 36–56, 63.

125. K. Holmstedt, *The Girls Come Marching Home: Stories of Women Warriors Returning from the War in Iraq* (Mechanicsburg, PA: Stackpole Books, 2009), 155.

126. Ibid., 288.

127. M. J. Friedman, C. L. Donnelly, and T. A. Mellman, "Pharmacotherapy for PTSD," *Psychiatric Annals* 33 (2003): 57–62, quotation at 58.

128. Yawar, "The Fool on the Hill."

129. R. Whitaker, *Mad in America: Bad Science, Bad Medicine, and the Enduring Mistreatment of the Mentally Ill* (New York: Perseus Books, 2002). See also J. Moncrieff, *The Myth of the Chemical Cure: A Critique of Psychiatric Drug Treatment* (Hampshire, UK: Palgrave Macmillan, 2008).

130. B. Stutz, "Self-nonmedication," *New York Times*, May 6, 2007, http://www.nytimes.com/2007/05/06/magazine/06antidepressant-t.html.

131. Serotonin is probably the one most frequently written about, but very little is known for certain about how serotonin works on its own and, as in the actual brain, in combination with a host of other chemicals.

132. R. Whitaker, *Anatomy of an Epidemic: Magic Bullets, Psychiatric Drugs, and the Astonishing Rise of Mental Illness in American* (New York: Crown, 2010).

133. S. Hyman, "Initiation and Adaptation: A Paradigm for Understanding Psychotropic Drug Action," *American Journal of Psychiatry* 153 (1996): 151–161.

134. G. I. Spielmans, S. A. Thielges, A. L. Dent, and R. P. Greenberg, "The Accuracy of Psychiatric Medication Advertisements in Medical Journals," *Journal of Nervous and Mental Disease* 196, no. 4 (2008): 267–273.

135. R. P. Greenberg, "Prescriptive Authority in the Face of Research Revelations," *American Psychologist* 65, no. 2 (2010): 136–137; and R. P. Greenberg and S. Fisher, "Examining Antidepressant Effectiveness," in *The Limits of Biological Treatments for Psychological Distress: Comparisons with Psychotherapy and Placebo*, ed. S. Fisher and R. P. Greenberg (Hillsdale, NJ: Lawrence Erlbaum, 1989), 1–37.

136. E. H. Turner, A. M. Matthews, E. Linardatos, R. A. Tell, and R. Rosenthal, "Selective Publication of Antidepressant Trials and Its Influence on Apparent Efficacy," *New England Journal of Medicine* 358, no. 3 (2008): 252–260.

137. J. M. Donohue, M. Cevasco, and M. B. Rosenthal, "A Decade of Direct-to-Consumer Advertising of Prescription Drugs," *New England Journal of Medicine* 357, no. 7 (2007): 673–681.

138. W. Bergera, M. V. Mendlowicza, C. Marques-Portellaa, G. Kinrysc, L. F. Fontenellea, C. R. Marmard, and I. Figueiraa, "Pharmacologic Alternatives to Antidepres-

sants in Posttraumatic Stress Disorder: A Systematic Review," *Progress in Neuro-Psychopharmacology and Biological Psychiatry* 33, no. 2 (2009): 169–180.

139. M. Thompson, "America's Medicated Army," *Time*, June 16, 2008, 38–42, quotation at 39.

140. C. R. Figley and W. P. Nash, *Combat Stress Injury: Theory, Research, and Management* (London: Routledge, 2006), 219.

141. Thompson, "America's Medicated Army."

142. Ibid.

143. Ibid., 42.

144. R. Verdon, ed., "Extensive Testing Is Precursor to Treatment," *Menninger Perspective*, no. 2 (2007): 10–11, at 10.

145. P. J. Caplan and E. H. Cohen, "Safety First," *New Scientist,* August 11, 2007, 19, published online as "Rules for New Drug Development Need a Serious Overhaul," http://www.newscientist.com/channel/health/mg19526165.900-rules-for-new-drug -development-need-a-serious-overhaul.html;jsessionid=APBDNHFNKHNB.

146. David Collier, personal communication, May 12, 2010.

Chapter 4

1. Paula J. Caplan, "Vets Aren't Crazy; War Is," *Tikkun*, September–October 2007, 44–48, http://www.tikkun.org/magazine/tik0709/frontpage/vets.

2. J. Gettleman, "Soldier Accused as Coward Says He Is Guilty Only of Panic Attack," *New York Times*, November 6, 2003, http://www.nytimes.com/2003/11/06/us/ soldier-accused-as-coward-says-he-is-guilty-only-of-panic-attack.html?pagewanted =1; and Associated Press, "Army Drops Cowardice Charge against Soldier," December 30, 2003, http://www.msnbc.msn.com/id/3840267.

3. M. Glassman, "The Changing Battlefield: When Grace Flees under Fire," *New York Times*, July 25, 2004. http://www.nytimes.com/2004/07/25/weekinreview/ the-changing-battlefield-when-grace-flees-under-fire.html.

4. J. Diedrich, "Carson Soldier Faces Charge of Cowardice," *Gazette* (Colorado Springs, CO), October 30, 2003.

5. René Robichaux, telephone conversation, May 13, 2010.

6. E. Schmit, "How to Stop the Killing When the Troops Come Home," *New York Times*, May 11, 2003, 4.

7. P. J. Caplan, "Ambiguity, Powerlessness, and the Psychologizing of Trauma: How Backlash Affects Work with Trauma Survivors," *Journal of Trauma Practice* 5 (2006): 5–24.

8. A. Ohman, A. Eriksson, and C. Olofsson, "One-Trial Learning and Superior Resistance to Extinction of Autonomic Responses Conditioned to Potentially Phobic Stimuli," *Journal of Comparative Physiology and Psychology* 88, no. 2 (1975): 619–627.

9. J. D. Holloway, "Psychologists Help Reduce Stress in the Military," *American Psychologist*, February 2004, 33.

10. S. Corbett, "The Permanent Scars of Iraq," *New York Times Magazine*, February 15, 2004, 34–41, 56, 60, 66.

11. R. G. Lande, B. A. Marin, J. I. Ruzek, et al., eds., *The Iraq War Clinician Guide*, 2nd ed. (Washington, DC: National Center for PTSD and the Department of Veterans Affairs, 2004), http://www.ptsd.va.gov/professional/manuals/iraq-war-clinician -guide.asp.

12. Ibid., 10.

13. Ibid., 18.

14. Ibid., 42.

15. W. Bergera, M. V. Mendlowicza, C. Marques-Portellaa, G. Kinrysc, L. F. Fontenellea, C. R. Marmard, and I. Figueiraa, "Pharmacologic Alternatives to Antidepressants in Posttraumatic Stress Disorder: A Systematic Review," *Progress in Neuro-Psychopharmacology and Biological Psychiatry* 33, no. 2 (2009): 169–180.

16. J. McManamy, "FDA Antidepressant Suicide Warning," McMan's Depression and Bipolar Web, http://www.mcmanweb.com/FDA_suicide.htm. See also P. J. Caplan, "The Pills That Make Us Fat," *New Scientist*, March 8, 2008, 18–19.

17. S. Shane, "A Flood of Troubled Soldiers Is in the Offing, Experts Predict," *New York Times*, December 16, 2004.

18. Ibid.

19. Ibid.

20. A. Albernaz, "Assessments Slated for Returning Soldiers," *New England Psychologist*, May 2005, 7.

21. Associated Press, "Army: Mental Health Better for Soldiers in Iraq," July 20, 2005, http://www.cnn.com/2005/HEALTH/07/20/military.health.ap/index.html.

22. D. Miles, "Officials Report Progress, Challenges in Treating Combat Stress," Armed Forces Information Service, Washington, DC, July 28, 2005.

23. Ibid.

24. C. Gage, "Harriet Tubman Visits a Therapist," in *Off-Off Broadway Festival Plays, Twenty-Third Series* (Samuel French, Inc., NYC, 1999).

25. M. Cramer, and J. Adam, "Screening Is Urged on Return from Iraq," *Boston Globe*, August 16, 2005, B3.

26. P. J. Caplan, *They Say You're Crazy: How the World's Most Powerful Psychiatrists Decide Who's Normal* (Reading, MA: Addison-Wesley, 1995).

27. S. F. Dingfelder, "Stigma: Alive and Well" (*Monitor on Psychology*, June 2009, 56–60), reports that despite decades of antistigma campaigns, people may be more fearful of those with mental illness than ever. At least a partial explanation for this is that the increased emphasis over time on emotional problems as *diseases* makes those diagnosed with mental illness even more stigmatized as before, even while antistigma campaigns have been carried out. I also wonder if the increased insistence on defining emotional problems as "broken brains" makes people even more frightened of those diagnosed with mental illnesses. See also E. Watters, "The Americanization of Mental Illness" (*New York Times Magazine*, January 8, 2010, http://www.nytimes.com/2010/01/10/magazine/10psyche-t.html?pagewanted=all), who reports that people are actually treated more harshly when their problems are described as diseases: "Even as we have congratulated ourselves for becoming more 'benevolent and supportive' of the mentally ill, we have steadily backed away from the sufferers themselves" (44).

28. N. Fick, "Coming Home—to What?," *Boston Globe*, August 28, 2005.

29. Ibid.

30. Ibid.

31. W. P. Nash, "Operational Stress Control and Readiness (OSCAR): The United States Marine Corps Initiative to Deliver Mental Health Services to Operating Forces," in *Human Dimensions in Military Operations—Military Leaders' Strategies for Addressing Stress and Psychological Support* (25-1-25–10), Meeting Proceedings RTO-MP-HFM-134, Paper 25 (Neuilly-sur-Seine, France: RTO, 2006), http://www.rto.nato.int/abstracts.asp.

32. B. Carey, "The Struggle to Gauge a War's Psychological Cost," *New York Times*, November 26, 2005.

33. Caplan, "Ambiguity, Powerlessness, and the Psychologizing of Trauma."

34. Jeffrey Poland, personal communication, May 6, 2010.

35. I. Pivar, "Traumatic Grief: Symptomatology and Treatment in the Iraq War Veteran," in *The Iraq War Clinician Guide*, 2nd ed., ed. R. G. Lande, B. A. Marin, J. I. Ruzek, et al. (Washington, DC: National Center for PTSD and the Department of Veterans Affairs), 75–78, http://www.ptsd.va.gov/professional/manuals/iraq-war-clinician-guide.asp.

36. C. Munsey, "Soldier Support," *Monitor on Psychology*, April 2006, 36–38.

37. D. Zwerdling, "Soldiers Face Obstacles to Mental Health Services," NPR, December 4, 2006. http://www.npr.org/templates/story/story,php?storyID=6575431.

38. L. Chedekel and M. Kaufman, "Army's Suicide Struggles Continue: 2006 Rate of Self-Inflicted Deaths in Iraq Could Exceed Record Set in 2005," *Hartford Courant*, July 31, 2007.

39. Ibid.

40. C. M. Sennott, "Told to Wait, a Marine Dies: VA Care in Spotlight after Iraq War Veteran's Suicide," *Boston Globe*, February 11, 2007, http://www.boston.com/news/nation/articles/2007/02/11/told_to_wait_a_marine_dies.

41. S. Borenstein, "Panel: Military System Needs Help," *Houston Chronicle*, February 26, 2007.

42. R. E. Gill, "Military Needs Civilian Psychologists," *National Psychologist* 16, no. 3 (2007), http://nationalpsychologist.com/articles/art_v16n3_2.htm.

43. S. Burnett, "Vets Visit Carson, Say Army Failing Traumatized Troops," *Rocky Mountain News*, May 17, 2007.

44. D. Gellene, "War Boosts `Baby Blues' Risk," *Los Angeles Times*, May 26, 2007, http://articles.latimes.com/2007/may/26/science/sci-postpartum26.

45. K. Edmonds, ed., *Dewhurst's Textbook of Obstetrics and Gynecology*, 7th ed. (Hoboken, NJ: Wiley-Blackwell, 2007).

46. P. Jeninek, "Army Plans to Hire More Psychiatrists," June 15, 2007, Associated Press.

47. Associated Press, "Pentagon May Drop Mental Health Question," June 18, 2007.

48. A. Hull and D. Priest, "Little Relief on Ward 53," *Washington Post*, June 18, 2007, http://www.washingtonpost.com/wp-dyn/content/article/2007/06/17/AR2007061701351.html.

49. K. Roberts, "Army Starts Stress Program But Lacks Resources," Reuters, July 17, 2007.

50. C. Munsey, "Helping and Healing," *Monitor on Psychology*, September 2007, 42–46.

51. Ibid., 42.

52. Ibid.,44.

53. J. Price, "U.S. Troops in Iraq More Willing to Seek Help for Stress," McClatchy-Tribune News Service, October 30, 2007.

54. G. Fuentes, "New Mental Health teams Set to Deploy with I MEF," *Marine Corps Times*, December 25, 2007.

55. C. Vanover, "Seeking Mental Health Help Shows Courage, Officials Say," American Forces Press Service, September 8, 2008.

56. P. Coleman, "Pentagon, Big Pharma: Drug Troops to Numb Them to Horrors of War," *Alternet.org*, January 10, 2008, http://www.democracymatters.org/site/apps/nlnet/content3.aspx?c=lgLUIXOwGnF&b=3793717&ct=4915929&notoc=1.

57. *MedicineNet.com*, "Medications and Drugs: Propranolol," http://www.medicinenet.com/propranolol/article.htm.

58. Pivar, "Traumatic Grief, Symptomatology and Treatment in the Iraq War Veteran," 75–78.

59. Coleman, "Pentagon, Big Pharma: Drug Troops."

60. Ibid.

61. Ibid.

62. Ibid.

63. M. Thompson, "America's Medicated Army," *Time*, June 5, 2008, http://www.time.com/time/nation/article/0,8599,1811858,00.html.

64. S. Liewer, "Virtual Reality Goes to War vs. Stress Disorder," *San Diego Tribune*, September 9, 2008, http://legacy.signonsandiego.com/news/military/20080909-9999-1n9virtual.html.

65. A. S. Tyson, "Army's Life-or-Death Drama: To Combat Suicides, Service Introduces Interactive Video," *Washington Post*, October 8, 2008, http://www.washingtonpost.com/wp-dyn/content/article/2008/10/07/AR2008100702780_pf.html

66. Ibid.

67. L. C. Daldor, "Bases Brace for Surge in Stress-Related Disorders," Associated Press, November 30, 2008.

68. Ibid.

69. J. Weissmann, "Veterans with PTSD Sue Federal Government over Disability Benefits," The BLT: The Blog of Legal Times, December 18, 2008, http://www.law.com/jsp/law/LawArticleFriendly.jsp?id=1202426843315.

70. A. Geracimos, "Military Marches toward Mental Health," *Washington Times*, December 3, 2008, http://www.washingtontimes.com/news/2008/dec/02/military-marches-toward-wellness.

71. G. Zoroya, "Army May End Counseling Notifications," *USA Today*, January 12, 2009, http://www.usatoday.com/news/military/2009-01-11-notifications_N.htm?csp=34.

72. R. Rogers, "Raising an Army of Counselors: Returning Combat Troops, New Vets, Families Targeted," *San Diego Union-Tribune*, January 3, 2009, http://tinyurl .com/9u7cvn.

73. For instance, as reported by L. Alvarez and D. Frosch, "A Focus on Violence by Returning G.I.'s" (*New York Times*, January 2, 2009, http://www.nytimes .com/2009/01/02/us/02veterans.html?_r=1): "Domestic violence among Fort Carson soldiers has become more prevalent since the Iraq war began in 2003. In 2006, Fort Carson soldiers were charged in 57 cases of domestic violence, according to figures released by the base. As of mid-December, the number had grown to 145. Rape and sexual assault cases against soldiers have also increased, from 10 in 2006 to 38 as of mid-December, the highest tally since the war began. Both domestic violence and rape are crimes that are traditionally underreported."

74. Ibid.

75. Ibid.

76. U.S. Department of Defense, "U.S. Army Releases 2008 Suicide Data, Highlights Efforts to Prevent Suicide," press release, January 29, 2009.

77. Ibid.

78. René Robichaux, telephone conversation, May 13, 2010.

79. J. J. Kruzel, "General Does Part to Reduce Mental Health Stigma," American Forces Press Service, February 4, 2009.

80. J. Schogol, "Pentagon Hopes Stories Help Troops with PTSD," *Stars and Stripes*, February 9, 2009, http://www.stripes.com/article.asp?section=104&article=60587.

81. M. LaPlante, "Suicide Has Claimed 10 Utah Guard Members since 2005," *Salt Lake City Tribune*, February 5, 2009, http://www.sltrib.com/news/ci_11620245.

82. Ibid.

83. U.S. Department of Defense, "Army Creates Suicide Prevention Task Force during 'Stand Down,'" press release, March 6, 2009.

84. U.S. Department of Defense, "'Super Coaches' to Assist Servicemembers with Psychological Problems," press release, March 24, 2009.

85. U.S. Department of Defense. "Program Offers Confidential Counseling for Troops, Families," press release, April 2, 2009.

86. M. Benjamin and M. de Yoanna, "Tales of the Secret Army Tape," *Salon.com*, April 9, 2009, http://www.salon.com/news/special/coming_home/2009/04/09/ptsd/ index.html.

87. Ibid.

88. J. Garamone, "Tragedy Highlights Need for Mental Health Help, Casey says," American Forces Press Service, May 14, 2009, http://www.militaryconnection.com/news%5Cmay-2009%5Ctragedy-mental-health.html.

89. R. H. Reid, "Army Fights Stigma of Mental Care in Iraq," Associated Press, May 18, 2009.

90. U.S. Department of Defense, "Army Leaders Struggle to Understand Record Suicides," press release, June 24, 2009.

91. G. Zoroya, "Troops' Kids Feel War Toll," USA Today, June 26, 2009.

92. B. Lewis, "New PTSD Program Answers Need for Comprehensive Treatment," Landstuhl Regional Medical Center Public Affairs, July 4, 2009. In a personal communication on May 14, 2010, Dr. Sharon Stewart, who works in the program, said they also use mindfulness techniques.

93. Sharon Stewart, personal communication, May 14, 2010.

94. Ibid.

95. Ibid.

96. Ibid.

97. G. Zoroya, "Monitoring Faulted in Rise of Soldier Suicides," USA Today, July 13, 2009, http://www.usatoday.com/news/military/2009-07-12-suicide_N.htm?csp=34.

98. Ibid.

99. S. Waterman, "Combat Psychology," Washington Times, July 23, 2009, http://www.washingtontimes.com/news/2009/jul/23/combat-psychology.

100. G. Zoroya, "Program Aims to Curb Marine Suicides," USA Today, July 28, 2009, http://www.usatoday.com/news/military/2009-07-27-marinesuicide_N.htm?csp=34.

101. U.S. Department of Defense, "Uncertainty about Military Suicides Frustrates Services," press release, July 30, 2009.

102. U.S. Department of Defense, "Army Releases July Suicide Data," press release, August 13, 2009.

103. U.S. Department of Defense, "DoD Establishes Suicide Prevention Task Force," press release, August 31, 2009.

104. U.S. Department of Defense, "Army Aims to Improve Soldiers' Mental Well-being," press release, September 16, 2009.

105. Ibid.

106. U.S. Department of Defense, "Army Continues Focus on Suicide Prevention," press release, October 13, 2009.

107. Ibid.

108. U.S. Department of Defense, "Mental Health Pros Meet to Consider Treatments," press release, November 3, 2009.

109. U.S. Department of Defense, "Center Assesses Psychological Trauma Treatments," press release, November 4, 2009.

110. B. Carey and D. Cave, "Who'll Counsel the Counselors? Military Faces Therapy Overload," *New York Times*, November 8, 2009, 1, 27.

111. Ibid., 27.

112. Ibid., 27.

113. G. Zoroya, "Therapists Deployed to War Zone to Fight Stress Disorders," *USA Today*, November 8, 2009, http://www.usatoday.com/news/military/2009-11-08-therapists-sent-into-war-zones_N.htm?csp=34#open-share-help.

114. A. Chang, "Military Experiment Seeks to Predict PTSD," *Washington Post*, November 20, 2009, http://bit.ly/4gXOhW.

115. K. M. Hall, "Brigade Teams Bring Mental Health to Fort Campbell," *Fresno Bee*, November 30, 2009, http://www.fresnobee.com/nation/story/1729587.html.

116. Ibid.

117. A. Adler, P. Bliese, D. McGurk, C. W. Hoge, and C. A. Castro, "Battlemind Debriefing and Battlemind Training as Early Interventions with Soldiers Returning from Iraq: Randomization by Platoon," *Journal of Consulting and Clinical Psychology* 77, no. 5 (2009): 928–940.

118. Walter Reed Army Institute of Research, U.S. Army Medical Research and Materiel Command, *Battlemind Training II: Continuing the Transition Home*, brochure, 2006,. http://www.behavioralhealth.army.mil/battlemind/BattlemindTrainingII.pdf.

119. K. Maurer, "Defense Dept. Probes Marine Mental Health Care," Associated Press, February 4, 2010.

120. Elspeth Ritchie, telephone conversation, May 20, 2010.

121. J. Dao and D. Frosch, "In Army's Trauma Care Units, Feeling Warehoused," *New York Times*, April 25, 2010, A1, A21, quotation at A21.

122. Ibid., A21.

123. Ibid., A21.

124. M. Mitka, "Military Medicating," *Journal of the American Medical Association* 303, no. 18 (2010): 1801.

125. G. Zoroya, "Mental Care Stays Are Up in Military," *USA Today*, May 14, 2010, http://www.usatoday.com/news/military/2010-05-14-mental-health_N.htm.

126. G. Zoroya, "Mental Health Hospitalizations Up for Troops, *USA Today*, May 14, 2010.

127. Ibid.

128. A. Tilghman and B. McGarry, "Accidental Overdoses Alarm Military Officials," *Air Force Times*, June 7, 2010.

129. J. Gould, "Video Shrinks Distance to Mental Health Care," *Army Times*, June 14, 2010.

130. U.S. Department of Defense, "Center Offers Hope to Heal War's 'Invisible Wounds,'" June 24, 2010, http://www.militaryfamilynetwork.com/article.php?aid=15388.

131. J. L. Thomas, J. E. Wilk, L. A. Riviere, D. McGurk, C. A. Castro, and C. W. Hoge, "Prevalence of Mental Health Problems and Functional Impairment among Active Component and National Guard Soldiers 3 and 12 Months Following Combat in Iraq," *Archives of General Psychiatry* 67, no. 6 (June 2010): 614–623.

132. G. Zoroya, "Mental Illness Costing Military Soldiers," *USA Today*, July 25, 2010, http://www.usatoday.com/news/military/2010-07-23-1Amentaldischarge23_ST_N.htm.

133. Ibid.

134. J. Griffith, "Citizens Coping as Soldiers: A Review of Deployment Stress Symptoms among Reservists, *Military Psychology* 22, no. 2 (August 2010): 176–206.

135. Ibid.

136. A. Tilghman, "Report Urges New Office for Suicide Prevention," *Army Times*, August 26, 2010, http://www.armytimes.com/news/2010/08/miltary-taskforce-defense-department-suicide-082410w.

137. Ibid.

138. B. Barrett, "Task Force: Military Suicide Prevention Efforts Inadequate," August 24, 2010, McClatchy Newspapers, http://www.truth-out.org/task-force-military-suicide-prevention-efforts-inadequate62658.

139. J. E. Barnes, "Soldiers' Suicide Rate Tied to Access to Problems at Home, *Wall Street Journal*, July 30, 2010.

140. G. Zoroya, "Leaders Criticized in Army Suicides, *USA Today*, July 30–August 1, 2010, 1.

141. United States Department of Defense, "Navy Suicide Prevention: It's an All-Hands Effort," press release, September 1, 2010, www.militaryavenue.com/.../Navy+Suicide+Prevention-+Its+an+All-Hands+Effort-34893.aspx.

142. R. W. Gunter and G. E. Bodner, "How Eye Movements Affect Unpleasant Memories: Support for a Working-Memory Account," *Behavior Research and Therapy* 46, no. 8 (2008): 913–931.

143. David Collier, personal communication, April 13, 2010.

144. A. Glantz, *The War Comes Home: Washington's Battle against America's Veterans* (Berkeley and Los Angeles: University of California Press, 2009).

Chapter 5

1. Bob Lange in D. E. Jones, *A Soldier's Story: The Power of Words* (Bloomington, IN: AuthorHouse, 2006), 131.

2. Barry Romo, telephone conversation, May 12, 2010.

3. A. Glantz, *The War Comes Home: Washington's Battle against America's Veterans* (Berkeley and Los Angeles: University of California Press, 2009).

4. J. E. Stiglitz and L. J. Bilmes, *The Three Trillion Dollar War: The True Cost of the Iraq Conflict* (New York: W. W. Norton, 2008).

5. Glantz, *The War Comes Home*, 115.

6. Ibid., 188.

7. D. Kersten, "Invisible Wounds," *Govexec.com*, July 1, 2005, http://www.govexec.com/features/0705-01/0705-01s3.htm.

8. Ibid.

9. Ibid.

10. Ibid.

11. Ibid.

12. R. Carroll, "VA to Review Veterans' PTSD Cases," August 30, 2005, Associated Press.

13. Ibid.

14. M. Brant, "The Fallout: The Things They Carry," *Newsweek*, August 29–September 5, 2005.

15. Harold Kudler, telephone conversation, September 16, 2005.

16. Ibid.

17. Harold Kudler, email communication, May 25, 2010.

18. Michelle Dillow, personal communication. January 24, 2007.

19. C. M. Sennott, "Told to Wait, a Marine Dies: VA Care in Spotlight after Iraq War Veteran's Suicide," *Boston Globe*, February 11, 2007, http://www.boston.com/news/nation/articles/2007/02/11/told_to_wait_a_marine_dies.

20. I. Katz, "Shh!," *Newsweek*, May 5, 2008, 27.

21. J. Graham, "Adding Insult to Injuries: Ill-Equipped VA Only Adds to the Pain, Vets Say," *Chicago Tribune*, April 9, 2007, http://www.chicagotribune.com/news/local/chi-veterans-graham,0,5888082.story.

22. A. Hull and D. Priest, "The War Inside," *Washington Post*, June 17, 2007, http://www.washingtonpost.com/wp-dyn/content/article/2007/06/16/AR2007061600866.html.

23. H. Yen, "US to Expand Veterans Mental Health Services; Wars Increasing Demand for Care," Associated Press, July 17, 2007.

24. S. J. Landers, "Suicide Hotline Lets Veterans—and Families—Dial for Help," *American Medical News*, August 25, 2008, http://www.ama-assn.org/amednews/2008/08/25/hlsc0825.htm.

25. S. Liewer, "VA Study Finds Mental-Health Care Is Lacking; Research Limiting Veterans' Treatment," *San Diego Union-Tribune*, September 5, 2008, http://www.signonsandiego.com/news/military/20080905-9999-1m5va.html.

26. U.S. Department of Defense, "Department of Defense Launches National Resource Directory for Wounded Warriors, Families and Caregivers," press release, November 17, 2008.

27. Ibid.

28. D. Zucchino, "Open Wound for Hurt Veterans," *Los Angeles Times*, November 25, 2008, http://articles.latimes.com/2008/nov/25/nation/na-combat25.

29. Ibid.

30. K. Maurer, "Veterans Still Waiting on Disability Appeals; Not a Single Case Has Been Heard," Associated Press, December 11, 2008, http://tinyurl.com/5d8np5.

31. A. Levin, "Evidence-Based Therapies Encounter Difficulty Transitioning into Practice," *Psychiatric News* 44, no. 3 (February 6, 2009), http://pn.psychiatryonline.org/content/44/3/15.2.full.

32. A. Levin, "Evidence-based Therapies Encounter Difficulty Transitioning into Practice, *Psychiatric News* 44, no. 3 (February 6, 2009): 15.

33. M. J. Carden, "Suicide Prevention Hotline Saves Veterans' Lives," American Forces Press Service, Washington, DC, February 13. 2009.

34. U.S. Department of Defense, "VA Budget Adds Mental-Health Services for Returning Combat Vets," press release, April 9, 2009.

35. M. Ma, "Seattle Hospital Teaches Meditation to Troubled Vets," *Seattle Times*, May 16, 2009, http://tinyurl.com/opyf34.

36. Harold Kudler, email communication, May 25, 2010.

37. D. J. Kearney, K. McDermott, M. Martinez, and T. Simpson, "Participation in Mindfulness-Based Stress Reduction Results in Health Benefits for Veterans with Posttraumatic Stress Disorder (PTSD): Results of a Randomized Controlled Trial," PowerPoint slide presentation, 2010.

38. David Kearney, telephone interview, May 12, 2010.

39. H. Bernton, "Soldiers' Emotional Battle Scars Put Doctors in Dilemma," *Seattle Times*, August 12, 2009, http://tinyurl.com/laufdc.

40. P. Barker, *Regeneration* (London: Penguin, 2008).

41. Bernton, "Soldiers' Emotional Battle Scars Put Doctors in Dilemma."

42. E. Goode, "Suicide's Rising Toll: After Combat, Victims of an Inner War," *New York Times*, August 1, 2009, http://www.nytimes.com/2009/08/02/us/02suicide.html?_r=1.

43. B. Bender, "Veterans Forsake Studies of Stress," *Boston Globe*, August 24, 2009, http://bit.ly/vE2uy.

44. D. Miles, "VA Strives to Prevent Veteran Suicides," American Forces Press Service, Washington, DC, April 23, 2010, http://www.defense.gov/news/newsarticle.aspx?id=58879.

45. Glantz, *The War Comes Home*.

46. K. Holmstedt, *The Girls Come Marching Home: Stories of Women Warriors Returning from the War in Iraq* (Mechanicsburg, PA: Stackpole Books, 2009).

47. U.S. Department of Defense, "VA Simplifies Compensation Rules for Post-Traumatic Stress," press release, August 24, 2009.

48. L. Daniel, "Services, VA Use Technology for Stress, Resilience Outreach," June 22, 2010, http://www.defense.gov/news/newsarticle.aspx?id=59736.

49. J. Dao, "VA to Ease Up on Benefits for Veterans with PTSD," *Seattle Times*, July 8, 2010. http://seattletimes.nwsource.com/html/nationworld/2012303491_vetstress08.html.

50. Associated Press, "Drug Prescribed for PTSD Raises Concerns," August 30, 2010, http://www.boston.com/news/nation/washington/articles/2010/08/30/drug_prescribed_for_ptsd_raises_concerns.

Chapter 6

1. W. Wasserstein, *The Heidi Chronicles* (New York: Dramatists Play Service, 1998).

2. E. M. Forster, *Howards End* (Mineola, NY: Dover, 2002).

3. D. E. Jones, from "War Drums," in *A Soldier's Story: The Power of Words* (Bloomington, IN: AuthorHouse, 2006), 61.

4. National Public Radio, "PTSD: A Marine's Story," November 17, 2010, http://onpointradio.org/2009/11/ptsd-a-marines-story.

5. D. Summerfield, "A Critique of Seven Assumptions behind Psychological Trauma Programmes in War-Affected Areas" (*Social Science & Medicine* 48 [1999]: 1449–1462), notes, "Death rates are two or three times higher in those with poor social connections" (1461), and also that during times of trauma, 95 percent of people in Bosnia and Croatia emphasized the need to be with other people and said that what helped the most were "nonspecific human warmth and acceptance" (1458).

6. E. Watters, "The Americanization of Mental Illness" (*New York Times Magazine*, January 8, 2010, http://www.nytimes.com/2010/01/10/magazine/10psyche-t.html?pagewanted=all), writes that many traditional cultures consider the person inseparable from the community, and this can help with healing when the focus is on helping the person get back into that community.

7. R. Whitaker, *Anatomy of an Epidemic: Magic Bullets, Psychiatric Drugs, and the Astonishing Rise of Mental Illness in America* (New York: Crown, 2010).

8. Jones, from "A Fight Within," in *A Soldier's Story*, 41.

9. A. Steptoe and A. V. Diez Roux, "Happiness, Social Networks, and Health," *British Medical Journal* 338, no. 7685 (2009).

10. E. Diener, "Subjective Well-Being: The Science of Happiness and a Proposal for a National Index," *American Psychology* 55, no. 1 (2000): 34–43.

11. J. C. Coyne and G. Downey, "Social Factors and Psychopathology: Stress, Social Support, and Coping Processes," *Annual Review of Psychology* 42 (1991): 401–425.

12. E. Watters, "The Way We Live Now: Idea Lab; Suffering Differently," *New York Times Magazine*, August 12, 2007, http://query.nytimes.com/gst/fullpage.html?res=9A05EEDD113BF931A2575BC0A9619C8B63&sec=&spon=&pagewanted=1.

13. D. Oaks, "On Military Veterans and Mental Health: Go Deeper," October 23, 2009, http://www.veteransforjustice.com/phpBB3/viewtopic.php?f=32&t=20.

14. C. Alexander, "Back from War, But Not Really Home," *New York Times*, November 8, 2009, 9.

15. "Gary Jacobson," message posted in response to "PTSD: A Marine's Story," NPR, November 17, 2010, http://onpointradio.org/2009/11/ptsd-a-marines-story.

16. W. Randall, *The Stories We Are: An Essay on Self-creation* (Toronto: University of Toronto Press, 1995).

17. D. Jacobs and D. Cohen, "Hidden in Plain Sight: *DSM–IV*'s Rejection of the Categorical Approach to Diagnosis," *Review of Existential Psychology and Psychiatry* 26 (2001): 81–96.

18. A. Yawar, "The Fool on the Hill," *Lancet* 373 (2009): 621–622, quotation at 622.

19. K. G. Howe, "Telling Our Mother's Story," in *Representations: Social Constructions of Gender*, ed. R. Unger (New York: Baywood, 1989).

20. J. Herman, *Trauma and Recovery* (New York: Basic Books 1997), 1.

21. J. Schogol, "Pentagon Hopes Stories Help Troops with PTSD," *Stars and Stripes*, February 9, 2009, http://www.stripes.com/article.asp?section=104&article=60587.

22. A. Fugard, Georgetown University commencement address, June 1984.

23. J. S. Gordon, "Cases without Borders: For Gaza Psychologist, Hope amid Despair," *New York Times*, January 13, 2009, http://tinyurl.com/94vf85.

24. P. Jeninek, "Army Plans to Hire More Psychiatrists," June 15, 2007, Associated Press.

25. M. Elias, "Post-traumatic Stress Is a War within the Body, for the Military and for Civilians," *USA Today*, October 27, 2008, http://www.usatoday.com/news/health/2008-10-26-PTSD-main_N.htm.

26. J. Kimberlin, "Out of the Darkness: Suicide and the Military," *Virginia Pilot*, July 8, 2007.

27. V. Frankl, *Man's Search for Meaning: An Introduction to Logotherapy* (New York: Washington Square Press, 1959).

28. Ibid. (lines 966–974 on Kindle).

29. S. Satel, "Measuring the Psychic Pain of War," *Slate.com*, http://www.slate.com/id/2148541/.

30. N. Fick, "Coming Home—to What?," *Boston Globe*, August 28, 2005, http://www.boston.com/news/globe/editorial_opinion/oped/articles/2005/08/28/coming_home____to_what. See also L. S. Brown, "From Alienation to Connection: Feminist Therapy with Post-traumatic Stress Disorder" (*Women & Therapy* 5 [1986]: 13–26), about the important role the community plays in helping people move past trauma.

31. B. T. Litz, M. J. Gray, R. A. Bryant, and A. B. Adler, "Early Intervention for Trauma: Current Status and Future Directions," *Clinical Psychology: Science and Practice* 9 (Summer 2002): 112–130, quotation at 128.

32. B. L. Litz and S. M. Orsillo, "The Returning Veteran of the Iraq War," in *The Iraq War Clinician Guide*, 2nd ed., ed. R. G. Lande, B. A. Marin, J. I. Ruzek, et al.

(Washington, DC: National Center for PTSD and the Department of Veterans Affairs, 2004), 21–32, quotation at 21. See also A. Glantz, *The War Comes Home: Washington's Battle against America's Veterans* (Berkeley and Los Angeles: University of California Press, 2009), who reports that veterans groups say that supporting service members "means listening to them when they get home" (153).

33. J. Tobin, *Ernie Pyle's War* (Lawrence: University Press of Kansas, 1997), 179.

34. B. Friedan, *The Feminine Mystique* (New York: W. W. Norton, 1963).

35. Alcoholics Anonymous, "Pass It On": The Story of Bill Wilson and How the A.A. Message Reached the World (New York: Alcoholics Anonymous World Services, 1984). A dramatization of the development of Alcoholics Anonymous and its dependence on human connection is the play, *BILL W. AND DR. BOB*, by S. Bergman and J. Surrey (Samuel French: New York, 2007).

36. S. Shane, "A Flood of Troubled Soldiers Is in the Offing, Experts Predict" (*New York Times*, December 16, 2004), writes that Dr. Thomas Burke, an Army psychiatrist, believes that if vets are told they are not crazy, they often get better rapidly.

37. M. Hill, "Reflections of an Experiential Feminist Therapist," *Women & Therapy* 5, no. 1 (1986): 27–32.

38. C. Cole and E. E. Barney, "Safeguards and the Therapeutic Window: A Group Treatment Strategy for Adult Incest Survivors," *American Journal of Orthopsychiatry* 57 (1987): 601–609.

39. David E. Jones, "Needless to Say," http://webspace.webring.com/people/ ll/11bravovet/thoughts.html.

40. Jones, from "Endings," in *A Soldier's Story*, 68.

41. R. G. Lande, B. A. Marin, J. I. Ruzek, et al., eds., *The Iraq War Clinician Guide*, 2nd ed. (Washington, DC: National Center for PTSD and the Department of Veterans Affairs, 2004), http://www.ptsd.va.gov/professional/manuals/iraq-war-clinician-guide .asp, quotation at 21.

42. S. Danish and B. Antonides, "What Counseling Psychologists Can Do to Help Returning Veterans," *Counseling Psychologist* 37, no. 8 (2009): 1076–1089.

43. David Collier, telephone conversation, April 13, 2010.

44. Graham Berman, telephone conversation, March 22, 2010.

45. G. Steinem, "Birthday Wishes," *Ms.*, Fall 2009, 42.

46. S. Simon, "Happier Vets, Lower Costs," *Wall Street Journal*, April 13, 2010, http:// online.wsj.com/article/SB10001424052748703909804575124451841717276.html.

47. Graham Berman, telephone interview, March 21, 2010.

48. Ibid.

49. David Collier telephone interview, April 13, 2010.

50. David Collier, telephone interview, May 12, 2010.

51. Glantz, *The War Comes Home,* 14–15.

52. Satel, Measuring the Psychic Pain of War"; K. Helliker, "You Might As Well Face It: You're Addicted to Success," *Wall Street Journal,* February 11, 2009, http://online.wsj.com/article/SB123423234983566171.html.

53. L. Kaufman, "After War, Love Can Be a Battlefield," *New York Times* (Sunday Styles section), April 6, 2008, 1.

54. Ray Parrish (telephone conversation, September 10, 2008) speaks of the ways he has seen some vets redeem themselves through these methods, each of which can involve increasing their connections with their previous community or with new ones.

55. See David E. Jones's Web site, http://webspace.webring.com/people/l1/11bravovet.

56. David E. Jones, personal communication, February 9, 2010. In the movie *Platoon,* a character says that those soldiers who made it owe it to the guys who didn't to use the rest of their lives to find goodness and meaning.

57. Quoted in T. McNally, interviews of S. Huze, P. Rieckhoff, and J. Massey, *Battlefield Iraq,* Interview transcript, January 20, 2006, http://www.uruknet.info/?p=19785.

58. X. Steen, "Escaping the Trauma Vortex," *Jerusalem Post,* January 2, 2009, http://www.jpost.com/Home/Article.aspx?id=127321. See also J. A. Livingston and J. M. Rankin, "Propping Up the Patriarchy: The Silenced Soldiering of Military Nurses" (*Women & Therapy* 5, no. 1 [1986]: 107–119), who say that an important part of the healing process for people who have been victimized—for all of us who have been victims—is to learn to take action.

59. David Collier, telephone interview, April 13, 2010.

60. Ibid.

61. David E. Jones's Web site is at http://webspace.webring.com/people/l1/11bravovet. Gary Jacobson's Web site is at http://pzzzz.tripod.com/namtour.html.

62. J. Dao, "Study Suggests Discussion of Killing to Help Veterans Cope with the Stress of War," *New York Times,* February 14, 2010, 21.

63. B. Carey, "The Struggle to Gauge a War's Psychological Cost," *New York Times,* November 26, 2005.

64. Helliker, "You Might As Well Face It," D1.

65. David Collier, telephone conversation, April 13, 2010.

66. David Collier, telephone conversation, May 12, 2010.

67. Glantz, *The War Comes Home*, 13.

68. Quoted in Whitaker, "Anatomy of an Epidemic," 349.

69. P. Barker, *The Ghost Road* (New York: Plume, 1995), 235.

70. N. Gerrard, "Guilt Is a Terminal Word: A Critical Analysis of Guilt in Relation to Women with a Focus on Mothers and Daughters," unpublished manuscript, Ontario Institute for Studies in Education, 1987 (available from the author at: 1904 Pembina Ave., Saskatoon, Saskatchewan, Canada S7K 1C3).

71. R. Mollica, "Trauma Care," *Boston Globe*, July 2, 2007, http://www.boston.com/news/globe/health_science/articles/2007/07/02/trauma_care.

72. Ibid.

73. Klein writes, "The only suffering which we cannot endure is that which has no meaning. An obsession is an attempt to get to meaning, to work something until we can let go of it" (1986, 36–37). When vets telling us their stories seem obsessed with particular events, it is helpful to remember what Klein said, because until they can discover or create some meaning about those events, they are likely to be stuck going over and over them.

74. Mollica ("Trauma Care"), a professor of psychiatry at Harvard Medical School and director of the Harvard Program in Refugee Trauma at Massachusetts General Hospital, says on the basis of twenty-five years of work with people who have suffered the worst kinds of trauma that

the three major social instruments of healing are altruism, work, and spirituality. These elements provide concrete methods and tools to promote recovery from trauma. They . . . assist in the construction of post-trauma attitudes and beliefs, and shift the survivor from isolation to rejoining the community. Unfortunately, it is common medical practice to neglect, ignore or even actively avoid addressing these social self-healing responses, especially spirituality.

75. P. A. Resick, "Post-traumatic Stress Disorder in a Vietnam Nurse" (*Women & Therapy* 5, no. 1 [1986]: 55–65), writes this: "Being popular, intelligent and a leader does not ensure ongoing social support following major life crises. It is not unusual for family and friends to become puzzled and impatient with the intensity of reactions and lack of recovery they witness in victims of trauma. They soon conclude that the victim's reaction and inability to forget and put it behind reflects some personal weakness or failure on the part of the victim. At a time when Ruth needed tremendous social support, others probably pulled back" (57).

76. Ibid.

77. Ibid.

78. Graham Berman, telephone conversation, March 21, 2010.

79. David Collier, telephone conversation, April 13, 2010.

80. S. Griffin, "On Wanting to Be the Mother I Wanted," *Ms.*, January 1977, 100.

81. See http://dictionary.reference.com/browse/sacred.

Chapter 7

1. J. Donne, *Devotions upon Emergent Occasions*, ed. A. Raspa (Oxford: Oxford University Press, 1987).

2. Quoted in B. Grigsby, "A Terrible Loyalty," *Montrose Daily Press*, March 4, 2010, http://www.montrosepress.com/articles/2010/03/04/opinion/columnists/doc4b8f1adee2897005118682.txt.

3. E. Wiesel, "Against Indifference: Reflections on 'Never Again,'" speech, Stanford University, May 21, 2006.

4. D. E. Jones, from "Perspectives," in *A Soldier's Story: The Power of Words* (Bloomington, IN: AuthorHouse, 2006), 27.

5. Jones, from "Scorners," in *A Soldier's Story*, 87.

6. K. Vonnegut, *Bluebeard* (New York: Dell, 1987), 140.

7. J. N. Shklar, "Putting Cruelty First," *Daedalus* 111, no. 3 (1982): 17–27.

8. C. Hoyt, "The Painful Images of War," *New York Times*, August 3, 2008, 10.

9. J. A. Livingston and J. M. Rankin, (1986). "Propping Up the Patriarchy: The Silenced Soldiering of Military Nurses," *Women & Therapy* 5, no. 1 (1986): 107–119.

10. Quoted in D. Kersten, "Invisible Wounds," *Govexec.com*, July 1, 2005. http://www.govexec.com/features/0705-01/0705-01s3.htm.

11. Quoted in J. Hoffman, "War's Other Enduring Videos," *New York Times* (Sunday Styles section), 2009, 1, 10.

12. For instance, see Hoffman, "War's Other Enduring Videos."

13. Gary Lord, email communication, April 23, 2010.

14. F. J. Partel, *A Wound in the Mind: The Court-Martial of Lance Corporal Cachora, USMC* (Fiction Publishing, Inc., 2009); and D. Grossman, *On Killing: The Psychological Cost of Learning to Kill in War and Society* (New York: Back Bay Books, 1996).

15. Partel, *A Wound in the Mind*; Grossman, *On Killing*. See also J. Shea, "A Novel of Turmoil, War, and Humanity," *Martha's Vineyard Times*, May 28, 2009, http://www

.mvtimes.com/marthas-vineyard/calendar/2009/05/28/in-print-wound-in
-the-mind.php.

16. S. Corbett, "The Permanent Scars of Iraq," *New York Times Magazine*, February
15, 2004, 34–41, 56, 60, 66.

17. J. M. Whiteley, "Counseling Psychology: A Historical Perspective," *Counseling
Psychologist* 12 (1984): 3–109.

18. Quoted in N. Genzlinger, "No Enchanted Evenings in This Pacific Warfare," *New
York Times* (Arts section), March 7, 2010, 1, 19.

19. J. E. Wibby, "Western Michigan Chapter Commemoration," *Bulge Bugle*, May
2010, 27.

20. D. Ephron and S. Childress, "Forgotten Heroes," *Newsweek*, March 5, 2007,
29–37.

Afterword

1. T. Perry, "Marine Corps Seeks to Use Buddy Ethic to Stem Rise in Suicides; 52
Marines Killed Themselves Last Year, Compared with 42 the Previous Year. The Corps
Wants Marines to Rescue Other Marines from the Edge, just as They Would Come
to Their Aid in Combat," *Los Angeles Times*, September 10, 2010, http://lat.ms/
cZKENPope.

2. A. Zavis, "Many Veterans with PTSD Struggle to Find Supportive Employment,"
Los Angeles Times, September 20, 2010, http://articles.latimes.com/2010/sep/19/
local/la-me-veterans-invisible-wounds-20100920.

3. United States Department of Defense, "Military Progresses in Identifying, Treating
Brain, Mental Injuries" press release, September 22, 2010, http://www.defencetalk
.com/military-progresses-in-identifying-treating-brain-mental-injuries-28961.

4. L. Shaughnessy, "Army's Largest Base Reeling from Four Apparent Suicides in One
Weekend," CNN, September 29, 2010, http://bit ly/yyKenPope.

5. J. C. McKinley, Jr., "Despite Army Efforts, Soldier Suicides Continue," *New York
Times*, October 11, 2010, http://www.nytimes.com/2010/10/11/us/11suicides.html.

6. M. Rosenberg, "Are We Giving Our Soldiers Drugs That May Make Them Kill
Themselves?," October 10, 2010, http://www.alternet.org/story/148444.

7. http://defensetech.org/2010/10/26/combat-stress-theres-an-app-for-that.

8. U.S. Department of Defense, "U.S. Defense Dept: Mental Health Issues Affecting
Troops and Their Families," October 28, 2010, http://www.defense.gov/transcripts/
transcript.aspx?transcriptid=4708.

9. Ibid.

10. Ibid.

11. Ibid.

12. libbyliberal, "Traumatized Troop Seeks Help: NCO Tells Him, \x91Get the Sand out of Your Vagina!,\x92" October 29, 2010, http://www.worldcantwait.net/index .php/home-mainmenu-289/6747-traumatized-troop-seeks-help-nco-tells-him-get -the-sand-out-of-your-vagina.

13. A. Glantz, "Investigation: Suicide Rates Soaring among WWII Vets," *New America Media*, November 11, 2010, http://newamericamedia.org/2010/11/suicide-rates-soar -among-wwii-vets-records-show.php.

14. Ibid.

Index